The History and Battlefields of the
CIVIL WAR

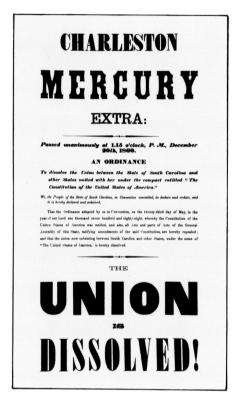

The History and Battlefields of the
CIVIL WAR

—— BY JOHN BOWEN ——

THE WELLFLEET PRESS
WELLFLEET

A QUINTET BOOK

Published by Wellfleet Press
110 Enterprise Avenue
Secaucus, New Jersey 07094

ISBN 1-55521-750-8

This book was designed and produced by
Quintet Publishing Limited
6 Blundell Street
London N7 9BH

Editorial Director: Sheila Buff
Designer: Graham Davis
Project Editor: Damian Thompson
Editor: Rosemary Booton

Typeset in Great Britain by
Profile Design, Bournemouth
Manufactured in Hong Kong by Regent Publishing Services Limited
Printed in Hong Kong by Leefung-Asco Printers Limited

This book incorporates material which first appeared in
Battlefields of the Civil War and *Civil War Days* -
both by John Bowen.

Part One

THE EASTERN THEATER 7

1   FORT SUMTER AND THE EARLY PERIOD 8

2   TWO PRESIDENTS: SIMILAR BUT DIFFERENT 22

3   FIRST MANASSAS (BULL RUN) 34

4   BILLY YANK AND JOHNNY REB 40

5   STONEWALL'S VALLEY 60

6   THE PENINSULAR CAMPAIGN 66

7   SECOND MANASSAS (BULL RUN) 76

8   ANTIETAM: THE WAR GOES NORTH 84

9   FREDERICKSBURG AND CHANCELLORSVILLE 90

10   GETTYSBURG 96

Part Two

THE CIVILIAN SIDE 103

11   GRANT'S DECISIVE CAMPAIGN 104

12   CIVILIAN LIFE: A WORLD TURNED UPSIDE-DOWN 124

13   MILITARY RULE: FREEDOM'S FOLLY 148

Part Three

THE WESTERN THEATER 165

14   WESTERN THEATER: OPENING SALVOS 166

15   SHILOH AND OTHER PIVOTAL BATTLES 178

16   SOLDIERS AT WAR : ENDURANCE AND DEATH 206

17   NEW ORLEANS AND SOUTHERN LOUISIANA 238

18   CLOSING THE MISSISSIPPI 246

19   THE WAR AT SEA: CAT AND MOUSE 260

20   CHICKAMAUGA, MOBILE AND SHERMAN'S FINAL PUSH 274

21   FINAL ACTS: HOOD MOVES NORTH, SHERMAN DRIVES EAST 302

22   AFTERMATH: A HUSH DESCENDS ON DIXIE 320

  INDEX 339

  PICTURE CREDITS 352

PART ONE

THE EASTERN THEATER

Astrange mixture of reluctance and anticipation pervaded the languid air of Charleston, South Carolina, on the night of April 12, 1861. The shoreline was ringed with deadly mortars and cannon, all pointed at the dark hulk of Fort Sumter on a man-made island at the narrow entrance to the harbor. War was imminent; citizens of both North and South exhibited a curious mixture of enthusiasm for conflict and the desire not to be blamed for starting it.

Great effort to avoid armed confrontation was coming to naught. Politicians in both North and South had exerted enormous efforts to resolve the conflict between two regions over slavery, economic competition and jealousy, and especially the divisive tariff issue which was, almost as abrasive as the more emotional slavery question. South Carolina had endured the affront to its sovereignty by 'foreign' forces stationed on its soil since December 20, 1860, when the State seceded from the United States and then joined the

Fort Sumter and the Early Period

Confederated States of America. Confederate President Jefferson Davis had sent word from Montgomery, Alabama, to exercise caution. U.S. officials likewise were hesitant to provoke the fight that seemed inevitable; when a relief ship sent to Fort Sumter in January by the outgoing President James Buchanan was fired upon by Confederate shore batteries, it turned back. Newly elected Abraham Lincoln backed up a tough Inaugural Address asserting Federal authority over the seceding States with almost a month of inaction. When he decided to send a relief expedition of three ships to the fort, he advised South Carolina Governor Francis Pickins that only supplies would be landed, not reinforcements, unless the expedition met resistance. All of this, however, was outweighed by mutual mistrust and strategic considerations.

DRIFT INTO WAR

Both sides had misled the other on occasion and those three small Federal ships now posed a major problem for the Confederacy. Fort Sumter was brand new (its present occupants were its first) and formidable, with 50 foot high brick walls, twelve feet thick at their base. It mounted 60 guns, but only a garrison of 85 men. The commander, Major Robert Anderson, had orders to remain, but admitted to Confederate emissaries that, without supplies, he could not resist the powerful array of 43 guns and mortars at Forts Johnson and Moultrie, located on either side of the entrance to the narrow harbor; Castle Pinckney, a small island in the inner harbor off the Battery; an innovative floating battery near Moultrieville; and temporary gun emplacements at other strategic locations along the shoreline. His supplies would be exhausted by April 15 and then he would have to capitulate. The three relief ships the steamship *Baltic*, the USS *Pawnee* and the five-gun revenue cutter *Harriet Lane* could alter the situation. If their mission succeeded, South Carolina officials foresaw the possibility of continued Federal occupation of the fort, which guarded one of the most important harbors in the new Confederacy; it could not remain in unfriendly hands.

By the spring, too, excitement had been building in Charleston for some time. State officials had been upset by Major Anderson's Christmas 1860 decision to occupy the fort, believing they had an agreement with President Buchanan that Federal troops would remain at the more vulnerable Forts Moultrie and Johnson. To many minds, the decision made war inevitable. Confederate forces had responded by moving into the former Federal mainland bases and began fortifying the entire shoreline. Crowds gathered to watch the emplacement of new cannon, and to look at the beleaguered fort.

BOMBARDMENT AT DAWN

When the Confederate cannon finally opened fire at 4.10 a.m. on April 13, it was like an early Fourth of July. Charleston's civilians, aroused from their slumbers by the booming of the guns, climbed to their roofs to watch the palpitating light of muzzle flashes and the explosion of shells. Spectators would be prominent through the 34 hours the fort was under siege. For men such as Brigadier General P.G.T. Beauregard of Louisiana, a former West Point commandant picked by Confederate President Davis to command the attack, there was less elation than a sense of relief that the waiting was over and that the final act of dissolution was occurring, mixed with the nagging uncertainty that affects all soldiers at such times.

A tragicomedy was being acted out. An ardent civilian secessionist from Virginia (still in the Union at that point), Edmund Ruffin, was accorded the honor of touching off the first shot, but may not have done so. Fort Sumter did no immediately return the fire, but waited until after daybreak. Major Anderson's soldiers leisurely breakfasted before manning their posts, and then spaced their firing to conserve ammunition. Confederate batteries, which opened the battle with an intense bombardment, alternated between sporadic firing and flurries during the 34 hours the fort

The Defender of Fort Sumter, Major Robert Anderson, remains a controversial figure. Did he break an agreement to maintain the status quo by moving his troops from Fort Moultrie to Fort Sumter? A Kentuckian with Confederate sympathies, he nevertheless honored his oath as a Union officer and defended Fort Sumter as long as he could.

Left Edmund Ruffin, shown here in the uniform of a private, was an ardent secessionist from Virginia; he was given the honor of firing the first shot in the assault on Fort Sumter.

held out. Their shells damaged Fort Sumter's wall and set fire to the officers' quarters and the barracks. In a day and half of firing, more than 2,000 rounds were fired from Fort Sumter, with the Confederates firing 3,500 more, but no one was killed and only eight men four on each side were wounded. The only fatality came as Major Anderson saluted the flag before evacuating the fort. A cartridge bag exploded, killing a gun-crew member, Private Daniel Hough.

COUNTER-ATTACK AND RECONQUEST

The relative light damage sustained by the fort in this first battle was just the beginning. As the war went on, re-possession of Fort Sumter became a Union obsession, partly because the naval blockade of the harbor was unsuccessful. There were three attacks from sea, all ending ingloriously, even the one in April 1863 that utilized a fleet of nine ironclad vessels. Union guns threw seven million pounds of metal at the fort, but, despite this, only 52 Confe-derate soldiers were killed. Action elsewhere on the Atlantic Coast and on Western rivers would find winning combinations of seapower and land forces against

forts, but Fort Sumter, even though subjected to sustained Union bombardment after 1863 from Morris Island, remained in Confederate hands until Charleston was taken from the rear on February 17, 1865, during Major General William T. Sherman's celebrated march to the sea. By that time, however, the fort was just a pile of broken bricks – a sign, also observed elsewhere during the war, that

Below A confederate flag flies over Fort Sumter in April 1861. Capture of the fort was the first major action of the war.

the advent of rifled cannon had made large, fixed fortifications obsolete.

THE LEGACY OF THE WAR

Fort Moultrie has been restored to reflect its entire martial history, starting with the Revolutionary War, but key features remain from its strategic role during the Civil War. The masonry fort that exists today had been given its basic shape by the time of the Civil War, but was reinforced with sand and wood to reduce the effect of explosions. The right section of the curved forward edge holds Civil War batteries, which indicate the alterations made by Confederates in response to technological changes in coast artillery. Along Cannon Walk, outside the walls of the fort, are a series of cannon which highlight the evolution of seacoast defense weaponry during and after the Civil War.

The site of old Fort Johnson, on the other side of the harbor, is now occupied by a research center and is not open to the public.

In a way, the historic area of Charleston was a part of the siege battlefield. From the Battery, the beautiful waterfront walkway now decorated with cannon, monuments, palmettoes and flowers, people watched history taking place. The streets of the old city retain the lowlands South Carolina atmosphere that existed, with the stories of such landmarks as the 1834 Gothic Huguenot Church, the 1770 Heyward-Washington House and the 1803 Joseph Manigault mansion recalling the era when General Beauregard was lionized by the ladies and gentlemen of South Carolinian society. Beauregard's statue is in the Washington Square. The Citadel, old and new, stands as an example of tradition of State military academies that exist in a number of Southern States. The college has moved from the historic 1822 structure to a more modern complex not far away. The graves of a number of Confederate soldiers are located in Magnolia Cemetery.

Hunley Museum emphasizes displays on Confederate naval history, including the CSS *Hunley*, the first submarine to sink a surface vessel. Named after its inventor, H.L. Hunley, who was killed in a practice dive, the submarine drove a spar torpedo into the hull of the USS *Housatonic* on February 17, 1864, and sent it to the bottom. However, in a cruel ironic twist, the *Hunley* itself was swamped by the wave created by the explosion and went down beside her victim.

The Parrott gun was one of the most popular cannon used during the Civil War. The rifled weapon, produced in various sizes, was used by both sides. This example is at Fort Gregg on Morris Island, South Carolina in 1865.

FORT SUMTER TODAY

Like others on the east coast, Fort Sumter has accretions from later wars, when the forts were used by coastal artillery; however, even today, it still shows the wear and tear of Civil War action. A tour boat from the mainland deposits visitors at a dock on the left flank from where they enter the fort through a sally port, built since the Civil War. Casemates or rooms in the walls of the fort demonstrate the practice of gunnery as it existed in the mid 1860s. Along the right flank are eleven 100-pound Parrott guns, a rifled cannon that was extremely popular throughout the Civil War. A mountain howitzer near the Right Gorge Angle, intended to defend the fort against a surprise landing by Union forces, shows how the Confederates had to improvise. Several projectiles still protrude from the wall of the left flank, reminders of the shelling by Union batteries in 1863.

The original shape of the five-sided brick fort, one of the series of fortifications authorized by Congress after the War of 1812 with Great Britain, remains. One of the flag-poles, replacing the one shot away during the Confederate bombardment, was erected in 1928 to honor Major Anderson and his men. The museum contains a variety of relics, and tells certain episodes of the fort's history in diorama and pictorial display form. A ground-level view from the esplanade along the Gorge exterior reveals the way the fort dominates the entrance to the harbor.

Fort Sumter's command of the entrance to Charleston harbor made Union control intolerable to the new Confederate States of America. Confederate bombardment started the Civil War. This view from the harbor, the one seen by most Charlestonians that fateful morning, is also familiar to visitors today.

Confederate ammunition and arms, stacked near an armory at Charleston, represent only a fraction of the quantities involved. More than 5,000 shells were fired by the two sides during the short siege of the city.

FORTS IN FLORIDA

The Confederate attack on Fort Sumter was not much of a contest; both sides were fatalistic about the outcome, and the action in retrospect seems more pro forma than contemporaries judged from news accounts at the time. The naval relief expedition, through a series of misunderstandings caused by secrecy and disagreement, waited just outside the harbor while Sumter was being forced to surrender. Indeed the spark that set off the Civil War could easily have happened in Florida, instead of South Carolina. Fort Pickens, on Santa Rosa Island off Pensacola, was one of the key coastal forts that President Buchanan promised not to reinforce and Lincoln was determined to hold. For a time it was a powder keg with a short fuse.

Professor J. Leitch Wright of Florida State University History Department is among those pointing to similarities between the little-known events in Florida on the eve of war and the famous events in South Carolina at Charleston. At the same time of Florida's vote on secession in early January 1861, Federal officials decided to destroy the Chattahoochee Arsenal and reinforce the Pensacola Forts. To prevents this, Florida seized the arsenal from a sergeant and three men, took possession of the navy yard and concentrated a sizable force near Fort Barrancas. Confederates also took control of Fort Marion (Castillo de San Marcos) in St. Augustine from a single caretaker.

Fort Pickens was unfinished at the time, but was more strategically located than Fort Barrancas on the mainland, which Lieutenant Adam J. Slemmer had orders to hold. Slemmer decided to move his 46 soldiers and 35 ordinary seaman to the more defensible fort on Santa Rosa Island, which also could be reinforced from the sea The same decision made by Major Anderson at Fort Sumter and a war of nerves with Confederate forces on the mainland began. President Buchanan, as fearful of starting a war at Pensacola as he was at Charleston, agreed to maintain the status quo and the Confederates held their fire. Lincoln, after taking office decided to reinforce the fort and, within a week after the bombardment of Fort Sumter, more than 2,000 soldiers had been sent to defend the position. Ironically the officer carrying orders to reinforce the fort had received a pass through the Confederate lines from the new commander of the Pensacola region, General Braxton Bragg. Confederates raided the island and guns from the fort battered Confederate Fort McRee, burned Warrington and Wolsey and fired at construction in the navy yard, but neither side had an advantage.

Fort Pickens is now part of the Gulf Islands National Seashore, a nature preserve and recreation area so delightful that it is difficult for even Civil War buffs to concentrate on historical objects. However, the ruins and museum relate the lively history of the fort,

which included imprisonment of the Indian Chief Geronimo after his capture. Fort Barrancas, located on the grounds of the Pensacola Naval Air Station, is restored and included with the Water Battery in a guided historical tour. Old Christ Church, the oldest-remaining church building in Florida which was used by Union soldiers as a barracks and hospital, houses the Pensacola Historical Museum. A number of other antebellum structures survive, including the 1810 Charles Lavalle House and the 1825 Lighthouse, still owned by the Coast Guard.

Fort Jefferson and Key West also remained

Fort Jefferson's strong walls were never tested in combat. The site now is better known for its rich marine and bird life. The old cannon still point seaward, but only as historical displays for visitors to the national park.

in Union hands throughout the war, the first because it was (and still is) inaccessible and the second because of the cleverness of Captain James M. Brannan, commanding the 44 soldiers on the island. Brannan's men were quartered away from Fort Taylor, the only place they could defend, so the captain moved them secretly in small groups and at night, through the hostile city to the fort. The East Martello Gallery and Museum is a wartime fortification built by the Union. The attempt to take the State capital at Tallahassee late in the war started from Key West. Fort Jefferson, the largest of the coastal forts built by the United States in the early nineteenth century, is now a national monument as well known for legends of pirates and sunken gold as for war stories.

THE VOLUNTEERS MUSTER

After the fall of Fort Sumter, President Lincoln issued a call for 75,000 volunteers and militia to restore the union, an action that precipitated further acts of secession, including those of Virginia and Tennessee which would become major Civil War battlegrounds. Baltimore citizens stoned troops being sent to protect the

Pensacola Bay, Florida, was heavily fortified throughout the Civil War, as this period photo shows.

national capital of Washington, but Maryland remained in the Union.

Neither side was prepared for war, but both acted quickly. On April 19, 1861, President Lincoln ordered a blockade of all Confederate ports. Alexandria, Virginia, across the Potomac River from the national capital at Washington, was occupied by Federal troops on May 28. The Union remained in control of Fortress Monroe in Hampton, Virginia, and began probing Confederate defensive positions. At Big Bethel, 4,000 untested Federals failed to dislodge 1,500 equally green Confederates on June 10, 1861. The first Confederate battle casualty was Henry Lawson Wyatt of North Carolina.

AMPHIBIOUS OPERATIONS

A Union strategy soon developed, with a major element being the attempt to control the coast of the South, through blockade and occupation of strategic points, and thereby to strangle the Confederacy. Accordingly, fighting on North Carolina soil began on the coast. In the first amphibious operation of the Civil War, in August 1861, Union troops took Cape Hatteras, a strategic elbow island on the North Carolina Outer Banks whose offshore waters were known for their peculiar currents and violent storms. During a two day battle, hastily constructed Forts Hatteras and Clark guarding Hatteras Inlet were reduced by gunfire from a fleet of eight warships. Then, the two troopships carried 900 of General Benjamin F. Butler's soldiers from Fortress Monroe in Virginia to capture the forts and take more than 600 Confederate prisoners. Loss of Hatteras was a blow to Confederate efforts to keep imports flowing through North Carolina because it deprived blockade runners of the entrance to Pamlico Sound.

Comments by Confederate prisoners after the battle indicate they placed too much confidence in newly invented water-mines placed at Hatteras Inlet, which were expected to deal with the Federal fleet, including the flagship USS *Minnesota*. A *Washington Star* article belittled the inventor, Matthew Fontaine

Fort Pickens at the entrance to Pensacola harbor had many similarities to Fort Sumter, and could easily have been the spark that set off the Civil War.

Maury, as a 'trickster' and Confederates as 'credulous enough to put faith in his pretentions to the extent of that by his wonderful submarine batteries and other kickshaws he could blow sky-high any of Uncle Sam's vessels that might seek an entrance into Hatteras Inlet.'

The Confederates chose Roanoke Island, lying behind the Outer Banks and between Pamlico and Albemarle Sounds as a substitute defensive position, hoping it would limit the effectiveness of Federal possession of Hatteras. They strongly fortified the island and the adjacent mainland with three forts and three independent batteries, holding more than 38 cannon of various sizes and types, and a squadron of eight gunboats. These were manned by 4,000 officers and men, and protected by a double row of stakes and some sunken ships across the inland passage, Croatan Sound. It was not enough when General McClellan, preparing for his Peninsular Campaign, decided that possession of Roanoke Island and thus complete Federal

control of the North Carolina Sounds would constitute a continuing threat to Richmond's lines of communication. An expedition of 12,000 men and 19 shallow-draft gunboats was delayed by damage in a mid January storm off Hatteras Inlet, but captured the objective on February 8, 1862, with forces under the command of Brigadier General Ambrose E. Burnside.

The occupation of Port Royal Sound and Hilton Head Island in South Carolina was another early achievement of Union arms. Remnants of Confederate Fort Walker, which succumbed to Union naval fire because it was improperly constructed and armed, survive on the fashionable resort island, which gives little indication of the isolation and harsh conditions there during the Civil War period. Hilton Head was headquarters of the Union Army Department of the South, commanded by Brigadier General Thomas W. Sherman (also known as 'The Other' Sherman), and thus a major staging base for the coastal operations in South Carolina, Georgia, and

Left Fortress (now Fort) Monroe. Lincoln stayed here in Quarters 1 during a wartime visit; the cell where Davis was imprisoned after the war is now part of the Casemate Museum.

Florida. The ruins of Confederate Fort White, defended successfully against several Federal attacks, are one of the attractions at Belle Island Gardens near Georgetown. During one attack on this fort, the Union flagship *Harvest Moon* was sunk by Confederate mines.

MOUNTAIN CAMPAIGNS

The Western counties of Virginia now the State of West Virginia became an early major area of contention. Mountainous West Virginia was divided by the war. These counties had always been suspicious of the lowlands, which controlled the Government in far-away Richmond. They were small-farmers and miners, for the most part, who owned few slaves and whose loyalty was to themselves more than to any cause or any government. Yet some of the Confederacy's greatest heroes came from the area. General Thomas J. 'Stonewall' Jackson was born at Clarksburg and raised at Jackson

Mill near Weston, and many mountain men followed him into Confederate gray. Confederate spies Belle Boyd and Nancy Hart were West Virginians.

Virginia tried to hold on to the area. The first fighting in West Virginia occurred when Union forces engaged Confederate artillery at Seawell's Point, but the distinction of staging the first battle goes to Philippi, where a splendid old covered bridge over the Tygart River used by both armies remains. The Battle of Philippi, on June 3, 1861, was an easy Union victory, as Union forces under Colonel B.F. Kelly surprised newly recruited Confederates under Colonel G.A. Porterfield and sent them scurrying. The 'Philippi races' helped pro-Unionists maintain control of West Virginia and may have given McDowell's army a feeling of overconfidence.

Jackson, in particular, thought the valleys along the forks of the Potomac had strategic

Below The Stonewall Jackson Shrine at Guinea Station preserves the plantation office in which Lee's 'right arm' died as a result of wounds received at Chancellorsville. The manor house, also used as a Confederate hospital, no longer exists.

Right General Thomas J. 'Stonewall' Jackson pushed his men, but shared their hardships. His Stonewall Brigade continued to serve with distinction after his death.

John Brown *(above)*, the fiery abolitionist from Kansas, led a raid on the arsenal at Harper's Ferry, West Virginia, in 1859. It resulted in his execution and martyrdom in the antislavery cause.

value. Even the dead of winter could not keep Jackson idle, and reinforced by 7,000 men under Brigadier General W.W. Loring, he moved to Romney, 35 miles from Winchester, which was defended by now-Brigadier General Kelley with 5,000 men. Jackson's move was hampered by the softness of his troops, a lack of equipment and the reluctance of Loring, but he never the less managed to destroy the Baltimore and Ohio Railway bridge over the Great Cacapon River and to occupy Romney,

which Kelley evacuated. Jackson left Loring to hold Romney and returned to Winchester with the Stonewall Brigade. Loring's imaginary fear that he would be cut off, fed by the grumbling of the officers at Romney, led Confederate Secretary of War Judah P. Benjamin to tell Jackson 'to order him back immediately.' Jackson dutifully obeyed orders, and submitted his resignation or alternatively requested to be returned to duty at the Virginia Military Institute. Neither was ac-

Harper's Ferry, taken and retaken several times during the Civil War, looks much the same today *(above)*, as it did in 1865, when the picture *(left)*, was taken. The community now is a national historic site explaining the development of weapons and its varied history as an arsenal.

cepted, but Benjamin was less eager to inject politics into military affairs thereafter.

HARPER'S FERRY AND GAULEY BRIDGE

The Federal arsenal at Harper's ferry, the object of John Brown's famous raid in 1859, was considered a prize. It was taken by the Confederates on several occasions, only to be abandoned to the Federals because the surrounding hills, looking down on the town, made it almost indefensible. Today, Harper's Ferry National Historical Park depicts a mid-nineteenth century community as well as a Civil War battlefield. The Master Armorer's House, a museum on gunmaking with a collection of weapons, and the late 18th century Harper House, the oldest surviving structure, are the leading display buildings. Bolivar and Loudoun Heights in West Virginia, Maryland Heights in Maryland and Short Hill in Virginia retain Civil War features.

The Gauley Bridge over the New River was the scene of heavy fighting in 1861, when troops under Brigadier General William S. Rosecrans defeated Confederates, who destroyed the bridge to protect their retreat. Another significant battle, on September 10, 1861, is remembered at Carnifex Ferry Battlefield near Summerfield on State Route 39.

A Confederacy short on manpower, as well as everything else, could not spare the means to hold West Virginia against a Federal army that numbered more than 27,000 at times. Federal interest was political, and in time West Virginians were induced to hold a constitutional convention in Wheeling and secede from Virginia. On July 14, 1862, Congress voted West Virginia into the Union as a separate State. West Virginians thus fought on both sides for most of the war, as the Confederate monument in Union, West Virginia, shows.

While the earliest fighting of the war occurred there, the 26 sparsely settled counties were later spared from becoming a major scene of battle by their difficult terrain, that restricted maneuvering by large units, their isolation and poverty.

This old covered bridge at Philippi, West Virginia, accommodated the crossing of armies from both sides during the war, but the nearby battle was a Union victory that helped pro- Unionists retain control of the State.

T he leadership of North and South reflected both the similarities and differences between them. Presidents Abraham Lincoln and Jefferson Davis were both Westerners, born only a hundred miles apart in Kentucky. Both were middle class in origin, and both were a complex mixture of idealism and opportunism, which affected their prosecution of the war.

DEDICATED TO THE UNION

Lincoln was a practical, ingenuous man who read utilitarian books and was not interested in intellectual pursuits for their own sake. His law partner, William H. Herndon, remembered a man who relished power and the management of people. Lincoln used humility as a tool, to obtain political advantage, and had confidence in his considerable abilities. His rural brand of shrewdness made him calculating and forward-looking, especially with regard to his political future; yet he preferred a simple, direct approach to prob-

Two Presidents: Similar but Different

lems and policies. Although Lincoln was not awkward in the social graces, he was never lionized by Washington society.

Lincoln had no experience as an administrator, but had latent ability and was a quick learner. His deliberate balancing within his administration of the diversity of prevalent ideologies with which he was not in conflict gave him access to talents he did not possess. Men such as Treasury Secretary Salmon P. Chase and Secretary of War Edwin Stanton exerted considerable influence. Friction would develop from every direction, but Lincoln controlled it through a policy of quiet manipulation – at which he excelled – or by direct exercise of authority.

Lincoln's political beliefs were as mixed as

President Abraham Lincoln (above left) retained his fatherly appearance despite the pressures of the Civil War. Jefferson Davis (above right) is pictured prior to taking office as president of the Confederacy.

his personality. He held offices in Illinois under Whig sponsorship. His service in the House of Representatives in the 30th Congress contributed to his selection to oppose Senator Stephen A. Douglas, a powerful Democrat with presidential ambitions, in 1858. The story of of how Lincoln backed Douglas into a corner on the issue of popular sovereignty in the Western territories in the celebrated Lincoln–N–Douglas debates has gone down as part of national folklore.

He did not win the election, but he received national exposure and an approving eye from the growing Abolitionist movement. Thus, Lincoln's political conversion was a combination of opportunism and ideological growth.

Lincoln believed the unity of the nation to

be sacred. He supported an anti-slavery policy, but its details were vague and was not in a hurry to enforce it at the expense of the Union. This changed as the War progressed, and he accepted the growing influence of the Abolitionist wing of the Republican Party on appointments and on shifts in policy.

A MAN OF THE SOUTH

Jefferson Davis's family moved south from Kentucky and in time attained a modest fortune. They became part of the Southern landed aristocracy, with all its pretensions and charm. Davis developed in a way quite different from Lincoln; he was not a self-made man but the product of a system producing a gracious living from managerial toil. He even experienced the tragedy so popular in Southern folklore when his wife of three months died after contracting malaria in Cuba.

A complex mixture of principle and ambition, Davis creatively mastered one challenge after another during a long career in

government. He was at home in the urbane and sophisticated atmosphere of Washington during a protracted period of public service, both in Congress and in the executive. He was elected to the United States House of Representatives, then to the Senate, then served a term as United States Secretary of War. At the time he was chosen to lead the fledgling Confederacy, Davis was widely regarded as the 'foremost man in the South.'

As president of the Confederacy Davis showed his diligence and attention to detail the fruits of the education he had received at West Point, which then as now was one of the best available. But in the long run, his insistence on handling even the smallest detail harmed his person, his reputation and the Confederate war effort. A courageous man, he did not let ill health – resulting from a congenital defect, aggravated by malaria – become an excuse for shirking responsibility or making tough decisions. He was moralistic, hard working and confident. His intense

The White House of the Confederacy in Richmond was Jefferson Davis's home while he led the Confederate States. It is now part of the Museum of the Confederacy.

loyalty proved to be both a strength and a weakness; he would not countenance criticism of those in whom he believed and was obstinate about his appointees and policies. The disastrous invasion of Tennessee in 1864 resulted primarily from these qualities.

Davis's belief in the rightness of the Southern cause and in States Rights never wavered. Indeed, it increased during the war. This did not prevent him from centralizing the Confederate Government when prosecution of the war demanded it. He was more flexible on the fundamental questions of State powers versus those of the national government than about the details of policies and relationships with people. Unlike others, Davis could see that the Southern way of life would be lost unless the war could be won.

The public perception of Davis was one of aloofness, but this was a misinterpretation of the dignified reserve and courtly manner which endeared him to the critical patricians of Richmond. Among friends and family, he was warm and devoted, and he loved children.

MANIPULATING POWER

Both men were given more power than any president to that time; Davis was less successful than Lincoln in using it. Davis was unable to negotiate a workable alliance between the conflicting ideologies in the South. Maybe no one could; the plantation mentality, which viewed any change in the political and social structure as treason, weakened the

Confederacy to the end of the war. Lincoln, too, was confronted by ideologues, while less sincerely motivated men wielded enormous power in the shadows behind him. The most influential members of his Cabinet were from the northeast and from the radical wing of the party, and their authority was enhanced by the outbreak of war. Lincoln maneuvered adroitly through currents from Peace Democrats on one edge to radical Abolitionists on the other by using both institutional inducements and personal prestige in whatever combinations were required.

The contrast between the two leaders shows clearly in the places which retain their memories. The log cabin in which President Lincoln is believed to have been born is preserved in a handsome marble structure on 100 acres of his father's farm near Hodgenville, Kentucky. Davis's birthplace no longer exists, but a 351-foot-high mon-ument to his memory has been erected at Fairfield. Lincoln's law office in Springfield, Illinois, from which he moved into a political career, is typical of the small, unpretentious midwest town office of the era. His home has a plain exterior and a homespun interior that matched

Above President Lincoln grew up in a log cabin very similar to this reconstruction on the farmstead of his father, Thomas Lincoln. The site is preserved as the Lincoln Boyhood National Memorial in Indiana.

Sarah Knox Taylor the daughter of President Zachary Taylor, was to become the first wife of Jefferson Davis. Their life together was cut short when she died of malaria three months after their marriage in June 1835.

Mary Todd Lincoln shared her husband's wartime trials, but has been harshly treated by some historians.

his personality. The agony Davis suffered after the war as a prisoner at Fort Monroe, Virginia, is reflected in the Casemate Museum there, while his tastes in home life are evident at both the White House of the Confederacy, his first official residence, in Montgomery, Alabama, and at Bellevue, near Mobile, where he spent the last years of his life.

The war destroyed both of them. Lincoln had been assassinated by the time Davis was captured. Davis survived vindictive imprisonment to provide his account of the ideological and economic conflict that ravaged whole States and sent at least half a million young men and uncounted numbers of civilians to their graves.

POLICY, POLITICS, FINANCES

The Confederacy, as a new nation, needed a complete set of laws and governmental institutions. Thus, as soon as possible, a convention was called in Montgomery, Alabama, at that time the capital of the Confederacy, to draft a constitution for the new nation. There, 50 representatives from seceded States participated in a 35-day meeting, which proceeded logically and carefully to determine the boundaries of its authority, create the framework of a provisional government and draft a permanent constitution while acting as a provisional Congress.

The United States Constitution was used as a framework for the Confederate Constitution, but modifications enthroned the Southern concept of government. States would possess a 'sovereign and independent character' even though a 'permanent federal government' was to be established. Obviously, the people elected to office would work out a compromise between the two. In some respects the Confederate document improved on the United States Constitution. It established item veto by the president and required two-thirds approval of appropriations not requested by the president; it provided for a district court structure and a procedure in the event of presidential disability; and it pro-

hibited tariffs. While it contained a prohibition against any new extension of the slave trade, it protected slavery in the States and territories of the Confederacy.

Confederate presidents would be elected for six-year terms but could not stand for re-election. Congress could, if desired, offer seats to members of the president's cabinet so that it could hear from them first hand.

In putting together a cabinet, President Jefferson Davis was constrained by the same type of regional considerations that had influenced American politics since the Revolution. His cabinet thus not only reflected various views but also many of the States including populous, front-line Virginia.

Constitutional issues also were important in the North. Lincoln assumed more power than any other president. By classifying secession as insurrection, he was able to assume emergency powers and commit the United States to war long before Congress acted. In the interest of national security, he followed a rule of 'military necessity' during the war, which suspended civil liberties and instituted summary arrest of persons suspected of opposing the war effort.

Although Lincoln was lenient toward malefactors charged under his proclamations, including those in the military, the suspension of habeas corpus and abrogation of constitutional rights by commanders of the military departments were controversial actions. Some constitutional issues were not settled until after the war. In the meantime, thousands were arrested and imprisoned, citizens were forced to take loyalty oaths, and simple economic rights were violated.

Lincoln did not aspire to dictatorship; his aggressive actions accomplished quickly what would have taken Congress months to do and Congress ultimately acquiesced in all of them. However, he was not above using military actions to serve political ends.

STRATEGY: JOMINI, CLAUSEWITZ OR MAHAN?

The Civil War began with neither side having a well developed strategy, and consequently the building process was long, and involved many shifts. Both sides moved from one strategy to another, in response to events and the grueling demands of the most destructive war in American history. Not even the rules of warfare were clearly understood at the start.

Railroads and the telegraph added new dimensions to warfare. They greatly expanded the battlefield by facilitating coordinated campaigns, increasing the area from which armies could draw supplies and creating a close working relationship between field commanders and their political superiors. While these elements shrank geography in one sense, they gave added importance to control of particular features such as rivers.

The leading strategists of the era were Antoine Henri Jomini and Karl von Clausewitz. While the concept of grand strategy was foreign to most West Point graduates who would assume the highest rank, they were familiar with the works of Swiss-born Jomini, the foremost authority on warfare in the period, when most of them were studying at 'the Point'. The influence of Jomini on the generals of both sides is still being debated by military analysts and historians, but intentional or not their actions followed his thinking on objectives, the offensive, mass, economy of force and the unity of command.

Jomini's concept of warfare, derived from the Napoleonic Wars, involved theaters of operation; the Union did not fully recognize until 1864 the interdependence of the Eastern and Western theaters. President Abraham Lincoln foresaw, in a primitive way heavily colored by political considerations, the need to coordinate actions on all fronts, but was mesmerized by the idea of a crushing blow to subjugate the South.

General Ulysses S. Grant was the first to make destruction of the opposing army and its civilian supports primary objectives. His coordinated advance on all fronts in 1864, which prevented Confederate armies from reinforcing each other, was aimed at destroying those armies, the supporting industrial infrastructure and civilian will to continue the war.

Confederate policy more closely reflected Jomini's views, but in limited ways and often for non-Jominian reasons. Jomini's concept of territorial objectives coincided with political realities in the Confederacy which dictated an attempt to defend every mile of its border and to maintain its influence in Border States, even if it did not have the ability to separate them from the Union.

The consequent dispersion of Southern forces reflected the pre-Jominian cordon system of defense and prevented the concentration that Jomini demanded. Here, again, conditions dictated the strategy of defense. The South, whose main objective was separation from the Union, entered the war with a strictly defensive policy. It did not want to force other States to leave the Union.

The Confederacy never really created a uniform strategy for both fronts. Only in the waning months of the war, when all was lost, did General Robert E. Lee reluctantly accept overall command.

Jomini's influence was greater on battle-

General Ulysses S. Grant poses for a photographer in front of his headquarters tent.

field tactics, where concentration of forces on interior lines was practised where feasible. His emphasis on defense as the strongest tactical position found a ready audience. General Lee was the foremost builder of defensive works during the war, but both he and President Jefferson Davis saw the tactical advantage of attacking, in the Napoleonic fashion, with divided armies and exposed flanks. Lee took calculated risks and divided his forces on numerous occasions; he subdivided an already divided army to achieve the brilliant flanking victory at Chancellorsville.

Clausewitz, whose book *On War* appeared in 1832, would eventually eclipse Jomini and others as military mentor to the world. However, he had not been widely studied in the United States and, thus, had limited influence on the Civil War. Nevertheless, the frustrations of a long war and the terrible toll of casualties produced definite Clausewitzian results, including the gradual deterioration of moral restraint.

Northern determination to win produced the 'total war' which Clausewitz had predicted, based on his interpretation of the Napoleonic Wars. The carnage caused by frontal assault and stand-and-fire tactics made many converts to his principle of maneuver. Even General Grant, who suffered 61,000 casualties in his Virginia campaign of 1864-5 (more than Lee's entire army), turned more and more to flanking maneuvers as the casualties mounted.

Clausewitz's dictum that war is an extension of policy—an 'affair of the people'—also gained importance as the war progressed. In the North, political objectives, including the Emancipation Proclamation, became so important that Lincoln came to believe they would determine the outcome of the conflict. The weaknesses of the Confederate political system, in which States vied with the central government for control of resources and events, were one of the causes of defeat. The psychological factors which Clausewitz cited played an increasingly important role in the decline of Southern resistance.

But Clausewitz stressed wars with limited objectives. While both sides entered the conflict with limited objectives, the North soon adopted a more comprehensive policy of crushing Confederate leadership and changing the political system in Southern States. This was enshrined into law by Congress as early as 1862. Grant took this to the ultimate—the ability of both the Confederate army and the Southern people to make war was to be crushed. He was so effective in achieving this end that an Italian general, writing in the twentieth century, listed the 'American War of Secession' among the 'wars of destruction.'

To achieve such results, according to Clausewitz, the North needed an army capable of defeating the enemy, avoiding self-exhaustion and holding off foreign intervention—all of which the Union achieved.

Grant and Lincoln were instinctively Clausewitzian when they advocated destruction of the enemy army, not the capture of territory, as the primary military objective. However, possession of Richmond, the Confederate capital, was an obsession that Lincoln could never overcome. As a result, Grant had to consider that in all his planning as general-in-chief.

Dennis H. Mahan, a respected professor of engineering, natural philosophy and the art of war at West Point in the pre-war years, exerted a powerful influence on his former students, especially early in the war. Mahan's *Outpost*—the official title was *Advanced-Guard, Outpost and Detachment Service of Troops, with the Essential Principles of Strategy and Grand Tactics for the Use of Officers of Militia and Volunteers*—was in the mind or knapsack of many officers and was felt often on the field of battle. Mahan's books were reproduced

during the Union and Confederacy.

Mahan emphasized a combat condition that influenced a number of Civil War battles —that commanders must make decisions based on incomplete information. One of Mahan's teachings, the value of speed in marches and maneuvers, was ably demonstrated by Confederate Lieutenant General Thomas J. 'Stonewall' Jackson. Many a Union general learned the validity of Mahan's judgement that 'the very elements of nature seem to array themselves against a slow and over prudent general.'

Books and observation can carry the soldier only so far. Invariably, experience is the greatest instructor. A great, and unhappy, learning opportunity awaited the eager minions of war.

This Kurz & Allison print depicts the struggle for Laurel Hill at Spotsylvania, where dismounted Confederate cavalry held off superior Union forces until Lee could once again place his army between General Grant and Richmond.

29

RELATIONS WITH THE OUTSIDE WORLD

The United States had diplomatic relations with most of the world at the outbreak of war and continued to maintain those relations. Policy was designed to keep foreign nations neutral, to prevent the sale of arms and materials helpful to the Confederate war effort and to block recognition of the Confederate States of America.

As a new nation, the Confederacy had first to build a diplomatic corps and then have its ambassadors accredited by governments around the world. While Confederate commissioners were received and more or less allowed to operate freely, accreditation was another matter. Confederate emissaries were successful in obtaining loans and sympathy but they could not persuade Great Britain and France, which were working in concert, to recognize the Confederacy. The Europeans waited to see whether the new nation could establish its freedom, while continuing their substantial trade with the United States.

Cotton was not king in the United States. Large stocks existed in Great Britain at the start of the war and these were supplemented by cotton grown in the new fields in Egypt and India. In some ways the shortages were welcome; they could be used as a scapegoat for the unemployment resulting from a recession in Great Britain and France.

The Trent affair late in 1861 raised Confederate hopes of foreign recognition to a high pitch. James M. Mason, a former senator from Virginia, and John Slidell of Louisiana boarded the British ship *Trent* in Havana on a trip to Europe as commissioners of the Confederacy. The vessel was halted on the high seas off the Bahamas coast by the United States sloop of war *San Jacinto* and the two commissioners were seized and taken first to Fort Monroe and then to Boston. The seizure put the United States in a spot; though the captain of the *San Jacinto*, Charles Wilkes, became a Union hero overnight, the British public was outraged. *The Times* in London demanded war with the United States. British forces in Canada were reinforced.

The South was elated; if Britain needed an excuse to intervene in the war, as most Confederates believed, that excuse now existed.

The restraint of the British government should have awakened the Confederacy to the reality that Britain would not intervene. Great Britain demanded an apology and the prisoners' release, but did not force the issue immediately. Lincoln finally released Mason and Slidell and sent them to England. The British lion went back to watching and waiting.

Great Britain's equivocation had both philosophical and pragmatic roots. The government of Lord Palmerston was philosophically opposed to slavery and, throughout the war, hesitated to alienate the anti-slavery movement at home. Furthermore Great Britain had a substantial stake in trade with the North; more than a third of its grain imports

The capture of two Confederate envoys, including James M. Mason, aboard a British vessel on the high seas—the famous Trent Affair—brought the Union close to war with Great Britain.

came from the plains States. Palmerston was also concerned about the possibility of war with the United States if the British recognized the Confederacy; a war that would not be in Great Britain's interests. However, the decisive factor was the unsettled conditions in Europe. Palmerston did not want to upset the fragile peace that existed.

FINANCING AND SUSTAINING THE WAR EFFORT

While internal problems in the Union during the war were primarily political, President Davis's were financial, as well. Both sides entered the war with assets. The Confederacy fell heir to those assets in its territory which formerly belonged to the United States; in February 1861, Louisiana turned over to the Confederate Congress $500,000 in specie obtained when it took over the New Orleans mint and Custom House, for example. The assets of the Union were much larger and its financial condition was good, despite an antiquated borrowing system and legal restraints on financing methods.

However, both governments turned heavily to borrowing to finance the war, especially in the early stages. At its first session, the Confederate Congress approved a $150 million loan paying eight per cent interest, fi-

'Greenbacks', printed by the Federal Treasury, helped preserve liquidity when precious metals could not be mined in sufficient quantities to meet wartime money needs.

nanced by a duty on cotton exports. An initial issue of paper currency was apparently aimed at providing a means of supplementing issues by State and local banks; the $50 denominations were too large to serve in every day commerce. However, a course had been set that would produce fiscal uncertainty and runaway inflation. The Confederacy continued to raise too many loans and issue too much paper money throughout the war. By 1863, rampant inflation in the Confederacy demanded action.

The Union took much the same course, but without the disastrous consequences because of its stronger financial condition and ultimate victory. President Lincoln called upon an agreeable Congress for an initial loan of $150 million in 1861. Although underwritten by banks, the notes were passed on to the public. Public subscription became the standard as other, and larger, loans were required. Congress approved an income tax of three per cent on incomes over $800 in 1861, but implementation was delayed until 1863. A shortage of gold and silver necessitated the printing of paper 'greenbacks,' which were declared legal tender by law but which were never popular with merchants or the public.

The Confederate government took the lead of industrializing the South. As the Union

The beautiful, hilltop Capitol designed by Thomas Jefferson dominates this 1862 photograph of Richmond. Ordnance lies in the foreground.

blockade tightened around the coast of the Confederacy, the nation was forced to develop internally the means of sustaining the war effort. Since the enormous amount of private capital needed for this development did not exist, the Confederate government built, owned and operated large factories to produce munitions and other military essentials.

Industrial capacity, which had been largely confined to Richmond before the war, was dispersed throughout the South. Gun-powder plants existed in six States, including a mammoth facility at Augusta, Georgia. More than 10,000 worked in the war factories of Selma, Alabama. New factories making cannon, rifles, pistols, carbines, lead shot, and shells were located in Macon, Augusta, and Columbus, Georgia, and elsewhere. A large leatherworks was built at Clarksville, Virginia. These developments were a credit to Pennsylvania-born Josiah Gorgas, the chief of ordnance, who created them. Munitions production was still going full-blast at the end of the war, despite Union cavalry raids designed to disrupt it.

THE MOWER.

We have battles to fight, we have foes to subdue,—
Time waits not for us, and we wait not for you!
The mower mows on, though the adder may writhe
And the copperhead coil round the blade of his scythe.

Designed & Lith by D.C.Fabronius.

Below The Confederacy built up enormous debts to finance the war. This $100 bond issued in 1863 carried 7 per cent interest.

Above Northern opponents of the war were derided as 'Copperheads'. This engraving shows Lincoln as 'The Mower' with a copperhead coiled on his blade.

Political infighting troubled the Confederacy all of its lifetime. The planter class resisted to the end any change to the pre-War status quo. Although Davis was able to maintain a fragile truce between contesting groups, the effort prevented him from building a core of political allies willing to take some of the heat off him. As a result, he was unpopular with Congress throughout the war. Only three persons served continuously in the Cabinet and only one of those, Secretary of Navy Stephen R. Mallory, held the same post throughout the war.

While Davis was placating conservatives, Lincoln was confronted by radicals on the one hand and a substantial peace movement on the other. A bitter contest between moderate and Radical Republicans resulted in the latter seizing control of the party. One of the by-products was the Committee on the Conduct of the War, which under the leadership of Ben Wade is accused by historians of causing intrigue (including discrimination against Democratic officers in promotions), rivalry, and dissension in the Union army.

3

A stern-faced statue of Major General Thomas J. 'Stonewall' Jackson, his taut muscles pressing against his uniform, perpetually surveys the battlefield of Manassas (Bull Run) from a vantage point on Henry Hill. The statue is a veritable symbol of power, and it stands on the ridge where the Confederate leader received, during the heat of battle, one of the most famous nicknames in history. But even such a heroic representation does not do justice to that imperturbable, demanding leader who inspired his men to prodigious feats. He was a superior tactician whose campaigns would later be studied by officers from many nations, and a firm believer that once he had done his best, the outcome of the battle rested in God's hands. Jackson's solidity was crucial to the Confederate victory in the first major land conflict of the Civil War because, at a critical moment, he provided a rallying point for Southern soldiers who only a few weeks earlier had been ploughing fields or toting accounts.

First Manassas
(Bull Run)

It was inevitable that fighting would occur at Manassas, barely 25 miles from Washington, D.C. Although Virginia had worked for reconciliation between the Union and seceding States, when President Lincoln issued a call for 75,000 militia and volunteers to put down the rebellion, she then cast her lot with the Confederacy. Her geographic location on the border made her a likely battleground, especially after Richmond became the Confederate capital. Manassas was a transportation hub astride the approaches to both Richmond and the fertile Shenandoah Valley; General Robert E. Lee, who had turned down command of United States forces to join his native State and initially served as adviser to Confederate President Davis, immedi-

ately recognized the importance of the junction. Federal forces posted there could pose a double-edged threat to Virginia while protecting the national capital, whose safety was one of President Abraham Lincoln's major concerns.

Neither side was prepared for war, but neither hesitated. The first battle of Manassas aroused the same enthusiasm and confidence, on both sides, that excited both populations before Fort Sumter. Federals were so confident of success that they openly boasted of driving Confederate forces back to Richmond. Curious civilians, including some members of Congress, mingled unhindered with the Union units, often visiting the camps. Many of them bought picnic baskets, as though

The Matthews or Stone House was twice engulfed by the fighting at Manassas, when it was used as a hospital, but it survived. Shells embedded in the walls may still be seen.

on a holiday, and some of the ladies had finery with them so that they could attend the victory ball which was to be held in Alexandria.

A TWO-PHASE BATTLE

The Battle of First Manassas on July 21, 1861, was the largest that had ever been fought up to that time in the Western Hemisphere. There were two distinct phases of battle. The morning phase basically involved a Union flanking movement that initiated the fighting while Confederate forces were forming to attack the Union army near Centreville. Confederates defended the Stone Bridge across Bull Run as a key point in their line. However, Union Brigadier General Irwin McDowell chose a flanking movement across fords of the stream. Sudley Ford was the principal crossing point, but became clogged as thirsty soldiers stopped for water on a hot day – one of numerous delays that affected the outcome of the battle. The crossing at Farm Pond, a little known ford which a loyalist farmer pointed out to Federal forces, went better. Confederate Colonel Nathan 'Shanks' Evans became one of the unsung heroes of the action by correctly diagnosing Union movements and moving his forces from the bridge to Mathews Hill to cope with the first Union assault. Mathews Hill quickly developed as the principal site of the morning fighting, with Confederates defending successive positions such as the unfinished railroad grade of the

Manassas Gap Independent Line. At Sudley Church, worshippers gathering for a church service were surprised to see Federal troops marching by; the church was used later as a Union hospital.

The Confederates gradually were forced back to Henry Hill, which has a spectacular view over Bull Run and to the mountains to the west. There, the second, and decisive, phase of the battle occurred in the afternoon. During see-saw fighting on the slope around the Henry House and the Robinson House, owned by a freed slave at the time of the fighting, Federal troops made five partially successful assaults only to be driven back each time by rallying Confederates. On the eastern edge of Henry Hill, Jackson earned the name 'Stonewall' from General Bernard Bee, who later was fatally wounded, as he exhorted his South Carolinians to rally around Jackson, who was standing like a 'stone wall.'

THE REBEL YELL

The Rebel Yell, which would remain a fixture throughout the war, came into being as Beauregard, Jackson and others brought their troops to an emotional pitch in the late afternoon. The final clash began at about 4 p.m. and ended in a disorderly defeat of the Federals. The bridge across Bull Run, regarded as a prize at the outset of the battle, became an obstacle as the Federals retreated in headlong disorder. As McDowell wrote later, 'the re-

After the Battle of First Manassas, Confederate forces occupied positions at Centreville, while the Union built a ring of forts around Washington. The Confederate defenses at Centreville looked like this in 1862.

Above left Groveton Cemetery holds the remains of 200 Confederate soldiers killed at Manassas, all but 40 of them unknown.

Below left The Stone Bridge (pictured today), provided a lane of retreat for Union forces at both First and Second Manassas, but was destroyed on several occasions.

Above This bigger-than-life statue of a stern-faced General Thomas J. Jackson dominates Henry Hill, where his performance in the Battle of First Manassas earned him the nickname 'Stonewall'.

THE BATTLEFIELD TODAY

Today, self-guided walking tours cover the principal features of the battlefield. The Stone Bridge, destroyed several times, has been reconstructed. The houses around which the fighting swirled were destroyed then or later, and were rebuilt. Adjacent to the new Henry House are the 1865 monument to the 'patriots who fell at Bull Run' and the grave of Mrs. Judith Carter Henry, the only civilian casualty of the battle, an elderly woman killed by Union shrapnel after she refused to leave her home. The neat, clean slope of Henry Hill, where the Park Service Visitors' Center is located, bears little resemblance to the rough terrain over which the armies fought, but the relative compactness of the battlefields permits visitors to reach major features on foot along established trails. The combination of trails and signs, memorials, reconstructions and strategically placed period cannon contribute to a mental picture of the progress of the battle.

Right The Federal army made innovative use of observation balloons early in the war, as this 1862 photograph shows. A Union general was the first to use a balloon to direct artillery fire.

Below Pontoon bridges played an important role in the Civil War. This crossing of Bull Run in 1862 was a forerunner of more important uses later, including the crossing of the broad Rappahannock River at Fredericksburg by the Union army.

Above Civil War commanders made extensive use of the telegraph in field communications, and often had to construct the lines that linked them to higher headquarters. These Union lines are being built in 1864.

treat soon became a rout, and this soon degenerated still further into a panic.' One who helped to create the panic was a firebrand who had been present at the siege of Fort Sumter: ardent secessionist Edmund Ruffin. He fired the final shot of the battle at soldiers fleeing across the Stone Bridge.

The flight toward Washington was panicky, with soldiers and civilians mingling on the dusty roads. What had started with such enthusiasm and promise had ended in disaster, and Washington itself was in jeopardy. It was saved by the exhaustion of the Confederate forces, and the uncertainty of Southerners about how their devotion to secession could justify an offensive stance.

Many of the intangibles that affect the outcome of combat were present at First Manassas. General McDowell's plan to flank the Confederate position was basically sound, but delays in moving units, faulty logistics and preparation, the inexperience of his troops and officers, and bad judgement during the

course of the battle proved costly. Confederate execution was not perfect, either, but was better, while the South possessed more effective intelligence and communications. The deference shown by the senior Brigadier General Joseph E. Johnston to Beauregard upon arriving on the scene, because Beauregard was familiar with the situation, was unusual in a war where the egos of the officers loomed large. After the war, Johnston and Beauregard would duel in print about what happened and its significance.

LESSONS FROM FIRST MANASSAS

First Manassas was the first clash in history between two civilian armies. The Confederacy, as a new nation, entered the war without a professional army, but with an officer corps drawn largely from the United States army; the Union army at the outset had only 16,000 regulars, most of them engaged in protecting the Western frontier or holed up in East coast forts. The battle was, in a way, an object lesson in the changes taking place in warfare – the emerging pre-eminence of firepower and maneuver. This first battle would turn on the strategic value of the railroads to move men and supplies quickly and prove their worth in modern warfare. It saw the first use of the telegraph in war, opening a new era in one of the major requirements in combat – communications. Confederate use of signal flags represented a new form of battlefield communication. Professor Thaddeus Lowe, who already had demonstrated to Union leaders how balloons could provide combat observation, encountered the hazards of the road as his partially inflated balloon snagged on trees along the road to Manassas. His balloon tracked the movement of Confederate forces after the battle. Balloons would be used often during the early stage of the war, and in May 1862 a Union general became the first to direct artillery fire from aloft.

More variations of weapons were used in the Civil War than in any previous conflict. While the Civil War did produce innovations in weapons and tactics – breech-loading rifles, rifled artillery, the first use of machine guns in combat, submarines, land and sea mines and hand grenades among them – it was basically a proving ground for existing technology and thus was of considerable interest to the European powers. Military writers in Great Britain, France and Germany would recognize it as the first total war, fought with the might produced by the Industrial Revolution, and as a glimpse of the warfare of the future.

Well into the twentieth century, military authors would draw on the tactical improvisation of Confederate and Union generals and the prodigious engineering feats performed by both sides. First Manassas produced the first winner of the Congressional Medal of Honor, an award created during the Civil War. The honor went to Adelbert Ames of East Thomaston, Maine, who commanded an artillery section, although he would not receive it until 33 years after the event.

Below This Rodman gun at Alexandria helped strengthen the ring of earthen forts around the District of Columbia. They were never successfully attacked, but only Alexandria's Fort Ward is preserved.

Left Tiny Centreville was a key Union position during both Manassas battles. This 1862 photograph shows Union soldiers on the edge of town.

Soldiers on both sides seemed to sense they were living through an exceptional period and many recorded their participation, so extensive and informative accounts of their activities exist.

Billy Yank and Johnny Reb were similar, but not cut of the same cloth. They came from the same native stock, with a sprinkling of immigrant blood, and they retained their attachment to their native States. Both rushed off to fight with romantic notions of war that soon were destroyed. Both were confident of success at the start, and both experienced periods of doubt but doggedly persevered in the face of adversity. The differences between Billy and Johnny lay in their backgrounds and attitudes and in the abilities of their governments to support them.

TYPICAL FEDERALS

The average Billy Yank was a youthful soldier. The enthusiastic first wave of volunteers came mostly from 18 to 21 years age-group. The

Billy Yank and Johnny Reb

average age of the Union Soldier was only about 26 at the end of the war: 98 per cent of those who fought were between 18 and 45. Most were under six feet tall and weighed under 150 pounds. Drummer boys, 13 years of age and younger, beat commands while shot and shell burst around them. Many of them died; one, named Johnny Clem, survived and ultimately became a general long after the war.

Officers were slightly older, on average. Senior officers were mostly in their forties – General Ulysses S. Grant was 39 when the war started, but General George A. McClellan was only 35. A few attained senior rank at a very early age. Arthur McArthur, Medal of Honor winner at Missionary Ridge and father of the celebrated Second World War general, was only 18 years of age when he was commissioned lieutenant colonel. The *enfant terrible* of the military, George Armstrong Custer, was only 24 when he received a general's star.

The 'Men in Blue' came from all jobs and professions – more than 300 in fact. Farmers were the largest group, followed by carpenters, shoemakers and clerks. There were rich, upper-crust socialites, and there were illiterates. One of the Indians who served was Lieutenant Ely S. Parker, a Seneca chief who was Grant's aide in the last stage of the war. About 200,000 blacks were enrolled, and at least 500,000 soldiers –nearly 20 per cent of the 2,865,028 men called into Federal service – were recent immigrants. The Irish Brigade was perhaps the most famous, but Germans, especially, also formed the rank and file of whole units.

Most men who entered the Federal service were not prepared for the different kind of life led by soldiers. Submission to military au-

European-style uniforms were popular with mid-nineteenth-century American soldiers. Colonel F.G. Utassy, left, and his brother were members of the Garibaldi Guards, 39th New York Infantry.

Right Recent immigrants, especially the Irish, made a substantial contribution to Union military strength. Thomas Francis Meagher was captain of Company K (Irish Zouaves), 69th Regiment, New York State Militia. An organizer of the 'Fighting Irish', Meagher was commissioned as brigadier general in 1862.

Above Drummer Gilbert A. Marbury, Company H, 22nd New York Infantry, poses beside a cannon. Although the youthful drummers did not carry weapons, they were in the thick of battle.

Right Confederate units, like Georgia's Sumter Light Guards, began the war with new uniforms, but keeping them properly clothed became a problem as the war progressed.

thority was hard for farm boys and city youth – often described in contemporary works as 'free, honest Americans' – accustomed to control only by loving family and the weather or constraints of the job. It was especially difficult for them to subdue their belief in meritocracy and give blind obedience to any men wearing shoulder straps, regardless of their ability and leadership qualities. They served best in units organized by their own States, to which they retained a strong attachment – regional affiliations were fostered whenever possible.

The Union soldier literally rushed to defend the national flag. While he opposed slavery in principle he had little knowledge of it and usually was surprised to discover it was not as bad as depicted in Northern publications. He was concerned mainly with an affront to the flag and with punishing those who caused it. The crusade against slavery was never popular with the soldiers at the front; some of them often denigrated blacks and, when the Emancipation Proclamation was issued, bitterly denounced the 'Negro war.'

'FOR SOUTHERN RIGHTS, HURRAH!'
Johnny Reb was young, too. Most Southern soldiers were between 18 and 30 years of age, and about three-fourths of them had rural backgrounds. Many were illiterate, and no effort was made by the military to educate them. The peculiar spellings in letters to the folks at home revealed an absence of dictionaries and general acceptance of phonetic spelling. Most Southern soldiers were unmarried but, like soldiers in every war, carried a photo or memory of a dream girl back home. Most were native Southerners with only about

Union Private D.W.C. Arnold *(top center)* was among the 'free, honest Americans' who had to adjust to the rigors of military life. For some, such as drummer boy Johnny Clem *(above center)* there was little adjustment to be made: a veteran at age 12, he had known no other life.
Most of the senior Union officers were in their forties at the start of the war–Major General George B. McClellan *(top left)* was, at age 35, slightly younger than average. Many units entered the war wearing fancy but unpractical uniforms. *(above left)*. As the war proceeded, uniforms like that worn by Private Emory Eugene Kingin *(top right)* of the 4th Michigan Infantry, USA, became standard issue. The kepi-style hat, as displayed by Sergeant Oscar Ryder of the 7th New York State Militia *(above right)* eventually became regulation.

four per cent being foreign born. The reason was simple. There were fewer immigrants in the South than in the North.

Foreign nationals sometimes took a hand. In New Orleans, foreigners who loved the city's robust ambience formed a unit to help defend the city. Indians – mostly Creeks, Cherokees, Chickasaws, Choctaws and Seminoles–served with distinction, and Stand Watie, a Cherokee, rose to the rank of general.

Johnny Reb was used to the outdoors and quite often had been a hunter. He exhibited a rare combination of independence and loyalty. The Southern soldier, one of the Confederacy's greatest assets, was an individualist who never really adjusted to military life. He chafed under camp routine and military discipline, and preferred to do things his own way; but he performed well in combat, where action replaced routine and individualism was rewarded.

The Southern soldier was not fighting for slavery; fewer than 25 per cent owned slaves or came from slave-owning families. To him, the attack on Fort Sumter was defensive because his 'nation' already had been invaded. His letters back home usually reflected a belief that he was fighting for 'freedom.' Most Southerners defended State's Rights as opposed to 'dictatorship' or, like General Robert E. Lee, elected to defend their home State.

THE FIRST VOLUNTEERS

Neither the North nor the South had an army of any consequence at the start of the war. The United States army at the time numbered about 16,000 men, most of them manning frontier posts or coastal forts. The Confederacy began from scratch, but was aided by a stronger tradition of military service. Many of the best qualified officers in the U.S. Army came from the South, and most of them resigned to enter Confederate service.

Thus, both armies had to depend on volunteers. Militia units were the first to be called to service in the war, sometimes augmented by new recruits on the eve of entering Federal service. Lincoln's initial call for three months was woefully inadequate, and later calls were for six months or a year. Trouble sometimes erupted because commanders would not let men go home at the end of their enlistment periods.

No matter how long they had been in existence, these units were unprepared for war. They had received only rudimentary training, were equipped with antiquated

Military units were organized within the States. In this fascinating sketch by Samuel Reader, a note inviting the artist to join a new company is reproduced and sketches of the uniform and the headquarters are shown.

Below Two types of
officers' uniforms and
the standard equipment
of Union enlisted men
are depicted in this
drawing. Swords
became less common
as the war
progressed.

weapons and were filled with romantic notions of warfare, which were reflected in their fanciful uniforms. Units marched off to war dressed in bright colors and unusual designs. Although impressive on parades, these uniforms were a hindrance on the battlefield. Billowing red Zouave-style pantaloons and fezes created easy targets at First Manassas and impeded the troops' movement when fording streams and climbing forested hills. While New York's Highlanders left their kilts and bonnets at home, they were ill-dressed for combat in tartan trews (trousers). The Emerald Guards of Mobile, Alabama,

wore bright green uniforms, and the Granville Rifles of North Carolina wore red flannel shirts and black trousers. A mixture of blue and gray in the uniforms of both armies was confusing. When the Orleans Grand Battalion of New Orleans, wearing blue uniforms, went into battle at Shiloh, they were mistaken by other Confederates as the enemy and fired upon.

THE BLUE AND THE GRAY

The fanciful uniforms were quickly discarded in both armies in favor of the more practical blue and gray. The legendary 'butternut gray' of the Confederates was an accident, it was nearest to the official cadet gray that could be achieved by home-made dyes when regular dyes could not be brought through the Union blockade. Although the double breasted jacket remained the official uniform for both sides, it was usually discarded in the field in favor of the more practical single-breasted style. Soldiers of both armies wore wool uniforms with frock coats or short jackets all year, a morale-sapping experience in hot summer weather in the South. The roadside often became strewn with abandoned clothing and equipment on a hot march. Even the popular kepi-style hat was found to be less practical than softer hats. In the winter, the soldiers wore overcoats or capes, but these were not always available to the men in the Confederate army. The men lived, marched, fought and were buried in the same uniforms. Annual cash payments were made to soldiers to replace lost or damaged components.

INSIGNIA AND BADGES

Rank insignia was slightly different in the two armies, but the table of organization was basically the same. The Confederate army

Right Corps badges, first employed in 1862 and made official a year later, were useful in keeping soldiers in the proper units. Divisions within corps were assigned different colors, as this 1865 poster shows.

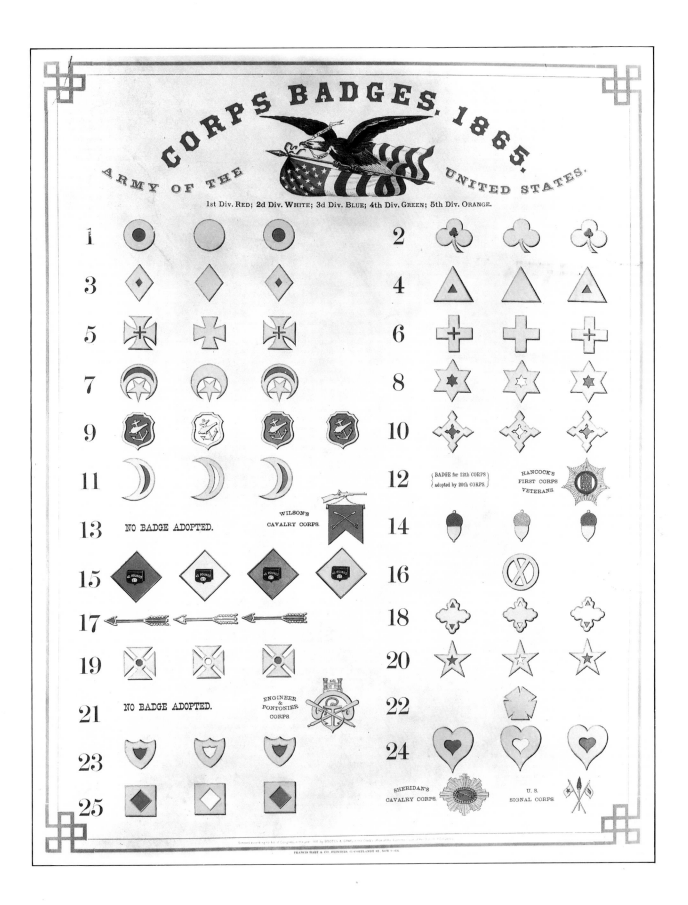

was created, mostly by West Point graduates, on the same pattern as the United States army. Union officers wore shoulder straps showing their rank, while noncommissioned officers wore chevrons on their sleeves. Senior Confederate officers sported collar insignia and wore sleeve piping.

Corps badges originated in the Union army in an attempt to alleviate confusion and identify stragglers. They first appeared in General Philip Kearny's Third Corps in 1862 and were made standard almost a year later by General Joseph Hooker, who assigned colors to divisions within each corps. Designs ranged from simple round patches to Maltese crosses, acorns and hearts.

In the first wave of enthusiasm, thousands enlisted for short periods without concern for rewards. However, as those short enlistments ended , it became necessary to offer inducements for longer periods of time and this lead to abuses. Girls who loved uniforms helped recruitment, made imaginative displays of flags and gave patriotic speeches at holiday picnics and in public squares. Bounties provided one of the most effective inducements, and sizable sums were offered. Some men made a career of enlisting, skipping out and then re-enlisting under another name many times over. Although a large number were caught, the practice continued.

States generally took the lead in forming new units. In most States, however, anyone who was persuasive or clever enough could form his own unit. Usually these were companies but ambitious individuals, who had enough prestige and money to get things started in a community, sometimes formed whole regiments.

The North, with its larger population and immigration, had an advantage under the volunteer system. The United States Congress authorized increasing the Regular Army to 40,000, but Federal recruiting officers were so ineffective that it never totaled more than 26,000 at any time during the war. Regular officers were appointed to most major field commands but were seldom placed in

Regulation uniforms of the two armies were similar, but of different colors. Union militia in gray uniforms and Confederate units in blue created confusion on some battlefields.

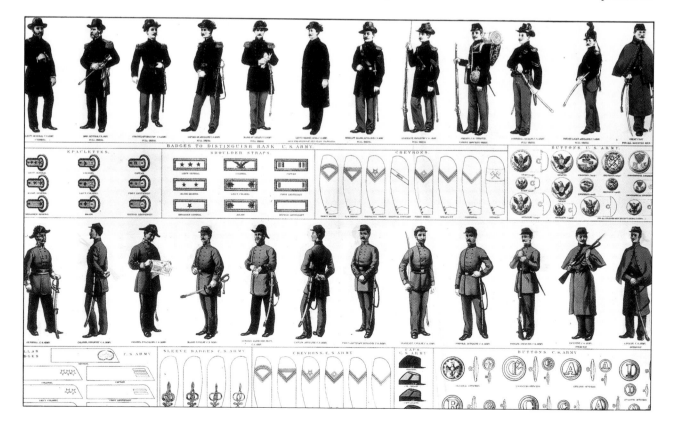

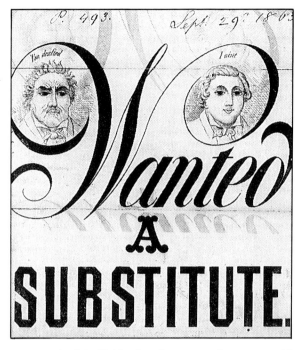

command of individual volunteer units or used to train volunteers.

INTRODUCTION OF CONSCRIPTION

Although the heritage of volunteering was strong in America – and was producing armies larger than the country had ever known before – it soon became obvious that even with financial inducements, the volunteer system could not provide the ever-increasing number of soldiers and sailors needed to satisfy the insatiable demands of war. Conscription, enacted first by the Confederate Congress on April 16, 1862, and a year later by the Union, added a new dimension to the war.

The Confederate draft, the first national conscription law in American history, authorized impressment of all males between 18 and 35 (later extended from 17 to 50) not legally exempt. The exception list was extensive, however, with State governors making liberal use of their powers to confer exemptions to satisfy domestic political needs. Furthermore, substitutes could be hired by those who could afford them – a controversial feature of the Act that was not cancelled until 1864.

The Union draft law permitted buying an exemption for $300, the amount usually paid as bounty. As a result, the initial draft call raised $15 million for the Federal Treasury. The law also allowed hiring a substitute, which created a perception (also prevalent in the South) that this was a 'rich man's war and a poor man's fight.'

RESISTING CONSCRIPTION

The laws were so unpopular that organized resistance movements came into being. Georgia's Governor Joe Brown made extensive use of his privilege of granting exemptions and even challenged the constitutionality of the law in court. The Federal draft sparked off serious riots in New York, Hartford, and other cities. Troops had to be pulled back from the fighting front to put down rioting in New York, which lasted for five days and cost 1,200 lives, many of them black.

Although many conscripts made good soldiers, just as many resented being forced to serve and were of questionable military value. Volunteers denigrated the conscripts so badly that serious tensions arose at times, and conscripts returned the dislike. Many hired substitutes, some of them immigrants seeking a start in a new country, performed admirable service, others, however quickly deserted.

The conscription laws permitted men to hire or send substitutes to the war–an unpopular arrangement that was attacked in song and in print on both sides. This Confederate drawing ridicules the quality of men provided by the system in the North.

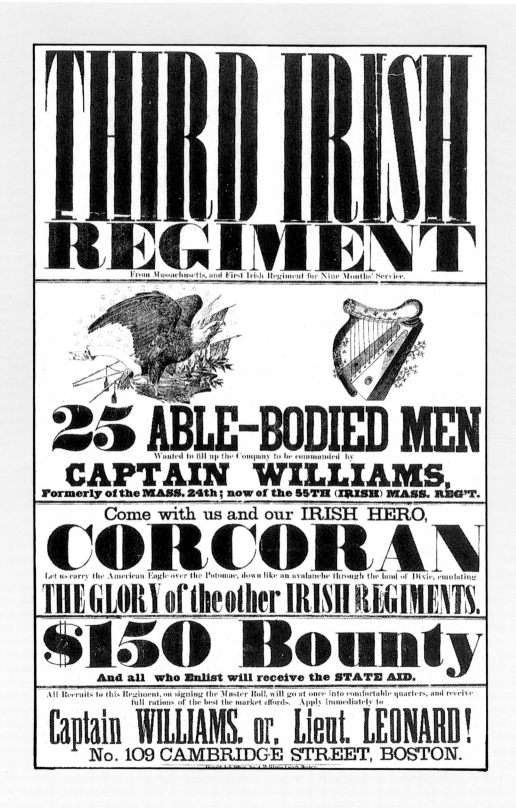

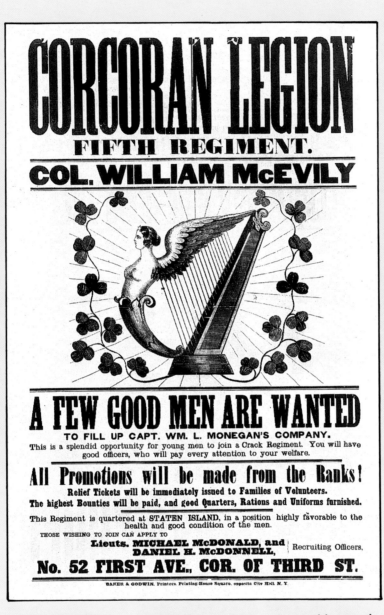

Volunteer armies fought the early years of the Civil War. Men were enticed by the promise of military glory from the recruiting officers of units such as the Third Irish Regiment of Boston (facing page). The Irish were among the most numerous of the immigrant groups to fight in the Union army, and in general they fought well, justifying William McEvily's claim that his was a 'crack' regiment (above).

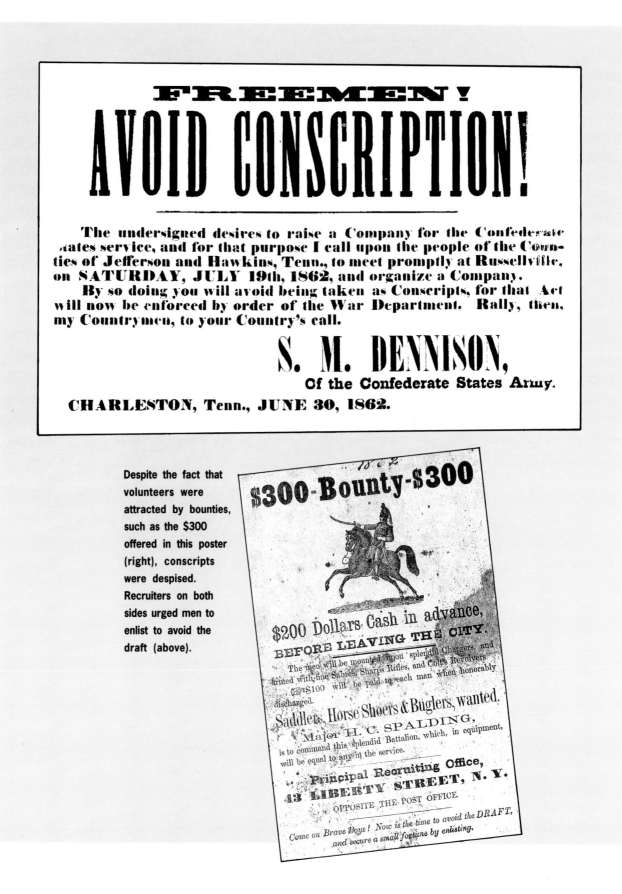

FREEMEN!
AVOID CONSCRIPTION!

The undersigned desires to raise a Company for the Confederate States service, and for that purpose I call upon the people of the Counties of Jefferson and Hawkins, Tenn., to meet promptly at Russellville, on SATURDAY, JULY 19th, 1862, and organize a Company.

By so doing you will avoid being taken as Conscripts, for that Act will now be enforced by order of the War Department. Rally, then, my Countrymen, to your Country's call.

S. M. DENNISON,
Of the Confederate States Army.

CHARLESTON, Tenn., JUNE 30, 1862.

Despite the fact that volunteers were attracted by bounties, such as the $300 offered in this poster (right), conscripts were despised. Recruiters on both sides urged men to enlist to avoid the draft (above).

$300-Bounty-$300

$200 Dollars Cash in advance, BEFORE LEAVING THE CITY.

The men will be mounted upon splendid Chargers, and armed with fine Sabres, Sharps Rifles, and Colt's Revolvers. $100 will be paid to each man when honorably discharged.

Saddlers, Horse Shoers & Buglers, wanted.

Major H. C. SPALDING, is to command this splendid Battalion, which, in equipment, will be equal to any in the service.

Principal Recruiting Office, 43 LIBERTY STREET, N. Y.

OPPOSITE THE POST OFFICE.

Come on Brave Boys! Now is the time to avoid the DRAFT, and secure a small fortune by enlisting.

The men were supposed to receive physicals before entering service, but these were often perfunctory. In some instances, inductees were simply asked by a doctor if they were in good health.

ELECTING OFFICERS

Company officers were elected by the men forming a unit, and so the person organizing the unit frequently was the man chosen to command it. These men naturally had little experience in drilling, much less in directing a unit on the battlefield, and they had to learn right along with those in the ranks. In some instances, officers marched alongside privates to learn drill from experienced sergeants, but most tried to tough it through by reading books, including Hardee's *Tactics* (used by both sides), and by personal bravery. In the Union army, regimental and brigade commanders were elected by the officers of the smaller units. Volunteer units were integrated into armies and corps under the command of professional soldiers appointed by presidents and war departments.

The practice of electing officers prevailed throughout the war. It worked better in the South, which had a strong military tradition, than in the North. Attrition, resignations and weeding out by senior military commanders solved some, but not all, of the worst problems. Incompetence plagued the Union army throughout the war, even at the corps level. Although some Confederate senior commanders were accused of incompetence, in general the quality of leadership was superior to that in the Union army.

The officers were a mixed lot. Vanity, politics, even personal greed interfered with the performance of their duties. Hot tempers sometimes created ludicrous – sometimes dangerous – situations; differences over authority or remarks about courage led to disputes and sometimes to duels. Union General William 'Old Bill' Nelson was shot by a general whom he had slapped during an argument. in September 1883, Confederate Brigadier General John S. Marmaduke challenged Brigadier General Lucius M. Walker to a duel and killed him; Walker allegedly had impugned his courage.

Although some officers were genuinely popular with their troops, most were regarded by enlisted men in both armies as pampered, overbearing, and dictatorial. Even the best officers sometimes were affected. In June 1863, General Nathan Bedford Forrest was shot by an aggrieved subordinate; but he stabbed his assailant fatally and himself recovered to continue to lead his cavalry in bold forays against the Union.

The war had a leveling effect. As it wore on, those who remained alive began advancing through the ranks so that many who enlisted as privates became lieutenants and higher-ranking officers.

TRAINING CAMPS AND LIFE AT THE FRONT

Once they entered national service, soldiers began a cycle of adventure and boredom so equally deadly that many wondered which would kill them first. The trip from home to their first assignment was exciting, partly because many had never traveled such distances on trains and steamships. A patriotic send off, with flags flying, bands playing, and friends and neighbors cheering, added to the romantic notions of war. The department of the Sixth Michigan Regiment from Kalamazoo rated a community celebration; the enlisted men rode in first-class railroad cars and the officers enjoyed the luxury of the directors' plush private car. New Orleans's Washington Artillery Battalion, which comprised men of wealth and high standing in the community, and served with great distinction throughout the war, was hailed at almost every stop along the long train trip to Richmond. But some new soldiers got a better introduction into what military life would be like; a San Augustine, Texas, company had to march several days to Alexandria, Louisiana, before it could ride eastward to Richmond on a train.

Camp life, whether for purposes of training or for duty, meant boring idleness and tedious chores. The men lived in tents in summer

Nathan Bedford Forrest, one of the Confederacy's most effective raiders, enlisted as a private in 1861. By 1862 he was a brigadier general: in 1863 he became a major general. At the end of the war he was a lieutenant general. He returned to farming and business after the war and died in 1877.

CONFEDERATE BUGLER.

An average soldier answered 19 bugle calls a day in camp; a cavalry or artillery soldier answered up to 25. Bugle calls on both sides were almost exactly the same.

and, when possible, drafty log huts in winter while they shed their disorganized civilian ways and learned the sometimes senseless but organized routine of the military life. Their days were occupied twice-a-day drilling, policing of the camp area, guard duty (the most despised of all activities), parading, inspections, and personal care. In the Union army, as many as 26 bugle calls might summon soldiers to duty during a day, although a dozen calls were normal for infantry, a few more for artillery and cavalry.

Since recreational activities were not officially sponsored, except in rare instances, soldiers in camp made their own diversions according to their interests. They read newspapers and cheap novels when they were available; gambled; played various sports in warm weather, and engaged in snowball fights in winter; staged impromptu theater performances; wrote letters home; sang traditional or off-color songs and recited poetry around the camp fires; organized literary associations and listened to band concerts. When they were near towns and cities, those who could attended lodge meetings, concerts and watched prize fights. They sometimes stole off to 'liberate' a chicken or pig from a nearby farmer. In Confederate army, soldiers occasionally would work nostalgically on a nearby farm during off-duty hours. Many Union divisions printed their own newspapers, an activity that was rare in the South because paper was in short supply. Cavalry units added horse racing and shooting contests to the usual activities.

Camp life was just as deadly as combat because soldiers from the farms had not been exposed to communicable diseases – such as measles, whooping cough and typhoid fever – or other diseases such as malaria and dysentery. A single measles epidemic at Camp Moore, training center in North Louisiana, killed 600 to 700 recruits.

FURLOUGHS AND FOOD

Furloughs were rare. Most often they were given to ill or wounded soldiers for convalescence at home, or before reporting for new duty after being exchanged. In the Union army, they sometimes were given for political reasons; General Sherman furloughed thousands of Indiana soldiers in 1863 so they could return home and vote for Lincoln in his bid for re-election. As both North and South recognized, any army marches on its stomach. In camps, company cooks generally prepared rations. When possible, bread was prepared by regimental cooks. The Union bakery ovens of Fort Monroe, Virginia, were famous during the 1862 Peninsular Campaign; and for a time, vaults in the Capitol Building in Washington were converted into ovens that produced

16,000 loaves a day in 1861. In the field, soldiers prepared their own food or in messes (small groups).

Official regulations in both armies prescribed adequate food, but the men did not always receive what the regulations stated. In the Union army, this was a matter of expediency and quality; in the Confederate, the result of shortages. Prescribed diets in the two armies were similar, but each included regional variations and preferences in methods of preparation. Staples were fresh and salt beef and pork (the latter were sometimes so briny

Below When soldiers were on the move, they cooked for themselves - not always with great success.

Right Patent medicines could not solve the enormous health problem that confronted both sides. Disease killed far more soldiers than bullets.

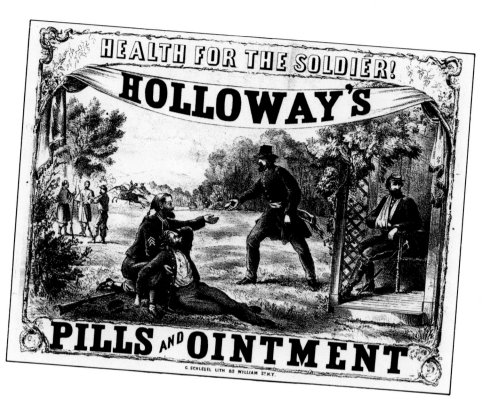

Right An effort was made to keep soldiers in the field in touch with their families, but most postal facilities were modest compared to this large Headquarters, Army of the Potomac, tent.

that soldiers soaked their rations in streams overnight to desalinate them), hardtack, softbread when in camp, and coffee and sugar, which experienced soldiers carried mixed together in cloth bags. Tobacco was prized.

Cornbread and beef were the mainstays of Johnny Reb's diet, supplemented as often as possible by pork, peas, flour, hardtack, potatoes, rice, molasses, coffee, sugar and fresh vegetables. Shortages were aggravated by the poor quality of food when it was available.

Troops and civilians shared hardships and good fortune. On one occasion, soldiers defending Richmond volunteered to share their rations with the poor of the city. Richmond returned the generosity while it was being besieged by sending a New Year's Day turkey to the soldiers, who drew lots to see which men should enjoy it.

Packages from home, usually shared with buddies, supplemented the fare of both armies. Union packages naturally were better stocked than those in the Confederacy, which generally contained only eggs, fresh or dried apples, apple butter, preserves and cakes. Sutlers, or merchants with semiofficial status, accompanied the Union armies and sold food and personal items to the soldiers at inflated

Below A horse-drawn delivery system offers a variety of newspapers to soldiers in a Union camp near Culpeper, Virginia. Newspapers were snapped up by soldiers when they were available.

prices. No sutlers were attached to the Confederate army, although itinerant merchants visited camps on occasion.

Equipment carried by soldiers varied according to their experience and the conditions. Essentials included blankets and rubber mat; canteen; dipper, tin, plate, knife, fork and spoon for mess; limited numbers of candles for lighting during winter encampment, often

Left In winter quarters, Civil War soldiers built wooden huts like these or log cabins to protect themselves. These soldiers made theirs more homelike by nameing it 'Pine Cottage'.

jammed into the mounting ring of a bayonet stuck into the ground; and personal grooming and sewing kits called 'housewives.'

TRAINING FOR BATTLE

Soldiers of both nations received inadequate training. The initial units to be called up were militia, which supposedly had been drilled and schooled, but their training quickly proved to be flawed. The mistakes made at First Manassas by both sides showed how green the troops were. Even as late as February 1862, when 10,000 Union soldiers overwhelmed Roanoke Island, North Carolina, a battery of Confederate cannon could not be fired because none of the men on the site knew how

Below Two soldiers take a boxing stance, but it was probably just a pose for the cameraman. Organized sports were rare in Civil War camps.

to service the weapons. A hastily summoned instructor from headquarters was giving instructions when the Union attack came.

Union and Confederate training camps were set up early in the war, but jurisdictional disputes limited their effectiveness. On both sides, States retained a major responsibility for training the soldiers they recruited. This consisted primarily of drilling at makeshift campsites, such as fairgrounds, often with wooden guns. When real weapons were available, they were often obsolete or unworkable. Infantrymen received basic instruction in loading musket or rifle, but seldom got

The Cavalry engagement.
Battle of Hickory Point K. T. Sept. 13, 18

Left A minor cavalry skirmish is depicted in a sketch by Samuel Reader. The sketch gives a good indication of the confusion of an engagement.

Below Firing a cannon–sketch drawn on the spot by Samuel Reader.

enough practice to master the complicated technique. Some units received training in firing by file or by company, but the availability of ammunition for practice was limited. Sometimes shooting contests were held, and an effort was made to improve accuracy, but marksmanship was never good during the war. Bayonet drill was perfunctory; an hour for an entire brigade was not unusual.

In the Union, Federal training began when the soldiers reached large assembly points near Washington or at Cairo in Illinois or other places. These camps gave only rudimentary instruction in drill and the use of shoulder firearms. Cavalry and artillery units generally drilled on foot until they reached the Federal camps, where they received horses and heavy weapons. Cavalry training was long and difficult. It required hours of mounted and

S.J.R.

Left The role of cavalry changed during the Civil War. Instead of charging into the ranks of infantry and fighting with swords and pistols, cavalrymen used their mobility to seize key points and then fought with rifles.

Below Medical care for soldiers was primitive and disorganized. A strong instinct for self-preservation led many soldiers to avoid the doctors and treat themselves. In this sketch by Samuel Reader, Tom McElroy takes his medicine.

unmounted practice, as well as training in the care and treatment of horses. Easterners who entered the cavalry to escape the infantry often failed to take care of their mounts and ended up on foot or back in camp.

Servicing an artillery piece was a complicated procedure that involved a team of men performing distinctive but coordinated tasks. If it were to be effective, there had to be considerable practice in maneuvering and unlimbering guns and in the aiming and firing. Training included target practice, using a tree or stump when such were available. In one instance, Battery B of the Rhode Island Light Artillery almost hit a town while aiming at a tree. The Tenth Massachusetts provoked the anger of a farmer by sighting on his pig pen.

The soldiers were supposed to receive further training in their permanent units, and often they did. Training continued during lax periods after units had been sent to the front, but this usually amounted to nothing more than refreshers in close-order drill. Officers who had to instruct were often inexperienced in the fundamentals themselves.

Despite the intentions of the training system, most soldiers went into battle ill prepared. On both sides, there were instances when green soldiers were sent into combat within a week or two of induction, some without any training at all. Many an infantryman, on the eve of battle, searched for an experienced comrade who would show him which end of a bullet to insert into the barrel of his rifle. It has been established that half of those who served had never fired their weapons until they reached the field. There, the most terrible teacher of all – combat itself – awaited them with a vengeance.

Left The end of the war in 1865 left row upon row of cannon, mortars and other field weapons, some captured from Confederates, some no longer needed by Union armies.

5

The Shenandoah Valley is 'Stonewall's Valley.' No other general is so closely identified with it, and not even Lee rivaled Jackson for the affection of its inhabitants. People sent letters to Confederate Secretary of War Judah P. Benjamin demanding that only Jackson defend the valley and then filled the ranks of Stonewall Brigade with their sons. Mennonites who refused to fight sent wagons with supplies to his army. Citizens of towns frequently occupied by Federals turned out on their porches to wave and cheer whenever the Confederates returned. Jackson lived up to their trust in him; his 1862 Valley Campaign 'whupped' an opponent three times his size so badly that Union armies were wary of valley defenders long after Jackson's death.

Jackson possessed an odd sort of charisma. He was dour and aloof, a quiet man whose life centered on his family and his Presbyterian religion. He was a gentle, affectionate father and his religion pervaded everything he did.

Stonewall's Valley

He once said that 'every thought should be a prayer.' He shared Lee's belief that duty was a calling, not an elective. Jackson was a professor at Virginia Military Institute in Lexington, Virginia, when the Civil War started, but volunteered for active duty immediately. His first command, at Harper's Ferry, was a rag-tag group of undisciplined newly enlisted civilians known as the Army of the Shenandoah, who at first resented his harsh discipline and dedication to year-round warfare. Jackson remained close to his men and suffered along with them, so that soldiers waking with snow on their blankets in the mountains of West Virginia might see their commander rise from the ground a few feet from them. If they had grumbled about their condition, and Jackson had heard it, he did not remonstrate. Neither did he relent; soldiers were supposed to endure hardships. They soon learned that combat and comfort did not coexist in Jackson's army and, while many thought him peculiar, they quickly came to trust and respect him. Jackson reciprocated by regarding no task beyond their capabilities.

THE STONEWALL BRIGADE

This group, the 1st Virginia, became the Stonewall Brigade, which fought with great distinction from First Manassas to Appomattox. The men cheered when Jackson rode past them, even on secret marches, and revered him like a father even after his death. Strangely, Jackson's most famous nickname never appealed to his troops; he was 'Old Jack' to most of them, and sometimes even 'Old Blue Light' or 'Hickory.' He was even known as 'Square Box' because of his large shoe size, but men of the 1st Brigade seldom referred to him as 'Stonewall.'

After First Manassas, where he acquired the nickname that helped make him a legend in his own time, Jackson was ordered to take command of Confederate forces in the Shenandoah Valley, which were part of the Army of Northern Virginia but operated independently most of the time. He was reluctant to leave the Stonewall Brigade, and a farewell address made at the request of his soldiers told something about him and his men. Rising in his stirrups before the massed brigade, he shouted:

'In the Army of the Shenandoah you were the First Brigade! In the Army of the Potomac you were the First Brigade! In the Second Corps of the army you are the First Brigade! You are the First Brigade in the affection of your general, and I hope by your future deeds and bearing you will be handed down as the First Brigade in this our Second War of Independence. Farewell!'

TRIUMPH IN VIRGINIA

Jackson's task in the Valley of Virginia was formidable. When he arrived at Winchester, he had only a force of militia to confront 27,000 Union troops spread out in western Virginia and another 18,000 camped on the banks of the Potomac River. Jackson's separation from his brigade was brief, for it was soon sent to reinforce him, bringing the size of his force to 4,000 men.

Jackson's tactics for the defense of the valley were so masterful they were studied

The only house 'Stonewall' Jackson ever owned is now a shrine to his memory in Lexington, Virginia, where he taught and where he is buried.

(along with some others from the Civil War) in the military academies of Europe for many generations. Well into the twentieth century, military scholars debated the campaigns in print in Great Britain, France and Germany. Field Marshal Erwin Rommel, who won fame in World War II as the 'Desert Fox,' was among those who visited the valley in the 1930s to study the subject at first-hand. Jackson's interest in holding the western counties of Virginia, which would break away during the war and form the State of Western Virginia, showed a sense of strategy as well. He could see those valleys pointing straight at the cities of Pittsburgh, Harrisburg and Philadelphia in Pennsylvania.

Jackson employed all his knowledge and wits in the 1862 Valley Campaign. He had 16,000 soldiers to counter three Union armies with a total of 65,000 men between them. His greatest danger was that the armies would unite against him, and his movements were designed to prevent that from happening. Jackson moved even before Brigadier General Richard S. Ewell's division arrived from east of the mountains to reinforce him. To deceive the Federals, he marched his units eastward through the Blue Ridge Mountains to Mechum's River station, where he put them on trains back to Staunton. He then moved northward along the Valley Pike, but veered westward to McDowell to rout two Union divisions. (This battlefield is largely intact, but is on private property thus not developed.)

'Old Jack' resumed his march up the Valley Pike to New Market, then turned east and disappeared into the small valley between the Massanutten and Blue Ridge Mountains. After a forced march, including 26 miles in one 16-hour day, he fell on Union forces at Port Royal, threatening to trap Major General Nathaniel P. Banks in the valley. Jackson's men marched all night and went into battle at Winchester with only an hour's rest. When they turned the Union right, the Federal line began to crumble, despite Bank's personal attempt to rally his men. The withdrawal soon turned into a Manassas-style rout, but the exhausted

Sometimes called the Great Valley or 'Stonewall's Valley' in recognition of his extraordinary exploits there, the Shenandoah Valley is first and foremost the 'daughter of the stars', the description first chosen by the Indians who were the first to see the fullness of the night skies and the beauty of the landscape.

Confederates could not pursue their defeated foes adequately. They advanced all the way to Harper's Ferry, impeded only by a short-lived skirmish at Charlestown.

Rebel control of the northern Shenandoah was brief because Jackson had to pull back to meet another threat from Major General John C. Fremont, with 16,000 troops, and Brigadier General James Shields, moving down from Manassas with 10,000. Cross Keys and Port Royal were two parts of a single battle, the first phase at Cross Keys featuring a furious counter-attack by Ewell's troops which punished Fremont. That success emboldened Jackson, who decided to hold off Fremont and attack Shields at Port Royal, then turn and deliver a decisive blow to Fremont. When the day was over, the Federals were in flight and the valley once again was in Confederate hands. Jackson's loss was the greatest of his five-week campaign – 800 men.

On June 17, Jackson's army answered a call to help defend Richmond against McClelland's Peninsular Campaign.

JACKSON'S 'FOOT CAVALRY'

Professional military interest in Jackson's 1862 Valley Campaign centers primarily on his mobility and deception. He moved infantry so fast his troops became known as 'foot cavalry.' His men were lean and lightly equipped; when Jackson had them leave their packs behind they knew he meant business. One historian believes his troops carried nothing but essentials, and preferred to carry their rations in their stomachs. Jackson was relentless in pursuing an objective, and he personally prodded malingerers. The sight of Jackson inspired both hope and dread in tired, hungry men, but even this personal bond would not have sufficed. Jackson's edge was that both he and his men knew the terrain, every wind gap, every creek. They had played and hunted on the hillsides and they had farmed the lowlands. They had excellent intelligence because they were among friends and neighbors who responded truthfully to the questions they asked. Furthermore, they knew how to use their advantage. More than once, Jackson moved his men away from his objective, only to turn up like magic before a surprised enemy.

The oldest state-supported military college in the nation, Virginia Military Institute is a National Historic District. The Cadet Barracks were built in the mid-nineteenth century in the Gothic Revival style.

SURVIVING MEMORIAL

Winchester is especially beautiful in late spring, when the surrounding apple orchards are in bloom, valley wildlife is brilliant and the distant hills are a hazy green. The 'Gateway to the Shenandoah Valley' bustles then more than at any other time of the year, as preparations are made for the annual Apple Blossom Festival and the arrival of the new influx of tourists along Interstate 81 and U.S. Route 11, which roughly follow the historic Valley Pike. During the Civil War, the influx was much more deadly. Winchester was the scene of more fighting than any other place in Virginia save Richmond. While war visited other places occasionally, it arrived in Winchester every year with the robins. The town changed hands more than 75 times, four of them in one fateful day. Understandably, only a shell of the neat, prosperous market community remained at the end of the war.

Jackson's headquarters, a handsome brick structure atop a knoll on North Braddock Street, holds a museum dedicated to the Confederate chieftain. Some of his personal effects are on display, along with other memorabilia.

Winchester, home to the famous Apple Blossom Festival, was taken and retaken 70 times during the Civil War–13 times in a single day.

6

O n to Richmond!' was the North's battle-cry in the East, but it was easier said than done. In their fortified line around Washington, Federal forces were only 100 miles from the Confederate capital over easy terrain with good roads. After First Manassas, however, it might as well have been the moon.

Richmond was in transition at the start of the Civil War. It was both a traditional Southern market-town and a developing industrial and rail center, with a sizable immigrant population. It was at the same time the capital of the cradle of constitutional government , where memories of George Washington and Thomas Jefferson were strong. The old still dominated the new. Although the iron industry alone employed 1,500 workers and achieved $2 million in business annually, planters, not industrialists, dominated the life of the city's 37,000 people. Whigs controlled the government, but Democrats had an intellectual following, as witnessed by the fact

The Peninsular Campaign

that the Richmond *Enquirer* was frequently called the 'Democratic bible.'

THE CONFEDERATE CAPITAL

Life in Richmond changed abruptly when Virginia joined the Confederacy. The city became a military center, with troops mustering, marching and massing. Relocation of the capital of the Confederacy to Richmond brought new civil servants of all grades, legislators and Cabinet officers into the city, creating shortages of housing and supplies. They were the vanguard of more than 70,000 who ultimately would work for the Confederate government. The city's 'floating population' overtaxed the hotels so badly that residents took temporary visitors into their homes.

Confederate President Jefferson Davis brought a new sense of urgency to a city used to leisurely living. Large crowds gathered on the streets when he arrived; within a few hours, he was on horseback inspecting the troops. A government which had been organized in Montgomery, Alabama, set up shop quickly and began issuing purchase orders, letters of marque and military commissions, dispatching commissioners to foreign countries and performing other tasks required of a sovereign nation.

The Confederate government also brought to Richmond a flood of 'pernicious characters'—speculators, gamblers and lawless rogues who made thievery, garroting and murder 'nightly employments.' A guard system was set up to protect the city at night, and people were challenged on almost every street corner. Gambling houses operated on Main Street and elsewhere, while brothels operated more or less openly. A 'Stranger's Guide' which appeared in a Richmond newspaper observed that 'very large numbers of men...frequently a very large number of bar-rooms in the city.' Soldiers appeared regularly in court on charges of drunkenness, beating women and attempted rape.

Women followed their husbands and fiancees to the city. One was a young woman from the Deep South en route to First Manassas because her betrothed had been ordered away before their wedding and she went to find him before it was too late. A young lieutenant from South Carolina, rejected by the girl he loved, killed himself by jumping out of a sixth-storey window.

Richmond played a larger role in the wartime Confederacy than any other city. It was not only the Confederate and State capitals, but was also a city of refuge for civilians driven from their homes by the war. It was a hospital center for the treatment of wounded; soldiers from all over the South said 'God bless the women of Virginia' for their saving work and enlifting presence in the hospitals.

Richmond became a prisoner-of-war center after the success at First Manassas. Union soldiers captured in that battle became the vanguard of thousands who would occupy crowded, makeshift quarters, and conditions became intolerable after the Union halted exchanges of prisoners. The citizens of Richmond consoled themselves that conditions there were no better than those being experienced by their own soldiers in the field.

RICHMONDERS AT WAR

Despite the influx of people, Richmonders remained clannish. They were protective, as they always have been, of the favorites in their society. The fall of strategic Roanoke Island, North Carolina, was a tragedy of the first order for the Confederacy, and General Henry A. Wise came under criticism for the defeat. Richmonders were confident it was not his fault since he had insisted it could be held only with reinforcements and had been ill at the time of the invasion. An investigation ultimately placed the blame on the then Secretary of War, Judah P. Benjamin.

Civilian life revolved around the military effort throughout the city's existence as capital of the Confederacy. Political, social, literary, scientific and religious circles were absorbed in the war. Writers of both prose and poetry were engrossed in war themes, and poets especially produced commendable works. Schools closed when classes were empty or

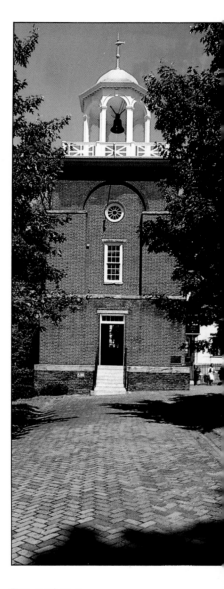

First used as a guardhouse, this 1824 bell tower on the grounds of the State Capitol in Richmond now provides additional government office space.

professors were not available. Scientists worked to develop new weapons and improve old ones. Editors and ministers appealed to both God and the public for assistance; some members of both groups felt so strongly they joined the army. The local government sent out agents in an effort to purchase food.

Children, who echoed the politics of their parents, reproached other children because their parents were 'Yankees' or expressed dislike for Great Britain and France because they did not recognize the Confederacy or come to its assistance.

Not everyone approved of the Confederacy, however. Union sympathizers spread graffiti on the walls of buildings, calling 'Union men to the rescue' and 'Now is the time to rally round the Old Flag' and 'God Bless the Stars and Stripes.' Occasional arrests were made and Unionists often banded together to protect each other. Those suspected of 'incomprehensible neutrality' were commonly known but some innocent people no doubt were unjustly tarred.

Attempts were made to continue usual pursuits. New Year's Day 1861 was bright and balmy, and President Davis's New Year's reception for government officials, military officers and civilian guests was a gala affair. This was the first New Year for the new Confederate nation and the people of Richmond were impressed by the grace and dignity, amiability, nobility of character and the absence of hauteur of their new president. Davis was especially taken by three children brought to the reception by their parents in defiance of protocol. Governor John Letcher also entertained, minus the usual champagne

Above Confederate General Joseph E. Johnston understood the capabilities of his army better than the political leaders in Richmond.

Below President Lincoln poses with General George B. McClellan and his staff after the Battle of Antietam halted the Confederate invasion of Maryland.

Victory did not prevent McClellan's dismissal.

which had been cut off by the Union blockade. The giant cut glass crystal punch bowl was filled with a steaming beverage derived from apples, while egg nog was also available.

Conditions steadily deteriorated. Holiday week at the close of 1861 was 'sad.' Supplies were short and it was patriotic to conserve, in recognition of the fact that the fare of the soldier in the field was not as bountiful as the turkey and fixings on the home table. Knitting for soldiers replaced pleasant evenings of chatting and repartee.

The nation needed new holidays. February 22, already observed as George Washington's birthday, was adopted as the national day of the Confederate States of America. Its first observance in 1862 was a formal occasion, with carriages bringing people into the city for a week prior to the event. The large square in front of the Capitol was crowded, but the address, like most delivered in those days, was heard by only those people within earshot of the speaker's voice.

Lincoln was kept aware of the conditions in the Confederate capital by a rapidly growing spy network. A few Union spies were discovered, including a War Department clerk who was hanged and his wife, who was expelled to the North, but some residents thought the attitude of officials toward spying was too lenient. When a woman attempted to send information to the North on how the man of the household in which she was a guest, who at the time was in Great Britain on assignment for the Confederacy, could be arrested, she was held captive in the infirmary of St. Francis instead of a prison.

THE PENINSULAR CAMPAIGN

Obviously, Richmond was a prime Federal target and Lincoln chose General George B. McClellan to build and field a Union army

General Lee was respected by both sides as a battle commander. He donned his best uniform for the surrender negotiations at Appomattox Court House, Virginia.

The Lincoln Gun, mounted on the ramparts of Fort Monroe, Virginia, in this 1864 photo, could hurl a 300-pound projectile a distance of four miles. The dismounted cannon now is displayed on the parade ground. It was the first gun cast by the Rodman process (in 1860) and was at that time the world's largest gun.

that could take the city. 'Little Mac' however, was better at building than marching, and devised a strategy for indirect action which would force the South to submit through control of strategic railroad junctions. He trained and paraded his troops, but he did not hasten to commit them to combat.

McClellan's success at turning the rabble which ran at First Manassas into the well-schooled and disciplined Army of the Potomac helped him overcome his natural caution and encouraged him into action. His optimism rapidly waned when his army of 150,000 was reduced to 105,000 men because Lincoln insisted on retaining 37,000 men, formed into the Army of Virginia, to defend Washington.

(In this campaign and others, McClellan over-estimated the size of the forces opposing him and doubted he had enough men of his own.) After continual prodding by Lincoln, McClellan set in motion a plan to approach Richmond indirectly through the Virginia Peninsula, an historic sliver of land lying between the James and York Rivers.

The Peninsular Campaign was an attempt to follow a line of least resistance. McClellan's plan had certain advantages. The rivers and naval superiority would protect his flanks during the advance on Richmond. Fort Monroe at the tip of the Peninsula, which, like Fort Sumter, was part of the coastal defenses constructed after the War of 1812, remained in Union hands to anchor a secure supply line. The Peninsula route reduced the distance on land to Richmond by 30 miles and was only lightly defended during the period when he formulated his plan.

Intermittent skirmishing had been indecisive, however; the first land battle of the war occurred when 4,000 untested Federals failed to dislodge 1,500 equally green Confederates at Big Bethel in Hampton. Furthermore, the slightest resistance heightened McClellan's anxiety. He moved slowly and cautiously; a Confederate line of trenches, dams and forts anchored on Yorktown and extending across the Peninsula delayed the Federal advance until Confederate General Joseph E. Johnston could bring 60,000 troops south from the Manassas line. Johnston's fighting retreat along the Peninsula included a one-day battle at Williamsburg, which enabled the bulk of his forces to settle into position and make ready for Richmond.

The fighting for Richmond began at Fair Oaks, and the intensity of the Seven Days Campaign that followed is witnessed by the national cemetery at near by Seven Pines, on the Williamsburg Road (U.S. Route 60). General Johnston was wounded in his attack on McClellan, and General Robert E. Lee replaced him. It was one of the most significant events of the war; as one historian has said, Lee in command was worth another army in the field.

LEE TAKES COMMAND

McClellan's army could hear the church bell ringing in Richmond, but Lee took the initiative with an imaginative and daring plan. McClellan's forces were divided by the rain-swollen Chickahominy River, which made his right flank under Brigadier General Fitz John Porter vulnerable. Lee's assault began in the Mechanicsville area northeast of Richmond. Lee watched the initial phase of the battle from the Chickahominy Bluff overlook, just off present U.S. Route 360 (Mechanicsville Road). At Beaver Dam Creek, massed Union artillery and musket fire halted the Confed-

Berkeley Plantation was the home of the Harrison family, which produced two presidents. The farm has been party to many historic moments, from the first Thanksgiving to Civil War battles.

erate attack, but the Confederates were successful at Gaines Mill on the second day. Today, vestiges of shallow Union trenches are visible along the nature trail to Breakthrough Point.

In his first action, Lee used many of the tactics he would employ throughout the remainder of the war. He left a light defensive force between the main enemy army and Richmond and sent the remainder of his army, together with Jackson's troops brought secretly from the valley, against the vulnerable flank. Delays prevented Jackson from arriving in time for the first battle, and the stiff resistance of Porter's units kept Lee from achieving his objective. Nevertheless, Porter's orderly withdrawal began the retrograde action that would take McClellan to the banks of the James River at Harrison's Landing on Berkeley Plantation, from which the army would ultimately be withdrawn. The army camped under the protection of the Union fleet in the river, left more than the Minie-balls and knapsack buckles which buffs with metal detectors seek after spring planting; it was during this time that the General Butterfield wrote the haunting 'Taps'. McClellan used eighteenth-century Berkeley mansion, ancestral home of the Harrison family which produced a signer of the Declaration of Independence and two presidents, as his headquarters, a use that is overshadowed by the other historical aspects of the mansion, now owned by a descendant of a Union bugler in the campaign.

BLOCKADING THE SOUTH

At sea, Union forces already had implemented a version of the Anaconda Plan, which called for occupation of the key points along the coast of the Confederacy. The Northern blockade proclaimed by Lincoln on April 19, less than a week after the fall of Fort Sumter, slowly strangled the foreign trade of the Confederacy and caused privation and hardship among soldiers and civilians alike. Breaking the blockade became a necessity for the South. South and North experimented with

AN INCONCLUSIVE BATTLE AND HISTORY IS CHANGED FOREVER

Nowhere was the disparity of assets during the Civil War more evident than in the naval forces. Not only did the Union possess virtually all of the pre-war Navy, it had an industrial base capable of coping with wartime demands. A massive construction program made the Union navy the most powerful afloat; by the end of the war, it surpassed in number of ships even the greatest maritime power in history, Great Britain.

The Confederacy made a valiant effort to build a navy, but had no hope of achieving parity. An inadequate industrial base forced the Navy Department to improvise. It experimented with many types of vessels, but achieved its best results with ironclads. Fifty were ordered and 22 actually saw service.

The use of ironclads helped compensate for the much larger Union fleets of wooden ships, but the vessels drew too much water and were too unwieldy to be the decisive weapon envisioned by their designers. Many of them performed poorly or broke down in combat because of engine problems.

The best-known Rebel ironclad was the *CSS Virginia*, the resurrected and converted former *USS Merrimack*, which fought only one major battle – with the *USS Monitor*, the 'cheesebox on a raft' designed by John Ericsson.

The battle, one of the most famous naval engagements in history, began on March 8, 1862, when the *Virginia* steamed out of Norfolk under command of Lieutenant George U. Morris to challenge the wooden Union fleet massing in Hampton Roads for General George B. McClellan's approaching Peninsular Campaign to take Richmond, the Confeder-

ate capital. The alarm caused by the easy sinking of the *USS Cumberland* and destruction of the grounded *USS Congress*, two powerful warships, extended all the way to Washington and raised Confederate hopes of breaking the Union blockade.

Fortunately for the Union, the strange-looking *Monitor* arrived at Fortress Monroe during the night, setting the stage for the first battle of ironclads. When the *Virginia* steamed into Hampton Roads the next day to resume destruction of the Union fleet, it was engaged by the *Monitor* in a four-hour battle at close quarters which ranged back and forth in the world's largest natural harbor. For the most part shells bounced off the thick hulls of both ships. Both received some damage, but re-

Above The defenses of the first ironclads were more than adequate protection against the seaborne artillery of the era. During her combat with the CSS Virginia at point-blank range, the USS Monitor suffered little more than dents in her armor plate

mained seaworthy; neither could gain the upper hand.

The shallow-draft *Monitor* retired to its anchorage under the protecting guns of Fort Monroe and the *Virginia* returned to its Norfolk base. They never met again; the *Virginia* was burned when the Confederates abandoned Norfolk and the *Monitor* sank in a storm off the North Carolina coast while being towed to a new base of operations.

The *Monitor* the first ship to mount a revolving turret, was the lead ship of a whole class produced during the war. Sister vessels would serve with distinction in several future engagements.

In other confrontations, the Confederacy used armament of any kind available, including bales of cotton, to strengthen its vessels against superior numbers and armament on Union ships. The cottonclad gunboats *Bayou City* and *Neptune* and the tenders *John F. Carr* and *Lady Gwin*, under army Major Leon Smith, helped recapture Galveston, Texas, on January 1, 1863. Union Commander William B. Renshaw's six wooden gunboats sank one of the cottonclads, but two Union vessels were lost. The others put to sea when Confederate soldiers occupied the city. Cottonclad vessels failed, however, to prevent the occupation of Roanoke Island and Elizabeth City, North Carolina.

Left Unfortunately the vessel was not so well defended against the elements: she eventually sank in a storm off North Carolina. This recent underwater photograph shows her turret, now encrusted with marine life.

ironclad vessels, and the inventions of the two sides met on March 9, 1862, in Hampton Roads. The CSS *Virginia* incorporated the hull of the USS *Merrimack* (burned to the water-line when the Union evacuated Norfolk in April 1861), beneath her above-water structure, which was plated with two inches of armor. The *Monitor*, in contrast, had been built in New York according to a radical design developed by inventor John Ericsson.

VIRGINIA AND MONITOR

Its first day out of Norfolk, the CSS *Virginia* had a field day against the wooden Federal warships anchored off Newport News, sinking the sloop *Cumberland* (part of its anchor chain is on display in Casino Park in Newport News) and destroying the grounded frigate *Congress*. The consternation among Federal naval and army officers exceeded the damage caused by the fighting; unchallenged, the *Virginia* could endanger the Union position on the Peninsula and break the blockade. The arrival of Ericcson's *Monitor* that night brought great relief, and the two iron monsters steamed out next morning to write naval history in the first battle of ironclad warships. The contest was a draw: the *Virginia* was slow, unwieldy and her draft was too deep for shallow water; the *Monitor* was unwieldy, too, had difficulty with her guns and equipment and was subject to flooding. At the end of the day the *Monitor* anchored under the protective guns of Fort Monroe and the *Virginia* returned to Norfolk.

They did not meet again and, although the existence of the *Virginia* inhibited McClellan's use of the James River in his Peninsular Campaign for a while, both the *Virginia* and *Monitor* met inglorious ends. The *Virginia* was sunk to prevent capture when Norfolk was evacuated by Confederate forces only two months after the historic battle of ironclads,

while the *Monitor* sank in a storm off Cape Hatteras. Efforts to locate the *Monitor* failed until, in 1973, modern technology spotted the vessel on the bottom of the ocean.

THE AFTERMATH OF BATTLE

Even the great victory in the Seven Days battles did not produce Confederate exultation. No bells were rung, no cheering mobs formed. People who tried to relax and resume their activities, unhampered by the noises and dangers of nearby warfare, were absorbed by the aftermath. Since many of the soldiers involved in the fighting lived in Richmond, mothers and wives eagerly sought news of their sons and husbands. When an officer rode up to tell a mother her son was alive but that his captain had been killed, the fiancée of the captain, who lived nearby, unhappily overheard the announcement.

Hospitals remained full of sick and wounded, some of them Union soldiers, and more were brought in. Grave diggers were overworked. Too many soldiers died to accord all of them military burial honors, but the ladies of Richmond provided flowers whenever they could. Private houses, whose tenants had fled the city to escape the war, were converted into impromptu hospitals to handle the masses of sick and wounded created by fighting near the city. Citizens volunteered to provide bedding and services, including the preparation of food. Women not only helped the surgeons, but made the men comfortable by reading to them, listening to their stories and providing words of kindness to dying soldiers who worried about their wives and 'little ones' back home.

Captured Union generals were paroled to walk unguarded through the city, while their less fortunate subordinates were herded into Libby Prison.

This cover of the *New York Illustrated News* from 1862 features an engraving of the US sailing frigate *Cumberland* being sunk by the Confederates' ironclad monster, *Merrimac*.

NEW YORK
ILLUSTRATED NEWS.

No. 125.—Vol. V.   NEW-YORK, SATURDAY, MARCH 29, 1862.   PRICE SIX CENTS.

SINKING OF THE UNITED STATES SAILING FRIGATE CUMBERLAND BY THE REBEL IRON-CLAD MONSTER MERRIMAC.—THE CREW OF THE CUMBERLAND FIGHTING TO THE LAST. SKETCHED BY OUR SPECIAL ARTIST. See page 330.

The battle of the Second Manassas from August 29 to September 1, 1862, was not a rerun of the first action, although it was fought over the same terrain. A great deal had changed in the year since two untried armies had met for the first time. The first battle was an isolated event expected to end the war quickly; the second was part of an ongoing campaign that followed the failure of Major General George B. McClellan's Peninsular Campaign. It would prove the genius of Confederate General Robert E. Lee in developing strategy, as well as tactics, and in using deception, and reveal his reluctance to impose his will on others, including recalcitrant generals. The carnival air that preceded the first battle was replaced by determination. The second battle was a contest between grim-faced veterans who saw no glory in war but still believed in their causes.

While the second battle did not produce the 'firsts' of First Manassas, it was just as important—and much larger and more costly. More than 100,000 troops were involved

Second Manassas (Bull Run)

19,514 were killed and wounded—four times the number in the first battle. Confederate victory paved the way for the first Southern invasion of the North.

Confronted with the threat to Richmond posed by the Peninsular Campaign, Confederate forces had pulled back from northern Virginia. Thus, the new Union Army of Virginia under Major General John Pope, numbering 45,000 men, pushed forward to the Rappahannock and Rapidan Rivers in a renewed attempt to reach the Confederate capital. General McClellan's refusal to attack Richmond from a Peninsula base without major reinforcements, after a severe pounding by Lee, led to the abandonment of the Peninsular Campaign and to Lee's decision to attack Pope before the two Union armies could unite. Jackson's division struck Pope's forces in the neat farmlands near Cedar Mountain, five miles south of Culpeper just off present U.S. Route 15. Jackson had won the Battle of Cedar Mountain by the time Lee arrived with fresh forces. Lee then used Jackson's well-known 'foot cavalry,' augmented by additional units, as though it were horse cavalry, sending Jackson with 24,000 men to cut Pope's communications with Washington. Lee, with main body, would follow and unite with Jackson to trap Pope.

It all came together on almost the same spot where the Battle of First Manassas had been fought. Pope, believing he faced only Jackson, threw caution to the wind in an effort to defeat the famous Confederate general and then mistook a tactical withdrawal for retreat. In pursuing Jackson, he was committing his army to the second battle of Manassas.

Union and Confederate forces occupied positions the reverse of their first encounter. Jackson's forces defended a strong position behind an unfinished railroad grade, still partly visible in wooded areas, until Lee's arrival. The heaviest Union assault occurred at a point known as the Deep Cut. Pope threw units piecemeal against Jackson's front, bending it but never breaking it. Jackson's veterans, low on ammunition, threw rocks to help repel one attack. The arrival of forces under Lee formed a V-shaped line with 160-degree angle. Major General James 'Old Pete' Longstreets's masterful use of artillery to support Jackson marked a turning point in the fighting, and when the Confederate wings moved forward they carried everything before them. Fletcher Webster, a grandson of Daniel Webster, died leading the 12th Massachusetts Infantry in the battle.

This time, it was Union soldiers who held Henry Hill, and their stubborn resistance provided the time for Pope's beaten army to retreat across Stone Bridge over Bull Run to the prepared defenses at Centreville. Behind the Centreville line, Washington was defended solely by a ring of 68 hastily constructed earthen forts.

WASHINGTON–BUCOLIC AND BUSTLING

Before the war, the national capital of Washington reflected its proximity to the Southern States in both population and outlook. The Southern drawl was more prominent than the sharper tones of the northeast and midwest on the streets and in the salons frequented by a structured, status-conscious society. Northerners often felt a little strange amid the Southern culture of the city.

The war did not change the atmosphere overnight. Although Southerners who left in droves for the Confederacy, including the senators and representatives of seceding States, were replaced by the aggressive and uncompromising Abolitionists of the new administration of Abraham Lincoln, many of the permanent residents of the city were Southerners by origin and temperament. Citizens of the border slave States, while remaining loyal to the Union, were sympathetic toward the Southern cause.

The first troops from New York to arrive to defend the capital, in advance of any fighting in the area, were met either with indifference or hostility by the public. Southern sympathizers naturally resented their presence, but others fumed at the inconveniences caused by the sudden influx of soldiers and civilians and

Union General John Pope was so confident at the Battle of Second Manassas that he mistook a realignment of Confederate forces for retreat and claimed a victory. The next day, he was decisively defeated.

the raw earthwork fortifications being raised on the occupied Virginia shore of the Potomac River. Police were increasingly involved in altercations with troops.

The inaugural of Abraham Lincoln as sixteenth President of the United States brought an unfamiliar mood to the city. The crowds of outsiders who lounged in hotels and milled about the streets, as well as pre-inaugural pomp at the Capitol and elsewhere, prompted a *Washington Star* reporter to write 'a day more un-Sabbath like than yesterday cannot well be imagined.' The hundreds of arrivees who could not find hotel accommodation used public fountains as 'al fresco toilet arrangements.' Masses of curious people crowded the entrance to Willard's Hotel, where Lincoln was staying. The crowd of spectators lining Pennsylvania Avenue for the parade was the greatest ever seen to that time. Lincoln's inaugural address was firm, but conciliatory.

Still, the loss of innocence took time. Crowds of excited citizens followed the Union army to Centreville and freely visited the army camps before the Battle of First Manassas. Many took picnic baskets to sustain them as they watched the 'festivities.' The rout and subsequent retreat to Washington was a sobering experience, which sowed the seeds of hatred toward the South that would grow in intensity with each defeat and not subside with later victories. Suspicion of the Southerners remaining in Washington replaced earlier cordiality, as stories of spying, real and fancied, made the rounds. This accelerated the departure of Southerners from Washington.

Martial ceremony was impressive but unthreatening. Reviews of troops drew large crowds. In November 1861, the *Washington Star* reported, droves of people spent half a day getting to Bailey's Crossroads south of the Potomac River to watch a military review. Salutes and salvoes greeted the arrival of the commandant, General McClellan, and as he rode along the line in review 'the roars of cheers that went up from seventy-five thousand throats of his army were nearly as deaf-

Above This derailed locomotive and cars was one of the relics of Union General John Pope's retreat after Second Manassas.

ening as the thunders of artillery.'

The bucolic side of the city of about 61,000 people persisted. Large fields surrounded the Gothic eminence known as the Smithsonian Institution. Cows grazed on the lawn of the unfinished Washington Monument, then a truncated beginning of the tall spire that ultimately was built. The *Washington Star* reported, but did not object to, an improvised dam on the tiny Tiber River north of New Jersey Avenue which was erected by soldiers defending the capital. The soldiers used the pool for bathing.

Work on the national Capitol went on because Lincoln viewed it as a symbol that 'we intend the Union to go on.' In 1864, the Goddess of Freedom was lowered into place on the dome. Ordinary events continued in the shadow of war. Picnics in Washington Park were a favorite personal and institutional pastime. Carriage accidents continued, and even Secretary of State Seward was involved when a nervous horse bolted while the driver was helping a woman board. In trying to get out of the moving carriage, Seward injured his face and fractured his right arm.

In June 1862, a baseball game was played

Below Fort Massachusetts, later renamed Fort Stevens, was one of the earthen forts defending Washington. In this 1863 photograph, its garrison is lined up in the sally port.

between the National and Washington clubs, with National winning by 40 runs–62 to 22. In May 1963, a headline fight between Joe Coburn and Mike McCordle for a $2,000 prize had sporting circles 'excited.' It went 68 rounds and ended with Coburn claiming to be American champion of the prize ring.

WHITE HOUSE RECEPTIONS

The social life of the nation's capital was especially pleasant when good news was heard from the front. Treasured invitations to the White House resulted in people arriving 'thick and fast.' A typical event began late, at 10 p.m., and included entertainment. Lincoln and other celebrities naturally were centers of attention. Dancing began at 11p.m. with Lincoln leading off with one of the ladies. Caterers loaded tables with food–pâté de foie gras, chicken, champagne, other wines and

liquors. Decorations of spun sugar might include a war helmet, Chinese pagodas, Roman temples, cornucopias and the Goddess of Liberty; even Fort Pickens.

Despite the war, the public had relatively free access to the White House. Lincoln held morning and afternoon receptions during winter, often twice a week, which were attended by civilians and military, including enlisted men. The women were elegantly dressed in silks and satins, with lace feather adornments, and the civilian men wore evening dress. Lincoln stood in the Blue Room or East Room to greet visitors with a handshake, but even close friends described the gesture as perfunctory, with Lincoln staring into space and not even recognizing them. These sessions usually gave Lincoln a swollen hand that would bother him for several hours.

Above The open field surrounding the Smithsonian Institution reveals the bucolic side of the nation capital during the nineteenth century.

Left The victorious Army of the Potomac marches in review down Pennsylvania Avenue in May 1865.

Music was not ignored. The Anchutz Opera Group from Germany entertained in September 1863. Human nature sometimes affected the course of intellectual pleasures; the efforts of a group of young men to serenade with musical instruments a young lady at the United States Hotel was interrupted by a bucket of water on their heads.

WASHINGTON AT WAR

The war effort intruded on everyday life in numerous ways, small and large. Soldiers were everywhere, with high-ranking officers bustling on duty and enjoying in a relaxed manner the restaurants and soirées of the capital at other times. So many army officers visited Congress in search of political promotions that an unsuccessful attempt was made to limit visitors to those on leave. On one visit to Ford's Theater, Lincoln could obtain seats only because the manager asked army office´rs to relinquish their box. When Lincoln requested the names of the officers, the manager said he did not know them because half of them were absent without leave and he did not want to cause trouble for them. At times, paroled Confederate officers walked the streets in their gray uniforms.

The once-quiet streets were crowded with traffic. Cavalry trotted along the thoroughfares, while artillery and quartermaster wagons churned up dust in dry weather and turned the streets into quagmires during inclement weather. Sloping streets sometimes became moving streams of mud, impregnated with litter and garbage.

Washington's five or six first-class gambling saloons and untold numbers of lesser quality establishments continued to be popular. Members of Congress and senior army officers were seen frequently at the faro and roulette tables of the first-class places. A *Chicago Tribune* reporter saw one of them lose $5,000 to $6,000 in a two-hour period one night in August 1862.

Madame Pauline Meyer's place of 'agreeable damsels' at 14th Street and N. Street was among the numerous institutions anchoring the lower end of the social ladder. Altercations with soldiers who lost watches and other such valuables at these pleasure palaces were not uncommon.

Even the unopposed occupation of Alexandria and the heights across the Potomac in

Below During wartime, Washington was teeming with high-ranking soldiers, enjoying the restaurants, society life and the chance to visit Congress. This view of the capital is seen from the president's house.

Virginia, included the former home of Robert E. Lee, Arlington, did not occur peacefully. The first Union officer to die in the war was New York Colonel Elmer Ephraim Ellsworth, who was shot by the proprietor when he charged into an Alexandria hotel to rip down a secessionist banner. It was a sign of the temperament of the times, and a prelude to the bloodletting as yet unanticipated. Alexandria was not integrated into the life of Washington, and passes were required to go back and forth.

In the period immediately following the defeat at First Manassas, near panic gripped Washington. Some newcomers departed and others made plans for a rapid retreat. The fear subsided as Confederates made no move to capture the city and the number of Union troops filling new earth and log forts grew.

Boarding houses and hotels were packed by government workers, businessmen seeking government contracts, relatives of soldiers and refugees. Citizens were called on for various kinds of support, from donating money to conserving water during times of drought.

'Drinking houses' posed a problem at times, especially during periods of tension. In September 1862, the military governor of Washington ordered the closure of all saloons because recent fighting had caused an 'unsettled state' in the population.

Excursions beyond the limits of the District of Columbia were not allowed and those who violated the ban were picked up and detained by military authorities— even a family on a picnic to the Prince George side of the Anacostia found themselves in trouble.

Sick and wounded from the battlefields poured into Washington throughout the war. The arrival at Sixth Street dock in May 1862 of the steamer *Louisiana* with 213 sick soldiers from the Peninsular Campaign brought the number of convalescents sent to Washington from the front to about 1,600. Some were dying of 'consumption.' In a few instances, the nearest relatives were on hand to greet them. The *Washington Star* noted that only the sick had been sent to Washington's hospitals; the wounded had been sent by boat to other Northern cities.

Washington had 21 hospitals to treat wounded soldiers, some of them located in the Patent Office, churches and public halls. Wounded by the hundreds came by train and boat from savage battles such as Fredericksburg and Chancellorsville in Virginia. The walking wounded, bandaged,

Right Carver General Hospital in Washington, D.C., helped care for the thousands of casualties from the bloody battlefields of Virginia. As new facilities were built, medical care improved.

disheveled and blackened with gunpowder smoke, often had to fend for themselves until they reached a hospital. They were 'so faint and longing for rest' that their plight softened the heart of a veteran newspaper reporter. On occasion, doctors were brought into the city from the nearby States of Pennsylvania, Maryland and Delaware in order to tend the sick and wounded.

Soldiers discharged from the hospitals were sent to Camp Convalescent in Alexandria, where deplorable conditions existed. Some of the 10,000 men often billeted there, including numerous stragglers, had to sleep in tents, even in winter.

SPIES AND SPY SCARES

Washington was the center of Southern spying. Security was lax during the Civil War period and military plans often were common knowledge well before they were executed. The society salons of the capital were fertile grounds for intelligence gathering and female spies of the Confederacy were especially effective in this work.

Mrs. Rose O'Neal Greenhow headed one of the numerous Confederate espionage groups in Washington. Her activities, including the information she provided on the Union plans at First Manassas, led to her arrest and brief imprisonment in the Old Capitol Prison in Washington before being deported to the South. The famous Belle Boyd was imprisoned for a time at the Old Capitol.

The capital was gripped by an uneasiness and a 'morbid sensationalism' that saw spies where there were none. The staid Smithsonian Institution came under suspicion of sending signals to the Confederacy because it burned lights late at night. An amused Lincoln, who was entertaining its director, Dr. Joseph Henry, when an informant came to him with the accusation, turned to the director and asked for an explanation. Weather instruments measuring wind speed, temperature and other data are checked at certain times every day, replied Dr. Henry.

The possibility of assassination was a con-tinuing concern. Even Lincoln got the jitters at times. When Noah Brooks, a newspaper reporter and a friend of the president, reported seeing flitting shadows behind trees during night walks, Lincoln began carrying a heavy cane. But even on expeditions to the front, he traveled without bodyguards. 'If anybody wants to kill me,' Lincoln said prophetically, ' he will do it.'

Holidays were generally festive and usually were used by the government to whip up patriotic fervor. The Washington's Birthday celebration in February 1862 featured the ringing of bells and firing of salutes from the navy yard and arsenal and the guns of fortifications around Washington. The Stars and Stripes was displayed from all public buildings and many private residences, and the city was partially illuminated.

Above Many famous Confederate spies, including Rose Greenhow and Belle Boyd (pictured), were imprisoned in the Old Capitol Prison in Washington.

It was a strange sight. Tough, battle-hardened veterans, lean from hunger and wearing tattered uniforms, sang 'Maryland, My Maryland' like recruits on the drill field as they stretched out for miles along dusty roads. There was good reason for their high spirits and the spring in their step; they were carrying the war to the North for the the first time.

Maryland was bitterly divided by the Civil War. Although the State remained in the Union, the decision was made as much by geography as sentiment. At the outbreak of the war, Union troops marching to the defense of Washington were stoned by civilians in Baltimore, which would remain a hotbed of secessionist sentiment throughout the war. Maryland units fought on both sides, but in general, eastern Maryland was more sympathetic to the Southern cause than western Maryland, which was populated by farmers proud of the accomplishments of their own hands and who owned few slaves. Most just wanted both armies to leave them alone to work their fields.

Antietam: The War Goes North

That was not to be. Invasion of the Confederate States by Union forces produced a sharp public reaction and a demand for retaliation. The idea of invasion had logistic and strategic appeal, too. An invasion of the North would enable the Southern army to draw supplies from what Lieutenant General James Longstreet called the 'bounteous land' of Maryland without further impoverishing areas of Virginia already well worked over. It would bring the war 'home' to Northerners who thus far had suffered few ill effects, and would soothe Southern feelings wounded by the deprivations of war. Success might produce good results abroad, too, in the form of recognition by one or more of the major European powers – and that would perhaps enable the South to break the blockade which was causing cotton and tobacco to pile up in warehouses and hindering the importation of badly needed munitions. General Lee further saw it as an opportunity for Confederate President Jefferson Davis to make a proposal for peace, which, 'being made when it is in our power to inflict injury upon our adversary, would show conclusively to the world that our sole object is the establishment of our independence and the attainment of an honorable peace.'

INVADING THE NORTH

Lee's victory at the second battle of Manassas (Bull-Run) provided the opportunity and the means to carry the war to the North. He moved cautiously across the Potomac near Leesburg, with J.E.B. Stuart's cavalry between his army and Washington. He planned to protect his other flank by clearing the Federal troops from Harper's Ferry and then bringing his army together to continue the invasion, perhaps into Pennsylvania.

Things did not go as well as Lee hoped. On September 13, 1862, while General 'Stonewall' Jackson was converging on Harper's Ferry, a lost copy of Lee's battle order was found by a Union private and reached General George McClellan in plenty of time to strike at Lee while his army was divided.

McClellan's affliction with the 'slows' enabled Lee, who learned from a Southern sympathizer that McClellan was in possession of the order, to move reinforcements to guard the passes of South Mountain. McClellan attacked the passes on September 14, and for a time Lee considered withdrawing from Maryland without further contest. He changed his mind when he received word that Jackson has captured Harper's Ferry, taken 11,000 Federal prisoners, and would soon be on his way to join Lee.

By then, Lee's army was concentrated on high ground west of Antietam Creek and across the angle formed by the junction of the creek and the Potomac River. Why Lee chose to fight from that position is a mystery; it was tactically strong, except that the streams blocked the avenue of retreat, but it was not a good position from which to continue an advance northward. Jackson's arrival on the eve of the September 17, 1862 battle brought Lee's strength to 40,000, far too few to press the invasion as long as McClellan's 87,000 blocked the way.

Antietam is one of the most beautiful Civil War battlefields. The view from the Visitors' Center on the present Maryland Route 65 looks back across rolling fields toward Sharpsburg; in the other direction lie more undulating fields, sometimes interrupted by sharp breaks that created problems for Union attackers and produced such colorful names as Bloody Lane. The terrain preserved in Antietam National Battlefield Park makes it easy to understand why the Union attack was not as coordinated a McClellan wished. But it is so beautiful and peaceful that the visitor has difficulty realizing that this was the scene of the bloodiest single day of the Civil War. As night fell on September 17, 1862, these fields were strewn with dead bodies and wounded men , pockmarked with shell holes, and littered with smashed equipment. The carnage was 'too fearful to contemplate' even for battle-wise General Longstreet. Federal losses came to 12,410 and Confederate losses were only slightly smaller, at 10,700.

General George B. McClellan commanded the Northern army at the Battle of Antietam. Although he stopped Lee's invasion of Maryland, he was later dismissed by Lincoln because of his bad case of the 'slows'

An eight-mile self-drive tour of the park covers all aspects of the battle. Cannon between the Visitors' Center and the restored Dunker Church stand on the spot from which Confederate artillery swept The Cornfield and East Woods as the Federals attacked. Photographs taken after the battle show clusters of dead Confederate gunners lying around some of their cannon. The cannonading during the battle was furious; indeed, some historians describe Antietam as principally a duel between artillery.

Below Monuments line Cornfield Avenue at Antietam, which cuts through the original field. The fighting was so heavy there that the cornstalks were cut down as though by scythes.

A THREE-PHASE BATTLE

The battle at Antietam had three distinct phases. It began with the dawn attack from Joseph Poffenberger's farm against 'Stonewall' Jackson's men in The Cornfield. Attackers and defenders charged between headhigh rows of corn, and the battle surged back and forth until, in the words of Union General Hooker, 'every stalk of corn in the northern and greater part of the field was cut as closely as could have been done with a knife, and the slain lay in rows as precisely as they had stood in their ranks a few moments before.' The fighting, the heaviest of the day, continued for three hours, and the field changed hands fourteen times. The costliest action of the bloodiest day was Union Major General John Sedgwick's attack from the East Woods against Jackson's defensive line in the West Woods. In less than half an hour, Sedgwick lost more than 2,200 men.

The second phase of the battle developed at the Sunken Road. Fighting between Union and Confederate infantry in this area lasted for four hours and caused so many casualties that the road was nicknamed Bloody Lane. The fighting finally petered out in a mixture of confusion and exhaustion.

The third phase of the battle reached a climax late in the afternoon at the Antietam Bridge, now named the Burnside Bridge after the Union general who commanded the assault against four hundred well-entrenched Georgia veterans guarding the crossing. The wooded ground around the bridge today is quite dif-

Confederates and Federals fought a four-hour, see-saw battle to possess the strategic point of Bloody Lane, clearly visible (left) from a postwar memorial tower. The picture above is a present-day view of the site.

Left Major General Ambrose E. Burnside took harsh action against political leaders and newspapers who opposed the war. He closed the *Chicago Tribune*, but Lincoln rescinded the order.

Above The contrast between the terrain at Antietam in 1862 and now is apparent. Antietam Bridge is now called the Burnside Bridge, after the Union general who captured it too late to affect the battle.

Top A small Confederate force held off a major Union attack at Antietam Bridge, protecting Lee's flank while the battle raged elsewhere.

Faulty cannon designs and misuse sometimes led to the disastrous result seen here. This artillery piece exploded in the Confederate defenses at Yorktown, Virginia in 1862.

ARTILLERY ADVANCES

Artillery advanced more off the battlefield than on. While smoothbore cannon continued to pour shot and shell onto battlefields, the problems of escaping gas and rotating the projectile that hindered the use of breech-loading weapons were slowly solved. The leading designs in breech-loading cannon came from Great Britain – the Armstrong cannon, adopted by both the Royal Navy and British Army, and the Whitworth. These breech-loading cannon were used to a limited extent by both sides.

Where used, advances in artillery forced military commanders to adjust their tactics. The growth in the size of garrison and siege cannon extended the depth of the battlefield and brought

cities packed with civilians under fire. They forced ships to fight at greater distances from the shoreline.
The 12 inch Blakely, designed for coast artillery service, weighed 27 tons. Fifteen-inch Rodmans and 32- and 42 - pounders became normal in forts around Washington.

Rifling and redesign gave added punch to former smoothbores, including the huge 24-pounders. These weapons were especially prized by the Union for their effect on the coastal forts in the South and, in 1862, were used to breech the thick, brick walls of Fort Pulaski, near Savannah, Georgia. The Rodman casting process, which ran water through the core as air cooled the barrel, and the reinforced Parrott chamber area provided the added strength required for such weapons.

The timely arrival of forces under General A.P. Hill protected Lee's line of retreat from Sharpsburg.

ferent from the open area which helped the sharpshooters keep Burnside's men from crossing for hours while the battle raged at the other end of the battlefield. At 1 p.m., Burnside finally forced a crossing and gradually pushed the Georgians back, but re-forming his lines for a frontal assault took two hours, during which Confederate reinforcements arrived.

Although the action in this area was minor compared to the carnage elsewhere, Burnside's crossing created a major threat to Lee's army. Control of Sharpsburg would cut of Lee's line of retreat. The ability of Confederate leaders to move men to the right place a the right time saved the day. About 4 p.m., Major General A.P. Hill's division, which had remained in Harper's Ferry to dispose of captured Federal property and parole prisoners, arrived the immediately drove Burnside back to the heights near the bridge.

The costly battle was over. The next day, Lee ended his first invasion of the North by withdrawing across the Potomac, none of his objectives having been fulfilled. The cautious McClellan licked his wounds and let him go, content to have held the field and forced a Confederate retreat.

President Lincoln inspected the battlefield, consoled the wounded and questioned McClellan about his slow pursuit. The photograph of Lincoln and McClellan sitting and talking in the command tent is one of the most famous of the war; what was said is a mystery.

POSITIVE RESULT FOR LINCOLN

The Battle of Antietam, the only major battle fought in Maryland, gave Lincoln many of the things he desired. McClellan has pressed the attack once he was ready, and his ability to hold the field ended the myth of Lee's invincibility. It also halted the invasion of Maryland at the outset, and so was a blow to Confederate hopes for recognition by European powers. Thus, although the battle was tactically a draw, it was a strategic victory for the North.

The victory created an atmosphere which permitted Lincoln to issue the Emancipation Proclamation. The proclamation was almost as controversial as suspension of civil rights. It caused political dispute on the home front and dissension in the ranks of the army. Not only did it affect property rights, as people of the period conceived them, but it tarnished the popular image of the war as one to save the Union. It also contained a fundamental paradox: while it abolished slavery in Confederate States, it did not do so in those States which remained in the Union. It was better received abroad, where anti-slavery forces maintained pressure on the governments of Great Britain and France not to recognize the Confederacy.

The positive results of the battle at Antietam were not enough to save McClellan, however; on November 3, Lincoln replaced him with General Ambrose E. Burnside.

The dead littered the fields and woods near the Dunker Church after the Battle of Antietam. The reconstructed church is now one of the principal landmarks of the battlefield.

9

A Great Battle Going On' declared a headline in the *Washington Star* on December 13, 1862. And indeed it was, but not from the Union standpoint. The Battle of Fredericksburg, which initiated a series of engagements along the Rappahannock River barrier almost halfway between Washington and Richmond, was such a disaster that it was the only one Major General E. Ambrose Burnside would lead as commander of the Army of the Potomac.

Burnside did not want the command because he lacked experience. Lincoln had doubts, too, but they were overcome by his exasperation at the slow movement of General-in-Chief George B. McClellan, who allowed Lee to withdraw his army uncontested from Maryland after the inconclusive Battle of Antietam. Burnside must have been influenced by Lincoln's impatience, for he pushed into hostile territory in wintertime and persisted in following his plan of attack even when confronted by Lee in possession of one of the

Fredericksburg
and
Chancellorsville

most defensible natural positions used in the Civil War, Marye's Heights and adjacent hills south of Fredericksburg.

The opening phase of the Battle of Fredericksburg might have been an omen for Burnside. Confederate sharpshooters hidden in the historic and until then peaceable city of less than 5,000 inhabitants prevented his engineers from completing pontoon bridges across the river – one of the innovations associated with the battle – even after he had devastated the town with artillery. Only by using pontoons in the manner of landing craft – another innovation that anticipated modern warfare – was he able to push sufficient forces across the river to clear the city of snipers and skirmishers. The worst was yet to come.

Union skirmishers moved through the narrow streets of the city, sometimes having to clear a street block by block. Ahead, lay snow-covered fields and Marye's Heights, which at that time were outside the city. Confederates were strongly entrenched along the base and along the ridge, while others entrenched behind the stone wall at the Sunken Road, mowed down Union lines attacking across open fields. They were aided by Confederate sharpshooters in the Innis House, which surprisingly survived the battle. The 'heroine of the Battle of Fredericksburg,' Martha Stevens, stayed in her house to tend the wounded; her grave, whose marker recounts her death almost 26 years to the day after the battle, can still be seen. Nearby is a monument to 'The Angel of Marye's Heights,' Richard Rowland Kirkland, the South Carolina soldier who risked his life to bring water to the thirsty wounded of both sides.

SLAUGHTER FROM THE HEIGHTS

The view from Marye's Heights shows how totally they command the surrounding terrain. The combination of strategically placed artillery units as Louisiana's acclaimed Washington Battery, which raked the attacking Union army. and infantry shooting from behind the Stone Wall was so effective that Colonel E.P. Alexander boasted 'a chicken could not

live on that field.' A second Union assault east of Marye's Heights, which should have been coordinated with the main effort but was not, was also unceremoniously beaten back by Lee's triumphant forces.

The heights, now a terraced national cemetery where more than 15,000 Union troops are buried amid memorials to many of the units involved, are mute testimony to the effectiveness of the Confederate defense. A tall column bearing an iron cross near the entrance, erected by Major General Daniel Butterfield, commemorates the valor of the Union V Corps and its 35,708 members who died during the Civil War. On the crest of the hill the 127th Regiment of the Pennsylvania Infantry is commemorated.

The Confederate commander watched the battle from a vantage point on what is now known as Lee Hill. It was there, when complete victory became obvious, that Lee allowed himself a little show of ebullience. 'It is well that war is so terrible - we should grow too fond of it,' he said.

FREDERICKSBURG TODAY

Today, an eight-mile drive self-drive tour begins at the base of the hill and moves through the wooded terrain to pass the well-preserved section of Confederate infantry trench; the point where Major General's George G. Meade's Federals briefly pierced the Confederate line; and Prospect Hill and Major John Pelham's Position, Confederate

From this hilltop, now decorated with cannon, General Lee watched the progress of the Battle of Fredericksburg.

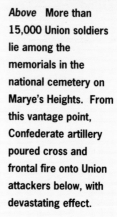

Above More than
15,000 Union soldiers
lie among the
memorials in the
national cemetery on
Marye's Heights. From
this vantage point,
Confederate artillery
poured cross and
frontal fire onto Union
attackers below, with
devastating effect.

Right 'The Angel of
Marye's Heights,'
Sergeant Richard R.
Kirkland, is
memorialized by this
monument near the
base of the hill. The
Confederate soldier
risked his life to carry
water to the thirsty
wounded of both sides.

ERECTED BY
THE STATE OF SOUTH CAROLINA
THE COMMONWEALTH OF VIRGINIA
COLLATERAL DESCENDANTS OF
RICHARD KIRKLAND AND
CITIZENS OF THE UNITED STATES
DR. RICHARD NUNN LANIER
EXECUTIVE DIRECTOR

IN MEMORI
RICHARD ROWLAND
CO: G, 2ND SOUTH CAROL
C.S.A

AT THE RISK OF HIS LIFE
SOLDIER OF SUBLIME COMP
WATER TO HIS WOUN
FREDERICKSBURG THE FIG

Capt. Russell Phot

Above Here, on December 13, 1862, was some of the bloodiest ground in history. Confederates massed in the sunken road at the foot of Marye's Heights, while Burnside hurled wave after wave of cannon against the stone wall. 6,000 Union soldiers fell that day.

IRKLAND
A VOLUNTEERS

IS AMERICAN
SION BROUGHT
D FOES AT
ING MEN ON

artillery strongpoints, still fortified with period cannon.

Fredericksburg has grown to incorporate the area of the December battle, so only essential parts of the battlefield are preserved. These are divided into three units, starting with a walking tour from Visitors' Center along the base of Marye's Heights.

CHANCELLORSVILLE

Confederates in the heights outside Fredericksburg were attacked again the following spring, and this time the Union forces were successful against the thin gray line. However, the battle was secondary to the main fighting around Chancellorsville, ten miles away. Chancellorsville is regarded as Lee's most masterful battle, but it was a costly one because it resulted in the death of 'Stonewall' Jackson.

Relics of the battle are strung out along present State Route 3 (the Orange Turnpike) west of Fredericksburg, but many features of the battlefield are contained within the national park. The Visitors' Center, located on ground where major fighting took place, is more important in this park than in most others because the circular driving tour does not adequately portray the master stroke that achieved another Confederate victory against far superior Union forces holding strong positions. The background obtained from a 12-minute slide presentation and the center's excellent museum makes more meaningful the stops at Hazel Grove, now fortified with a few of the three dozen Confederate cannon crowded there at the time, and a painting depicting the artillery duel with massed Union cannon at Fairview, and the trenches and earthworks visible at both sites. Even the foundations of Chancellorsville Tavern, which gave the battle its name, are still visible.

In a way the Battle of Chancellorsville was a follow-up to the Union defeat at Fredericksburg the previous December. Major General Joseph 'Fighting Joe' Hooker, who succeeded Burnside as commander of the 130,000 man Army of the Potomac, made his winter camp near Fredericksburg and resumed the 'On to Richmond' drive in the spring. With the lesson of the futile attack on Marye's Heights burned into his mind, Hooker chose to combine a flanking movement against Lee with a new assault on the hills south of Fredericksburg. Lee anticipated his plan and, although outnumbered nearly three-to-one, took the initiative on May 1. Hooker's units fell back from positions which were crucial to the outcome of the battle. Hazel Grove was one of the few open places in the wooded countryside where cannon had clear fields of fire, but the key to success was Jackson's brilliant surprise flanking attack that collapsed the right wing of Hooker's army. Jackson's winding flank march from the bivouac where he and Lee agreed on the tactic can be duplicated by following the Furnace Road and Jackson Trail, part of it unpaved, to State Routes 613 and 3.

A TRAGIC ACCIDENT

Jackson was determined to push his success the next day so he rode out at night with a small staff party to reconnoiter. The group was mistaken for enemy scouts on their return and Jackson was badly wounded in the left arm, which was amputated in the field. The loss of Jackson was serious, but the next morning Lee threw his army against the fortified Union line, driving Hooker back to new positions a mile north of Chancellorsville.

The thin gray line left to defend the heights near Fredericksburg had been breached by the Federals, however, and Lee was forced to once again split his army. At Salem Church, seven miles east of Chancellorsville, now restored as part of the battlefield park, the reinforced Confederates halted this Union drive and pushed it back across the Rappahannock River.

Meanwhile, the wounded Jackson was taken 27 miles to T.C. Chandler's Fairfield Plantation at Guiney (now Guinea) Station, a key supply center on the Richmond, Fredericksburg and Potomac Railway line, where it was thought he could receive proper

Left General Joseph 'Fighting Joe' Hooker commanded the Union army at Chancellorsville.

Above The wounded at Chancellorsville were treated at field stations.

More seriously wounded men were taken to field hospitals, which usually occupied a nearby farmhouse. Despite advances during the war, military medical practice remained primitive on both sides.

care. The main house was already filled with wounded from the fighting, so Jackson was placed in the nearby white frame plantation office. The days that followed marked alternately optimism and despair as pneumonia set in. On the afternoon of May 10, eight days after his greatest victory, Jackson became delirious and began shouting military commands. Finally he quietened, and then he drew on his knowledge of the Bible as he said: 'Let us cross over the river, and rest under the shade of the trees.'

Death had claimed the general Lee had called his right arm; Lee would miss Jackson sorely in the battles to come. Many years later, British statesman David Lloyd George would remark 'In this little house the Confederacy also died.' The frame house where 'Stonewall' died is the main feature of the Jackson Shrine, which is five miles off Interstate 95 via State Routes 606 and 607. It is furnished plainly inside, with the bed and blanket and the clock on the mantel (which still works) being original. Another room is outfitted as the doctor's room. A painting, with a recorded commentary, at the entrance to the small park depicts the plantation at the time of Jackson's death. Only the foundations of the brick manor house remain.

CHAPTER 10

Everything about the Gettysburg battlefield is grand. It is the largest contiguous battlefield park in the nation, the most developed and commercialized, and the one which accommodates the greatest number of visitors. It has more than 1,000 monuments and cannon along 40 miles of scenic roads, and has the most impressive monuments – all of which make it easy to follow and understand the decisive battle that occurred there from July 1 to 3, 1863.

The grandeur is justified. Gettysburg was a watershed in the Civil War. It halted the last invasion of the North by the South, and it ended for all time the hope that European powers would recognize the independence of the Confederacy. The war would last almost two more years, and General Lee would lead his Army of Northern Virginia to victory again, but the tide of the Confederacy began ebbing when the bravery of Major General George E. Pickett's men could not break the Union center at The Angle and the Copse of Trees.

Gettysburg

Union soldiers who died at Gettysburg are commemorated by the Soldier's National Monument in the cemetery where President Lincoln delivered his famous Gettysburg Address.

Yet, Gettysburg became a battlefield more by chance than by design. On June 3, after his stunning victory at Chancellorsville against a vastly superior force, Lee marched north again in an attempt to take pressure of Vicksburg, then under siege. He passed through western Maryland and into Pennsylvania, with Harrisburg, its capital, as the objective. Union forces under General Hooker paralleled his route to protect Washington and Baltimore, but Hooker resigned as commander of the Army of the Potomac and was succeeded by General George G. Meade. Lee ordered his army, by then almost at the Susquehanna River, to turn back to Cashtown, and units of the two armies met by chance at Gettysburg on June 30. The next day the battle scene was set as Confederates drove the Federals through Gettysburg to a line formed by Culps Hill, Cemetery Ridge and Little Round Top south of town. Lee moved his forces to Seminary Ridge almost a mile from the Union line, placing them in a north-south arc that stretched almost five miles.

The fighting started late on July 2 and continued until 10 p.m. at night as Lee sought to turn the Union flanks before Meade could concentrate all his forces. General Longstreet, who was to attack the critical left flank, would spend the remainder of his life denying that his delays cost the Confederacy a victory at Gettysburg; but it was not until 4 p.m. that his cannon roared into action preceding the attack. By then, fresh Union troops had moved into the Wheatfield and Devil's Den, names that by nightfall would become immortalized by the blood of thousands of dead and wounded soldiers. Nor was General Richard Ewell's attack on the other flank wholly successful; it lacked coordination and bogged down as

Below General George Gordon was in command at Gettysburg. He was the fifth commander of the Union army in less than 12 months.

Above The yard of the Trostle Farmhouse is littered with dead animals after the Battle of Gettysburg. The 9th Massachusetts battery, which set up there, lost most of its horses.

additional infantry units and cannon moved into Meade's line of blue. Delays had cost Lee a decisive victory.

A DAY TOO LATE

The third day, July 3, was a classic example of infantry attack. Union regulars regained ground on their right flank, putting both flanks in almost impregnable positions. This forced Lee to make a frontal assault on the center of the line, where a breakthrough would divide the Union army and win the battle. Longstreet had objections, as he always did, but Lee was determined. 'The enemy is there, and I am going to strike him,' he said, pointing at Cemetery Ridge. What followed has gone down in history as a symbol of Southern courage, under the name Pickett's Charge.

Seen from either side of the battlefield, from The Angle and the Copse of Trees—at which the charge was aimed—or from the Virginia Monument near the Confederate center, the heroism of the charge is evident. Almost a mile of open field slopes gradually down from one ridge and up to the other. There is no protection, no place to pause. The 12,000-man gray wave led by soldiers carrying bright regimental flags advanced at walking pace most of the distance, their lines shredded by double cannister shells and sharpshooting riflemen in the Union defenses. The rebels charged at a run only the last quarter-mile, into a barrier of smoke created by the deadly firing from the ridge ahead. It was a magnificient effort that almost worked. The Confederates breached the Union line near the Copse of Trees but were too few and too exhausted to hold the ground. As they drew back across the open field, their casualties continued to mount; and when the 50 minutes of combat was over, 10,000 of them had fallen.

The next day was the Fourth of July, the birthday of the United States, and the battle did not resume. Lee's losses during the three days of fighting, a staggering 28,000, represented 38 per cent of his 75,000-man army, and he could no longer press the fight. Meade, who had lost 23,000 of his 97,000 men, pursued, but the chase was rendered ineffective by Confederate rear guards and by rain. Lee's retreat was made even more bitter by 'dispiriting news' that Vicksburg had fallen and the South was cut in two.

GETTYSBURG TODAY

Gettysburg today is the most visible American battlefield. It can be viewed in electric map and static display form at the Visitors' Center, on a cyclorama housed in its own building, and from an observation tower. Airplanes carry visitors on regular flights over the 25 square miles of the battlefield. The most popular method of visitation remains the drive-through tour, which follows both lines of the last two days of the battles and major points involved in the initial day's combat.

The drive begins at the cyclorama and follows a road named consecutively after Union Generals Hancock, Sedgwick, Sykes, Warren, and Crawford, running among dozens of monuments, large and small. General Meade is memorialized by a large equestrian statue, while a nearby small monument recognizes the 1st Pennsylvania Cavalry. Pennsylvania and other Union States have raised impressive memorials along this part of the drive.

An artillery battery at The Angle (sometimes called the Bloody Angle) looks out on

At the Gettysburg National Battlefield, memorials in the Wheatfield and Death Valley recall the terrible loss of life.

the ground covered by Pickett's Charge. A copse of trees stands nearby, as it did in 1863, and a tablet identifies the spot as the High Water Mark of the Confederacy. That was where Pickett's men were halted and, although they did not realize it at the time, the days of the Confederacy were numbered.

The drive crosses Little Round Top and skirts Big Round Top, where a one-hour circular walking trail winds through a typical Pennsylvania hardwood forest and passes a stone wall built for defense by Union troops. Then, the driving tour meanders through terrain occupied on the second day by Union units while the Confederates dallied.

Memorials in the Wheatfield and Death Valley recall the terrible toll of the day's fighting, and a path leads onto the rocks called Devil's Den from which sharpshooters poured deadly fire.

Confederate Avenue along Lee's battle-line has fewer memorials and cannon, but the ones there are among the most expressive on the battlefield. Alabama mourns her fallen sons at Biesecker Woods. A feature on the Virginia Memorial, which stands on the spot

near the center of the line from which Lee watched Pickett's Charge, is an equestrian statue of Lee on a high pedestal. Figures around the base of the statue, all in action, represent various types of workers who left civilian life to become soldiers. The smaller, but equally impressive, North Carolina Memorial is to Lee's left, in the area where they marshalled to join Pickett's Charge.

The park road also runs along McPherson and Oak Ridges, where the battle began as a chance encounter, to the Eternal Light Peace Memorial, dedicated in 1938 on the 75th anniversary of the battle to 'Peace Eternal in a Nation Unified.'

A short drive through Gettysburg reveals privately owned attractions ranging from the National Civil War Wax Museum to the Lincoln Train Museum. Life styles of the Civil War era are recreated during Heritage Days each July. The driving tour then reaches Culp's Hill and Spangler Spring, where see-saw fighting occurred on the second day of the battle.

Gettysburg National Cemetery, across the street from the Visitors' Center, has 3,585 plain white headstones and a tall, lean Soldiers Monument acknowledging their supreme sacrifice. But by a curious twist of fate, the cemetery is better known for a speech that contains ten sentences. President Lincoln was not the principal speaker at the dedication of the national cemetery on November 19, 1863, and was invited only as a formality. Edward Everett, considered one of the greatest orators of the day, spoke for almost two hours – and nobody today remembers what he said. Lincoln's address, which took only two minutes to deliver and was heard by few in the audience, not only is engraved on a memorial in the cemetery but is world famous as an expression of hope that good can arise from the sacrifices of war.

A medical tent serves as a field hospital for an emergency amputation at Gettysburg.

CAVALRY ACTIONS

Two major cavalry actions are related to the Gettysburg battle. On June 9, 1863, the greatest cavalry battle of the war occurred at Brandy Station, Virginia, five miles north of Culpeper, as Union forces surprised Confederates preparing for the invasion of the North. More than 10,000 riders were involved. The site looks much as it did during the 12-hour battle, but is undeveloped. General Stuart's cavalry then moved independently into Pennsylvania, east

of both Lee and Meade, and was shadowed as far as Hanover by Union cavalry. Unable to locate the main Confederate force, Stuart pushed on to Carlisle, where he hoped to obtain rations. When he learned that Union troops were lying in ambush in Carlisle homes, he sent a flag of truce offering surrender or bombardment, and began shelling the town when the offer was refused. Stuart then ordered his men to set fire to the United States cavalry barracks, which were rebuilt in 1864 and are still part of an active army base.

Blacksmiths were an essential adjunct to any cavalry division. The need to ride through rough and rocky terrain often meant that horseshoes were a necessity.

PART TWO

THE CIVILIAN SIDE

I n May 1864, a year after his triumph at Chancellorsville, General Lee met General Ulysses S. Grant on the field of battle for the first time. The Wilderness Battlefield, part of the battleground complex around Fredericksburg, preserves the site where Grant, as General-in-Chief of all Union armies, began the costly strike-and-flank campaign of attrition that would end the war.

A drive around the portion of the battlefield owned by the park service shows why the dense thickets and tangled overgrowth deserved the name Wilderness, and why the fighting was so confused that whole units became lost. Heavy firing that set fire to dry underbrush added to the confusion.

The national park lies roughly south of State Route 20, along which Lee moved part of his forces to meet Grant. The Wilderness Exhibit Center has paintings and written commentaries on the battle, and the road through the park passes landmark farms and remnants of Confederate trenches dug for the

Grant's Decisive Campaign

Lieutenant General
Ulysses S. Grant
poses in front of his
tent at Cold Harbor,

Virginia, in June
1864. Cold Harbor
was one of his most
costly battles.

battle of May 5-6, 1864. A monument to Hood's Texans, who fought at the Wilderness as part of Longstreet's Corps, recalls an incident which formed a bond between Lee and the Texans in the Army of Northern Virginia that would outlive the war. At a critical point in the fighting near the Widow Trapp Farm, Lee determined to rally his forces by leading a charge himself. The Texans there were appalled, and shouted to Lee that they would not go unless Lee moved back to safety.

'Go back, General, go back!' shouted the Texan soldiers.

'Hooray for Texas!' shouted Lee, waving his hat.

Lee retreated, and the Texans charged. This was not the first time Confederate soldiers had shown concern for their leaders, but ever afterward Lee retained a special affection for the Texans under his command.

The Wilderness battle was a draw. The Federals abandoned the field, but this time they did not retreat across the Rappahannock. They turned southward in another flanking movement that would renew the fighting at Spotsylvania Courthouse. From the Wilderness, the drive follows the Brock Road (State Route 613), along which many Federals walked, and turns onto Grant Drive at the entrance to the park.

There is a good view from the exhibit shelter of the Laurel Hill area, where on May 8, 1864, dismounted Confederate cavalrymen fought a determined holding action against a superior Federal force until Confederate infantrymen, hastening from the Wilderness, reinforced them and put Lee once again between Grant and Richmond. Paintings and commentaries at and near the shelter provide a good introduction to both the seven-mile

Lieutenant General Ulysses S. Grant poses in front of his tent at Cold Harbor, Virginia, in June 1864. Cold Harbor was one of his most costly battles.

walking tour of the battlefield, which begins there, and the drive through the park. The principal feature of the park is the Bloody Angle, a salient where the firing was so heavy that it severed the trunk of an oak tree 22 inches in diameter. Monuments to New Jersey, New York, and Ohio troops who assaulted the salient, and a walking trail now occupy the site where some of the most savage hand-to-hand fighting of the war occurred. At the McCoull House site within the salient, Lee once again prepared to lead a charge but was dissuaded by Virginians and Georgians. The incredible bravery displayed by soldiers on both sides did not determine the outcome at the Bloody Angle; not until a new line had been prepared across the base of the salient did the Confederates pull back to Lee's last line, almost parallel to Brock Road. A strong Union assault on this line was crushed by infantry and 30 massed cannon.

Sporadic fighting went on around Spotsylvania Courthouse for almost 2 weeks, and the battle cost Grant 18,000 men. The number of Southern casualties is unknown, but some of those killed are buried in the Confederate Cemetery off State Route 208 east of Spotsylvania. The battle was another draw, and Grant again abandoned the field to maneuver southward. More bloody battles in the war of attrition lay ahead; it was still far from being over.

A WAR OF ATTRITION

Cold Harbor, a few miles from Mechanicsville, in June became one of the bloodiest battlefields of the war as General Grant maintained his grinding war of attrition on Confederate forces. In one 30-minute period, the Army of the Potomac sustained 7,000 casualties assault-

This Kurz & Allison print depicts the struggle for Laurel Hill at Spotsylvania, where dismounted Confederate cavalry held off superior Union forces until Lee could once again place his army between General Grant and Richmond.

The well-preserved Fort Harrison lies 10 miles south-east of Richmond, capital of the Confederacy (as well as of Virginia).

ing Confederate defenses. The battlefield area within the national park has good examples of the types of earthworks raised by the Confederates, which originally stretched for six miles. A path leads through the works and over small connecting bridges. Other major features are the Gathright House, the Watt House, and walking trails with interpretive signs.

A string of forts lies west of Malvern Hill. Drewry's Bluff, or Fort Darling, was a Confederate strongpoint on the James River south of Richmond. Exhibits and markers at the scenic site provide an account of the unsuccessful attack on the fort in 1862 by four Union gunboats, including the ironclad *Monitor*, and a revenue steamer. Fort Brady

was constructed by the Union to neutralize Drewry's Bluff. Fort Harrison, the largest and best preserved, was built by the Confederates and enlarged and strengthened by the Federals after they captured it in 1864. A footpath through the fort and visual displays show the unusual design of the fort, which was divided into segments to minimize shell bursts. The smaller Fort Gilmore, although heavily attacked, remained in Confederate hands until Richmond was evacuated. The even smaller Fort Hoke became a strategic strongpoint.

Parker's Battery was a Confederate artillery strongpoint that helped immobilize General Benjamin F. Butler's Army of the James in 1864. Hopewell, east of Richmond on the James River, was named City Point in

The Gathright House (above left), a short distance from Cold Harbor, was used as a hospital during the bloodiest half-hour of the war. A frontal assault cost Grant 7,000 casualties. The restored Watt House (above right) is a landmark of the 1862 Battle of Gaines Mill near Richmond. Fort Harrison (left), strengthened and enlarged by the Union after its capture, is an excellent example of an earthen Civil War fort.

The big guns at Drewry's Bluff, called Fort Darling by the Union, dominated the James River south of Richmond so completely that even an attack by Union ironclads was beaten off.

those days. Its strategic location is recognized by the remains of Fort Abbott.

The battle for Richmond finally was fought at Petersburg, an important rail and highway center 25 miles south of the Confederate capital. Unsuccessful in direct assaults on Richmond, Grant resumed his efforts to outflank Lee and cut off his communications to the south and west. Petersburg National Battlefield's 1,531 acres preserve relics of all the phases of the ten-month siege of the city,

which brought great hardship to Confederate soldiers and Petersburg civilians alike, and proved the overwhelming industrial and financial capacity of the North.

Unsuccessful in direct assaults on Richmond, Grant resumed his efforts to outflank Lee and cut off his communications to the south and west. His initial attack on Petersburg was successful. Even though the Dimmock Line had been constructed after the Peninsular Campaign, it was too lightly manned.

different scene in 1865 — well defended raw earthworks against which Confederate units were hurled, only to be forced back by superior forces.

The Crater, the best known feature of the battlefield, recalls an incident that, tragic though it was, had little effect on the war. There are remnants of a tunnel dug by men of the 48th Pennsylvania Infantry Regiment, many of them coal miners in civilian life, and of the crater created when 8,000 pounds of

Above The Dictator lobbed 200-pound explosive shells more than two miles into Petersburg during the Union siege.

Top left Union soldiers dug a tunnel under the Confederate line at Petersburg in an effort to breach it.

Above This grass-covered crater in Petersburg National Battlefield Park was once a gaping hole into which 15,000 Union troops rushed, only to be trapped by a Confederate counter-attack.

Battery 5, located at the rear of the battlefield park Visitors' Center, was one of the nine original strongpoints in the line. It is a good example of the earthworks fort used in the war, and is now outfitted with the period cannon. Nearby, in a shaded glen, is the Dictator, replica of the 2,000-pound Federal mortar that was used to lob 200-pound explosive shells into Petersburg, then two miles away.

Fort Stedman, the scene of the Lee's desperate attempt to break Grant's siege, is now shaded by trees. A nearby painting shows a

black powder exploded under the Confederate strongpoint known as Elliott's Salient. Then, 15,000 Federal troops attacked through and around the gaping, smoking hole in the ground which destroyed more than 100 feet of the Confederate line; but many were trapped as a Confederate counterattack, led by Major General William Mahone, forced them back into the crater. By the time it was over, 5,500 men had been killed, wounded or captured, 4,000 of them Federals. Ironically, the Confederates had suspected something was afoot

Waiting was as difficult for Civil War soldiers in the trenches as it was for men in other wars. The exposed position of the officers indicates a lull in the fighting. Such opportunities did not occur often at Petersburg, where this picture was taken.

and dug an exploratory tunnel themselves, missing the Union tunnel by only a few feet.

Petersburg battlefield has other outstanding relics, including Battery 9, which was captured by black troops, and Meade Station, an important supply point for Grant's army. A replica of an earthworks system complete with log structures and trenches, located at the entrance to this stop on the self-drive tour of the battlefield, gives a good indication of how primitive life in the field was. The replica is used in living history demonstrations.

Grant's superiority in manpower, transportation, and logistics decided the battle — and the fate of the Army of Northern Virginia. As Grant lengthened his lines, Lee's forces were stretched thinner and thinner. Grant began to cut the rail and road approaches to Petersburg from the south, one by one, and a final assault on April 2, 1865, compelled Lee

to abandon Petersburg. Confederate President Davis received the sad news while attending church in Richmond's St. Paul's Episcopal Church. The event is recalled by pew plaques and the Lee memorial window.

The day would become even sadder for the Confederacy. People who for the most part had borne up under years of danger and months of siege went wild as the Confederate army began pulling out. To prevent violence, whisky barrels were emptied into the streets; but people scooped it up in pails and sopped it up with cloths. Distribution of food in the government commissary turned into a near-riot. An attempt to burn the tobacco at Shockoe Slip to keep it from falling into Union hands set the city ablaze. The fire spread unchecked until Union forces entered the city and demolished buildings to create fire breaks. Shockoe Slip was reborn after the war as an

industrial zone, but today is mainly a chic area of restaurants and speciality shops.

LEE'S RETREAT FROM PETERSBURG

Lee evacuated Petersburg at night to gain time, a ruse that Union forces did not discover until 3 a.m. and Grant then occupied Petersburg without resistance. But the ten-month siege had cost him 42,000 casualties and prisoners, and Confederate losses numbered 28,000 men who could not be replaced.

Lee's retreat was southwesterly, with Amelia Courthouse designated as the assembly point, but Lee's lack of supplies proved costly; the need to forage enabled General Philip H. Sheridan's cavalry to get between Lee and Danville, through which Davis passed on the way south, and forced Lee to choose Lynchburg as an alternative. Fear that Lee would escape and unite with the western Confederate army, then falling back through the Carolinas before Sherman's drive, gave Grant extra incentive.

Lee's retreat was marred by the kind of mistakes made by tired officers overwhelmed by the problems confronting them, a combination of events that caused the normally imperturbable Lee to question aloud whether his army was 'disintegrating.' Sayler's Creek

Monument Avenue in Richmond is named for its equestrian statues of Virginia's heroes, including this one of General Lee.

RICHMOND: THE WAR BETWEEN THE STATES RECALLED

Like Charleston, Richmond has many places which recall the War Between the States. In the State Capitol, whose central building was designed by Thomas Jefferson, the Confederate Congress met. General Lee received command of Virginia forces there. Statues in Capitol Square memorialize 'Stonewall' Jackson, one of the State governors during the Civil War and Dr. Hunter McGuire, Confederate surgeon.

The White House of the Confederacy, Jefferson Davis's residence when he was president, is incorporated into the Confederate Museum, which has the largest collection of Confederate artifacts, including the field uniforms of Lee, Jackson, General Joseph E. Johnston, and General Stuart. Monument Avenue is so named because of its impressive monuments to Confederate heroes Lee, Jackson, Stuart, Davis, and the Virginian who became known as the 'Pathfinder of the Seas,' Matthew Fontaine Maury.

Within the bounds of Hollywood Cemetery, along with two United States presidents and Confederate President Davis, lie the remains of 15,000 Confederate dead.

Battlefield Historical State Park, off State Highway 307 and U.S. Route 306 a few miles east of Appomattox, commemorates the last full-scale battle fought by the Army of Northern Virginia, a battle that occurred only because Lee's rear guard mistakenly followed the wagon train along another route and the rain-swollen creek delayed passage of the Confederate main body. The site, overlooking the small stream where Ewell's Corps successfully drove back the Union center but became surrounded, has paintings, maps, and recordings that explain the tragic battle, which resulted in the surrender of 7,000 Confederate soldiers. Hillsman House, situated on the hilltop from which Union forces attacked, dates from the 1770s and is restored outside to its Civil War appearance.

In an engagement not far away, Major General John B. Gordon lost most of the Confederate wagon train and two-thirds of Lee's cannon but was able to prevent capture of his troops.

The loss of such quantities of men and supplies, along with the straggling and desertions resulting from a disjointed retreat, put Lee in an untenable position, but he still hoped his ragged and hungry soldiers could break through Grant's tightening ring and unite with the Army of Tennessee under Johnston. The combined force could strike first one and then the other of the Union armies and gain more time for the Confederacy. Lee's last chance dissipated when General Gordon's attempt to create an escape route west of Appomattox could not be sustained without reinforcements–a situation that made the loss of 7,000 men at Sayler's Creek critical.

Lee considered courting death by leading a breakout charge, but this appealing alternative to surrender was overcome by his sense of duty. The South would need the leaders that remained to rebuild after four years of destructive warfare; the South could not afford to sacrifice brave men in a futile gesture. Lee swallowed his pride and agreed to meet with Grant to discuss terms.

'Sheridan's Ride' has gone down in Civil War history as an outstanding example of leadership. Union General Phil Sheridan (1831–88) was surprised by a counter-attack at Cedar Creek; he rode to the battlefield, rallied his troops and won a decisive victory.

COMMANDERS:
SOME GLAMOROUS,
SOME NOT

The Union suffered throughout the war from the appointment of political generals and as a rule had military leadership inferior to that of the Confederacy. Its superiority in manpower and *matériel* more than made up for such shortcomings, although ineffective leadership contributed to major debacles.

Lincoln's first choice, General George B. McClellan, was the best of the early commanders. McClellan created and trained the army which ultimately achieved victory, but believed less in military conquest than in a policy of strangulation by control of strategic 'choke points' in the South. His Peninsular Campaign, an attempt to use favorable terrain to attack a weak point, was a disaster, but his army held the field well at Antietam. An impatient Lincoln relieved him from his post for having the 'slows.'

Lincoln finally entrusted the future of the war to General Ulysses S. Grant, whose willingness to 'fight' was attractive. Ironically, on several occasions before being named general-in-chief, Grant was as close to eclipse as to ascendency. His initial offer of service was ignored, perhaps because of an earlier problem with drinking which influenced his resignation from the army. After initial wartime service as a colonel of volunteers in Missouri, Grant won fame for his 'unconditional surrender' demand at Fort Donelson. Had Confederates continued the push at Shiloh after the death of General Albert Sydney Johnston, Grant might well have lost the battle that attracted Lincoln's attention. He was constantly criticized for heavy losses of men and his initial campaign against Vicksburg was unspectacular.

General Grant has been described as the first modern general. His policy of total war used the advantages of superior armies to weaken the Confederate forces, while reducing the South's ability to wage war by devastating whole sections of the country. While early Union interest in the Shenandoah Valley had been tactical – a back door to Richmond – Grant's interest was strategic, the devastation of the 'breadbasket' of Lee's Army of Northern Virginia.

Grant's devotion to devastation and death was strategic, not personal. He did not display personal bitterness toward the South, as many Union leaders did. Indeed, on several occasions, he showed a developed sense of ethics. After the war, when radicals sought to try General Lee in court, Grant threatened to resign his commission if the surrender terms he had signed were subverted.

Grant chose General William Tecumseh Sherman to command the final push on the western front. A tactician with daredevil tendencies, he was ruthless to the point of being accused of committing atrocities. He once had Confederate prisoners of war marched over areas to test them for mines, for example. Sherman's ruthlessness had a purpose. He told a Southern woman complaining of being robbed by his soldiers that the crueler the war, the sooner it would be over. He understood that Southerners had to be convinced that continued fighting was hopeless, and sought to make war so 'terrible' they would submit.

Sherman was respected by his subordinates and had the good fortune to have excellent commanders of his armies—the unspectacular

Opposite This portrait of General Grant hangs at Appomattox Court House National Historical Park, where the Confederate Army of Northern Virginia surrendered.

117

Right Major General
William T. Sherman
commanded the final
push on the Western
front and cut a path to
the sea through
Georgia.

Union Major General
George B. Thomas
(above) was known as
the 'Rock of
Chickamauga' for his
heroic stand in that
battle. Major General
Alexander McDowell
McCook (right) was
one of 14 'Fighting
McCooks' who served
in the Union army.

but steady General George H. Thomas; the
brilliant General James B. McPherson; and
General John M. Schofield, who after the war
would become general-in-chief. Sherman
frequently feuded with the press, which led to
periodic calls for his ouster, because he felt
that too much was published that could be
used by the enemy.

Both Grant and Sherman were fortunate
choices. Although their personalities had
major flaws, their military perception was
superb and their confidence in their strategy
to end the war was steadfast. Both would

continue to make mistakes, and both benefitted from being called to high duty as the fortunes of the Confederacy waned, but they had ability and determination. Neither criticism, civilian suffering nor appalling losses of men could deter them from their policy of attrition.

One of the 1,900 Union generals who served in the war, 583 with full rank and 1,367 with breveted rank, was General Alexander M. McCook, the highest-ranking member of the 14 'Fighting McCooks' of Ohio who served in the war.

CONFEDERATE GENERALS

Among those who resigned from the United States Army to enter Confederate service were some of the highest-ranking and most respected officers, including Robert E. Lee, who had been informally offered command of the Union forces.

No other commander on either side would approach Lee in the admiration and respect of his troops and the civilian population. Lee was even respected in the North for his imaginative and enlightened leadership. A Virginia gentleman from a distinguished family which included Revolutionary War heroes, he was a bold and resourceful tactician whose ability to inspire his men was as well known as his tolerance of misfeasance by his subordinates. As has been said, Lee in command was like another army in the field. His Army of Northern Virginia was always inferior in size to the opposing Union forces, but was never outfought. Lee's value to the Army of Northern Virginia was appreciated in the ranks; at The Wilderness, when Lee attempted to lead a charge, Texans refused to move until he went to the rear.

Lee was as inspiring in defeat as in victory. He accepted full responsibility for the failure at Gettysburg, although General Longstreet's delay was fatal and General Pickett blamed himself for not breaking the Federal line during his costly charge. Lee did not sacrifice the lives of his hopelessly outnumbered men at Appomattox Court House, as he might have done, because he recognized the futility of the

effort and foresaw the value of these young men in the recovery of the South from wartime ravages. So great was his prestige that no one blamed him for the capitulation of his army.

General Thomas J. 'Stonewall' Jackson, a deeply religious, strict disciplinarian who imposed as harsh a regimen on himself as on his men, is often regarded as the foremost combat commander of the war. Jackson's masterful 1862 campaign in the Shenandoah Valley has been studied by succeeding generations of military officers. Jackson conceived the turn-

This full-length portrait of Robert E. Lee was taken by Matthew Brady shortly after the end of the war. Lee posed reluctantly, concerned that it might violate his parole.

119

The aggressive but unsuccessful Confederate General John Bell Hood (above) and the dashing cavalier J.E.B.('Jeb') Stuart, Lee's most trusted cavalry leader (left).

utilizing terrain to his advantage, resulted in his dismissal. He was returned to the command of an army decimated by his successor, General John B. Hood, but successfully confronted Sherman at Bentonville, North Carolina, before surrendering at Bennett's Farm, now a State historical park.

As a group, Confederate commanders were more glamorous than Union generals. The cavalry leaders were at the top—the dashing J.E.B. 'Jeb' Stuart, bold and brash General John Hunt Morgan, the energetic General Jubal A. Early and even those of lesser rank, including the Gray Ghost, Major John S. Mosby. By far the most popular with the ladies was General P.G.T. Beauregard, the Louisiana aristocrat who commanded the attack on Fort Sumter and was a hero at First Manassas. He was besieged with requests for locks of his hair, eagerly sought for personal appearances, and remembered in the names of untold numbers of babies and pets.

ing movement at Chancellorsville which drove the Union army from the field in confusion. His death in that battle deprived Lee of his 'right arm.' Jackson had an odd sort of charisma; his men often joked among themselves about his appearance and manner, but they responded to him on the battlefield. The Stonewall

Brigade, which he founded, served with distinction to the end; after the war, when his body was interred in Lexington, Virginia. Cemetery, many of them went to bivouac once more with Old Jack.

General Joseph E. Johnston was warm and unpretentious, popular with his troops and well schooled in tactics. He understood both the capabilities of his army and the strategic necessities on the western front much better than did the politicians in Richmond. His lack of popularity outside the army resulted primarily from the impossible task assigned to him. The war in the West did not receive the attention in Richmond it deserved, and he was forced to engage a Union army twice the size of his in terrain which made maneuvering difficult. His delay and fall-back tactics,

Right The Court House hosts the Visitors' Center and museum at Appomattox National Historical Park, a recreation of the Civil War community.

Opposite Handsome General P.G.T. Beauregard was popular among the ladies in the Southern States.

THE FINAL SURRENDER

Appomattox Court House National Historical Park recreates the scene of the surrender site. Lee and Grant met in McLean House, which by an ironic twist was owned by a farmer who resettled there after his home at Manassas had been endangered by warfare. The present house is a reconstruction on the original foundations and is authentically restored inside. (The original was taken apart after the war, exhibited and then stored at the Smithsonian Institution, where it deteriorated.) The replica of the room where the signing of the surrender took place on Palm Sunday 1865 is so expertly arranged one can almost see the two generals, flanked by aides, sitting at the tables across the room from each other.

Lee's intention was to get the best terms possible and to prevent his Army of Northern Virginia from being marched into captivity. Grant, still haunted by the fear that Lee might somehow escape, was generous: Lee's men were paroled to return to their homes, and the officers kept their sidearms to help preserve law and order. Grant also provided 25,000 rations for Lee's starving men. Lee and Grant would honor both the letter and the spirit of the agreement; Lee would never permit an unkind word about Grant in his presence, and Grant would threaten to resign his command if Lee were arrested and tried for treason. Lee also defended Grant's military record against postwar detractors; 'I have carefully searched the military records of both ancient and modern history, and have never found Grant's superior as a general,' he said.

The paths at Appomattox National Park lead through a village that looks much as it did in 1865. The reconstructed courthouse, which houses the Visitors' Center, museum, and slide presentation about the surrender, is the centerpiece of the restored village. Clustered around it are more than a dozen structures, including Clover Hill Tavern, the oldest surviving structure; Meek's Store and Woodson law office; and the Kelly and Isbel houses, which depict two quite different lifestyles of the period. The Old Richmond-Lynchburg Stage Road, along which the Union forces lined up to receive the Confederate surrender, leads past an area known as Surrender Triangle, where static displays and a recorded explanation recreate the surrender scene.

It was an electric moment when Confederate forces, led by General John B. Gordon, a capable and loyal Georgian, marched up the hill and along the road bordered by Union troops. The Union line was called to attention in salute to the bravery of the men surrendering.

The crestfallen Gordon immediately straightened and returned the salute. There was minimal public display or exultation or rancor as the Confederates stacked arms and laid down their banners. Confederates who had existed for days on handfuls of parched corn wept and broke ranks to kiss the flags they were surrendering, but they obeyed Lee's eloquent surrender order, General Order No. 9, which put into words the thoughts of many of them: 'I need not tell the brave survivors of so many hard fought battles, who have remained steadfast to the last, that I have consented to this result from no distrust of them; but feeling that valor and devotion could accomplish nothing that could compensate for the loss that must have attended the continuance of the contest, I determined to avoid the useless sacrifice of those whose past services have endeared them to their countrymen.'

Men on both sides were relieved that the bloodshed was over. Grant was already in Washington receiving the adulation of its citizens when Lee mounted Traveler and,

Right Appomattox, an obscure village when General Robert E. Lee surrendered the Army of Northern Virginia, was typical of the hundreds of hamlets throughout the South.

Left The last photograph of Confederate General Robert E. Lee, taken in 1870. Both he and 'Stonewall' Jackson are buried in Lexington, Virginia.

Right The McLean House at Appomattox where Lee surrendered on Palm Sunday, 1865; this photo was taken shortly after that historic day.

with a few aides, rode to Richmond to rejoin his family as a private citizen. The cause of the restoration that prevented the final defiant charge at Appomattox occupied the five years that remained to him. He accepted the presidency of Washington College only after ascertaining that his association with the college would harm neither the institution nor its students; after his death, it was renamed Washington and Lee University in his honor.

123

The attack on Fort Sumter produced a surge of patriotism throughout the North. In New York City and elsewhere, mobs formed spontaneously and roamed the streets to impose their rule. Newspapers and private homes suspected of Southern sympathies were forced to fly the Stars and Stripes or suffer the consequences. In Bangor, Maine, schoolgirls grabbed a Palmetto flag from a young man and destroyed it. Suspected Southern sympathizers everywhere were pelted with rotten eggs or subjected to insults. In the Brandywine region of Delaware, church bells were rung, flags were proudly raised, and mass meetings were organized in schoolhouses.

Much the same happened in the new Confederacy. The citizens of the seceding States had revelled in their freedom. President Lincoln's call for troops to suppress the new nation reawakened the old fears and chauvinism. Men who believed deeply in State's rights rallied to the defense of their new

Civilian Life: A World Turned Upside-down

country. One of the great surprises of the war was the speed with which a sense of nationhood developed in the Confederacy, a region where particularism and individualism were deep seated.

This surge of patriotism was not the only thing the citizens of the two nations shared. The war changed the tempo of life more than anyone suspected at the start, intruding on the ways of a people accustomed to feeling secure in their homes and jobs, whether they were farmers or store clerks. Roles changed as the two nations shifted from normal pursuits to wartime economies and benefitted from the surge in industrial activity. Men had to decide whether to join the great crusades gathering or to remain at home, to be derided by those who volunteered for military service. Inconveniences ranged from minor irritations of crowding on public transportation to shortages of essentials.

The war modified social customs. Women in both countries were proud of the men marching off to war and immediately began organizing knitting and sewing groups to provide extra comforts for the troops. Fewer men were available for dances and other social functions and women went unescorted to places they would have avoided before. Women took a more active role in agriculture, business, and government. Of necessity, they adapted quickly to tasks that had been unfamiliar to them. On the other hand, marriage rates rose perceptibly. Once away from familiar places, the men longed for the comfort of the soft arms of their wives or girlfriends; when soldiers came home on leave, they wanted to make up for lost time by courting.

Cultural life, good and bad, expanded as the need for escape from wartime conditions grew. Crowds filled theaters and opera houses, gardens, skating carnivals, and billiard tournaments. They also frequented saloons, burlesque shows, and cock fights, engaged in drunken brawls and frequented houses of ill repute in greater numbers than before.

The appearance of society changed as much as its tone. The congregations at some

churches were now mostly female. Civilians for the first time saw cannon and other weapons of war dragged through their streets with serious intent. Men in uniforms were more apparent than at any previous time in American history and even dominated the life of some cities. As the conflict wore on, more and more men using crutches or wearing folded sleeves or pants legs lounged on home porches. The system of raising volunteer units in a particular community or State accentuated both the numbers of men away and the losses to certain families and at times resulted in the death of most of the male members of a family.

Professor Nicola Marschall designed the first Confederate flag, the Stars and Bars. It was adopted by the Confederate Congress in March, 1861.

Right This topical
patent medicine
broadside makes up in
impact what it may
lack in ethics.

Below Armed civilians
in New York City
skirmish with a
military unit following
the imposition of
conscription.

GREAT EXCITEMENT
IN
South Carolina!

Was being caused before the war by the wonderful cures of Bronchitis, Asthma, Sore Throat, Consumption, &c., &c., effected by Wishart's Pine Tree Tar Cordial, in and around Charleston.

BEAUREGARD

himself might as well be

A PRISONER!

as to be confined with a distressing Cough or Sore Throat and not be able to obtain Wishart's Pine Tree Tar Cordial, which is known to cure all Complaints of the Throat, Consumption, &c.

Depot, No. 10 North Second Street.

THE NORTH: LIFE GOES ON

There were major differences between civilian life in the North and that in the South. The economic dislocation in the Union was minor compared to that which occurred in the Confederacy. New England was hard hit for a time, as mills closed down for lack of cotton to spin and weave. At one point Mayor Fernando Wood proposed that New York City and Long Island secede from the Union so they could trade with both sides. Overall, though, the North experienced a boom in manufacturing and trading. The Union already was industrialzed and the peacetime economy was quickly converted to a wartime footing. For example, Revere Cooper Company of

Canton, Massachusetts, turned from household items to cannon. Grover and Baker of Roxbury, which manufactured sewing machines in peacetime, began making the Springfield rifles that ultimately would become the dominant shoulder weapon carried by the Union soldier.

War contracts were lucrative sources of profits. Harlan and Hollingsworth on the Christina River in Delaware began building warships. In Wilmington, wagons were ordered from A. Flaglor & Company and ambulances from Gregg and Bowe. Dean and Company, textile manufacturers in Newark, Delaware, received contracts for woolen blankets and

PRESS COVERAGE FROM THE FRONT

Northern citizens were kept informed by newspapers' and magazines' prodigious and costly effort to cover the war. Reporters and artists who went along with the troops sent back a constant stream of detailed reports. They had access to government transportation and communications systems, but their treatment varied. Those who enjoyed the confidence of generals and admirals were able to obtain complete and accurate information; others were forced to overcome or live with the hostility of commanders. The articles about individual activities and heroism and the numerous drawings, engravings, and photographs of battles, marches, and camp life show they did not ignore the common soldier.

Although military commanders had a right to censor newspapers, press freedom was generally observed – so much so that newspapers on both sides became conduits of intelligence. General Lee regularly read a number of Northern newspapers in an attempt to glean information from apparently innocuous articles.

Above Civilians showed their patriotism in a variety of ways, including this Volunteer Refreshment Saloon in Philadelphia providing water, coffee and food to soldiers on the move. Small views at the bottom of the engraving show interior accommodations.

George Alfred Townsend (far left) of the *New York Herald*, was one of the first journalists to reach Richmond after it surrendered. Artist Frank Vizetelly (near left) was among the small army of reporters and artists who covered the war on both sides.

The receipts from the Great Central Fair held in Philadelphia's Logan Square from June 7 to June 28, 1864, went to the Sanitary Commission for the benefit of sick and wounded soldiers and sailors. President Lincoln visited the fair on June 16.

cloth. Du Pont Company, which pre-war did a large business with the South in blasting and sports powder, immediately became one of the North's largest producers and ultimately would produce more than 40 per cent of all gunpowder used by the Union. Stock shares of companies receiving government contracts soared; that of the Erie Railroad rose from 17 to $126\frac{1}{2}$ in three years. Money changers and war profiteers grew rich, but at the same time good business organization obtained and transported mountains of supplies to the men in the field.

THE RISE OF THE LABOR UNIONS

The war improved the status of the labor unions as high profits and strikes created leverage for skilled workers. However, wages rose only 50 to 60 percent during the war compared to a 100 percent increase in prices. Strikes occurred frequently – more than 100 in 1864 alone. White workers in Cincinnati and Brooklyn rioted when manufacturers began employing blacks.

The most serious incident involved the 1863 draft law. Its passage brought out rioters in New York. They lynched a dozen blacks, burned the draft office, a black orphanage, and the homes of a few prominent Republicans and tried unsuccessfully to destroy the building of the *New York Tribune*. In four days of rioting, much of it aimed at blacks, about 1,200 people were killed and property amounting to millions was damaged. Some of the dead were rioters shot by troops recalled from Gettysburg to end the violence. Nineteen

rioters later were imprisoned. Other resistance occurred in the Northeast and Midwest, where some draft officials were murdered.

NORTHERN PATRIOTISM

Most Northerners were eager to show their patriotism, however. They sponsored public programs to raise money for humanitarian purposes, and overall contributions reached astounding figures. Individual patriots took on unselfish tasks like knitting socks for strangers and working long hours in hospital. Families sent food and supplies and letters of hope to the soldiers in the field. Merchants decorated their windows with patriotic displays. War souvenirs brought or sent home by soldiers attracted community-wide attention. Even non-violent Quaker merchants displayed captured swords in their windows—which got them into trouble with their fellow church members. A Rebel flag was flown over city hall—upside-down and under the Stars and Stripes. Schoolchildern sponsored such public displays of patriotism as song fests and speeches, and drilled as junior home guards.

Self-appointed organizations like the United States Sanitary Commission and the United States Christian Commission donated large amounts of money and devoted great effort to improving conditions for the combat soldiers. They raised money from their members and at public programs. The Great Central Fair in Philadelphia was attended by President Lincoln: a four-acre site at Logan

Newspapers made prodigious efforts to cover all aspects of the Civil War. The *New York Herald* sent this mobile team into the field.

Square was covered with activities – a large art museum, Indian dancing, plays, book stalls, raffles, bazaars, and even ladies selling strands of hair. Volunteers like Clara Barton created new outlets for humanitarian efforts, while the government itself provided improved hospital treatment for the sick and wounded.

Despite the enlistment of hundreds of thousands of farmers, crop production was maintained. The production of wool was stimulated by the loss of cotton from the

Left Most 'contrabands' or former slaves gravitated to Union camps after leaving their former owners.

Below The masthead of the newspaper *The Liberator*, edited by abolitionist William Lloyd Garrison, shows Christ breaking the bonds of slavery.

South. Flax and hemp also were used as substitutes for cotton, and sugar was imported from Cuba.

MORALE IN THE NORTH

Morale at home rose and fell with success at the front and with the degree of personal tragedy. In general, morale was low in the North during the early years of the war as heavy casualties produced few results. Confidence was so low after the defeat at Fredericksburg, in fact, that Quartermaster General Montgomery Meigs warned that 'exhaustion steals over the country.' Lincoln was visibly shaken by the defeat and by demands in Congress that he change his Cabinet: but he regained composure within a few days and skillfully faced down congressional leaders in a personal confrontation. Later victories, es-

pecially the Battle of Gettysburg, greatly improved morale in the North.

Northern suffering was mostly individualistic because nearly all the fighting occurred in the South and Border States. Except for brief raids, only western Maryland, southern Pennsylvania, Missouri, Kentucky, and the New Mexico Territory were invaded by Southern troops, and these incursions were brief. The Confederate army foraged, but by and large left the civilians alone. In these invasions, the public rallied round the flag both during and after the fighting. Communities near prison camps were momentarily frightened when groups of captives escaped in an effort to return to the South.

The families of soldiers sometimes encountered dire straits, and continuing efforts were made to provide food, clothing, and fuel. Local campaigns raised most of the money for these efforts. The benefit Mardi Gras sponsored by the Brandywine communities was typical in form, but not in results, of the hundreds held throughout the North. The Mardi Gras included a grand ball in a hall hung with patriotic bunting and the portraits of military and naval heroes. The ladies wore red, white, and blue dresses. However, the cost of the ball ate up much of the profit and only $80 was left to provide for the poor.

REFUGEE PROBLEM

The Union had a minor refugee problem. At the start of the war, thousands of Northerners who had been living in the South, for one reason or another, and Southerners who opposed secession moved northward. Southern whites trapped behind Union lines often sought to distance themselves from the front by going

Right George N. Barnard's photographic laboratory in the field near Atlanta in 1864 attracts curious off-duty soldiers.

Right As the Federal armies drove south through the Confederate States many slaves voted with their feet. Here a black family with a loaded cart enters the Union lines to find freedom–of a sort.

Above Although there were few refugees in the North, they were a massive problem in the South late in the war. Whole families would take to the road with their possessions as the war engulfed their homes.

North, where they were not always welcome. Few procedures existed for caring for these refugees; usually they were dependent on relatives and friends for assistance.

Blacks were a constant refugee problem as they took advantage of Union advances to escape the institution of slavery. Many of them gravitated to military posts, where commanders usually made an attempt to take care of them. Former slaves were hired for menial tasks and many were accepted as soldiers. Private associations, which also aided liberated blacks, were especially prominent in the educational field. More than a thousand teachers, including a few black ones, were recruited and sent into occupied areas of the South.

ROCKY MOUNTAINS AND WEST

Civilian life in the territories and States in and west of the Rocky Mountains was sporadically affected by the war. Many of the regular soldiers on station there were moved east; others resigned to enter Confederate service. Union recruiters enrolled men from Colorado, Utah, and other areas for service in the East,

but most of the men went into local units raised to replace the departing regulars and to block the considerable Southern influence in the region.

Citizens in New Mexico and Arizona were briefly affected by the war. Farmers and townspeople along the Rio Grande River witnessed a short invasion by Texas units, as well as their retreat after defeat at the Battle of Glorieta Pass near Santa Fe. For the most part, the citizens of Albuquerque and Santa Fe, both of which were occupied by Confederate forces, took little part in the conflict. Scarce supplies in the towns were requisitioned for military purposes, but foraging in the countryside was limited by the unproductive nature of the terrain.

Small bands of Confederates operated in sparsely-settled Arizona, a part of the New Mexico territory which preferred the Confederacy. They occasionally captured wagons of Union wheat and burned Union hay, but their presence was mostly a show of force to encourage those sympathetic toward the South. Confederate troops were welcomed by the inhabitants of Mesilla who, in March 1861, had called a convention to declare the southern part of New Mexico a Confederate territory.

A mass meeting in Tucson in August of the same year declared the area ready to join the Confederacy, and a Confederate outpost was established there about six months later amid the cheers of the population. But a few months after the Confederates surrendered the town to the much stronger California Column, comprising loyalist infantry, cavalry, and artillery from the West Coast State. The experience was traumatic for Tucson. A few nationalist citizens left when the Confederates arrived, and a much larger group accompanied the retreating Confederates. Indeed, Tucson was virtually a ghost town when the California Column entered because the citizens feared reprisals for their support of the Confederacy. They slowly drifted back as it became apparent that was not the case, and life in the town returned to normal.

California troops were sent into Utah, as much to watch the Mormons—who were distrusted by Washington and most military

Below Recruiting blacks into the Union army solved two problems—manpower and their hindering presence near military camps.

Pony Express rider Frank E. Webner helped maintain the fragile communications link between St. Joseph and the West Coast until the telegraph line was completed.

officers—as to control the Indians. Soldiers were also sent to Nevada, where the Confederate sympathies of perhaps a third of the people in Carson City and Virginia City spawned rumors of plots and concern about the safety of the Comstock Lode, an abundant source of silver and a major factor in helping the Union finance the war.

California citizens were inconvenienced in other ways. Persistent rumors of a Confederate threat from within the city or from Pacific Ocean raiders caused the cost of maritime insurance and manufactured goods to rise. Letters from the East were delayed by Indian attacks on Pony Express riders, who connected the telegraph terminal at St. Louis and the West Coast, or by wartime demands on communications. Southern sympathizers formed secret societies to further their cause and tried to stir up trouble in the mines and among the Spanish Californians whose families had stayed on after California became independent from Mexico.

CALIFORNIA AND THE SOUTHERN COUNTIES

Confederate support was strongest in the southern counties, where a divided population coexisted fitfully throughout the war. As Southern sympathizers departed to take an active part in the fighting, a reservoir of sympathy for the South remained among citizens who opposed coercion of seceding States. Quarrels and fights between factions occurred regularly. Anti-coercionists elected candidates to local offices and to the State legislature. A score of newspapers opposed coercion editorially. The *Tulare Post* called those who favored forced unionism 'blood-hounds of Zion.' The publishers were arrested but both were set free, even though one would not take a loyalty oath. They resumed publication, but the newspaper was destroyed by Union troops angered by the death of two volunteers in quarrels between factions.

The editor of the *Los Angeles Star* also was detained for some time for articles favoring nonintervention.

A popular San Francisco minister who asked for God's blessing on the presidents of these American States, instead of the President of the United States, and who opposed loyalist resolutions at a church meeting was hanged in effigy. Loyalists raised the Stars and Stripes on the steeple of his church and on lampposts near the entrance. He resigned and took an extended trip to Europe, with a handsome donation from the congregation.

Unionist sympathizers worked hard to keep the State loyal by organizing to seize control of the reins of power. They took over the State militia under a law, passed by the State legislature, which required re-appointment of all officers. The election of Leland Stanford, one of the founders of the Republican Party in California, as governor in 1861 boosted the nationalist cause. He embarked upon a campaign of mass meetings and other activities to maintain morale and increase the numbers and influence of the loyalists. That was no easy task during the early failures of Union arms in the East, but one parade and rally in San Francisco attracted 25,000 people. Journalists, judges, clergymen, businessmen, and army officers all were enlisted in the effort. General E.V. Sumner, who had been sent by Lincoln with orders to keep California loyal, participated fully in these activities.

The Federal Congress required men arriving in California from the East to carry

passports. This had a two-fold purpose: so many recruits reached the Confederacy through Southern California that strong measures were employed to stop the flow; passports also were effective in preventing Southerners from embarking from California for Great Britain and France.

The Union units authorized in California were easily filled and their influence was pervasive. A succession of commanders imposed the odious loyalty oath on people suspected of Southern leanings. Civilians were arrested and held without trial under Lincoln's suspension of the writ of habeas corpus. The first use of San Francisco's island fort of

Left and below
Alcatraz Island, in San Francisco Harbor, was a safe storage area for ordnance. Arrested Southern sympathizers also were held there.

The Great Seal of the Confederacy is on display today in the entrance hall of the White House of the Confederacy in Montgomery, Alabama.

or the vigor of the State's growing commerce.

The assassination of President Lincoln released Southern sympathies that had been suppressed throughout the war. General Irwin McDowell, by then commander of the Department of the Pacific, was able to handle this situation better than he did the Union army at First Manassas. General Order 27, issued on April 15, 1865, declared that persons exulting over the assassination 'become virtually accessories after the fact and will at once be arrested by any officer or provost-marshal or member of the police having knowledge of the case.' Thirty-nine men were sent to Alcatraz under that order.

CIVIL AND UNCIVIL SOUTH

The comfortable way of life that existed in the South was transformed gradually by the Civil War into one of shortages and suffering. The war consumed everything the few factories in the South could produce, as well as most of the produce of the farms. Cotton and tobacco rotted on the docks because it could not be shipped aboard, while blockade runners maximized profits by returning with luxuries that would bring the highest prices.

In the first flush of patriotism, the sacrifices did not seem hard; the prevailing mood in the antebellum South was of essential equality among white citizens. Since nearly everyone expected a short war, inconveniences could be tolerated as contributions by those at home to the war effort. There were other compensations; farmers could easily sell their crops and employees in cities had an abundance of cash. Cultural life went on and in some cases improved. Theater, musical concerts, and receptions remained vigorous. Some Negro minstrels became famous. Creative energies flowed in other areas, especially science and technology.

In the Confederate capital of Richmond, the new government brought in a new era of parties and dances. Taxes were raised but not enough to arouse political opposition.

Newspapers and magazines were eagerly sought. The *Southern Illustrated News* and

Alcatraz as a prison was to hold civilian internees. Starting in late 1862, 36 civilians were incarcerated on Alcatraz for 'treasonous utterances.' Most of them were guilty of making provocative statements, but at least one was jailed for a drunken toast which mentioned Jefferson Davis.

These steps were effective. Everyday life went on undisturbed in most parts of California. The war did not interrupt the flow of metals from the mines, the productivity of the farms,

Above Major General Irvin McDowell, who commanded the Department of the Pacific, threatened to jail anyone exulting in the assassination of Lincoln.

Right Many patriotic songs were composed on both sides. This anthem by a Richmond composer seeks the salvation of the Confederacy.

other publications carried colorful accounts written on the battlefield. Newspaper editorials were full of passion and righteous indignation. Patriotic songs were popular, including the 'Bonnie Blue Flag,' 'Just Before the Battle, Mother,' and 'All Quiet Along the Potomac To-night.' Diversions included candy pullings, quilting parties, spinning bees, picnics, and religious services. Bazaars, bake sales, suppers, and other devices were used to raise money to support the war.

But each year, the shortages grew worse and the war seemed no nearer an end. The Confederate government was forced to impress food, clothing, livestock, machinery, and transportation equipment to prosecute the war, further increasing civilian shortages and arousing resentment. Impressment created hardship on small farms, many of which were poorly tended because the men were in the army. Inflation was a heavy burden on the poor; their plight was largely ignored by the Confederate and State governments until it became explosive. Efforts to adjust government salaries to compensate for the inflationary spiral were usually late. Even well-to-do people complained at times about the pinch of prices.

Increasing centralization of government worried State's Rightists, while the system of purchasing exemptions raised cries of discrimination against people of poor and modest means. Then, as the final insult, Union armies devastated whole sections of the South, visiting physical and mental hardships of one kind or another on nearly every citizen.

IMPACT OF WAR IN RURAL AND URBAN AREAS

Most battles were fought in rural areas, but towns and cities did not escape. Homes and churches in war zones were used as field hospitals. Churches also were used as billets for men—who desecrated the buildings and burned pews and altars as firewood—and even to stable horses. After big battles, hotels, homes, schools, and other buildings were pressed into service to handle the wounded. The owner of Carnton's plantation took it upon

himself to retrieve hundreds of Confederate dead after the Battle at Franklin, Tennessee, and bury them in a cemetery on his land.

For those removed from the military foragers and battlefields, food was less a problem in the countryside than in the cities. An exchange economy developed, with grain being milled on a share basis. Neighbors took turns slaughtering and sharing when a severe shortage of salt eliminated the possibility of preserving meat; near the coast, people extracted salt from seawater. Molasses often was used as a substitute for sugar.

Farm families suffered from a shortage of supplies and equipment. Makeshift scythes with cradles were used for harvesting, and threshing often was done by hand. In order to make ends meet, rural slaves sometimes were hired out to businesses in the cities, which were short of manpower because of enlistments and the draft.

City life in the South was affected by a shortage of currency and by the variations in legal tender. At first the Confederacy issued only big bills, depending on States, banks, localities, and corporations to provide additional liquidity. Then all of them printed too much. Gold and silver were seldom seen. Debtors paid off old debts in depreciated currency, and inflation became so bad that the urban economy turned to barter when possible. Doctors preferred goods to cash, and schools asked for tuition in the form of edibles. By 1865, a gold dollar would buy 70 paper dollars.

Coffee, sugar, baking soda, and spices were in short supply. Staples such as paper, and indispensable items like needles and locks, were simply not available for purchase. Oil for lamps, which formerly had come from the North, and rubber, quickly disappeared from markets. The leading publications in Richmond, among the best in the United States before the war, declined in quality or went out of business.

Southerners, forced to become ever more self sufficient, showed a genius for make-do in discovering substitutes for scarce items.

The cities of the South were military targets. Here artillery pieces are set up in front of the Tennessee State House in Nashville.

Roasted cereals and peanuts were used to make coffee. Tea was made from sassafras and blackberry leaves. Women made shirts for their husbands from petticoats. Shoes were made from carpets, and some women even fashioned homemade silk stockings. Women learned to knit and crochet beside open fireplaces or in the dark when they could not burn lamps. Letters were written in homemade ink on coarse paper and wallpaper was used to make envelopes; envelopes were reversed so they could be used a second time. Palmetto leaves were turned into fans, soot was used to make shoe polish, twigs became toothbrushes and pulverized charcoal became tooth powder, combs were made of wood and cow horns, soap was the strong sort made with lye, and roots and herbs were substituted for prepared medicines.

When rubber became unavailable, bands to drive machinery were made from cotton cords. Lard and bacon drippings were used to grease machines and axles. Most handicrafts shops, on which the South depended heavily, closed because the owners and workers went off to war.

But Southern vanity showed, too; one woman, when she could not obtain silk stockings, went to bed and stayed there!

HELPING THE MEN AT THE FRONT

Women worked at home to make life more comfortable at the front for the men in arms. Mrs. A. H. Gay of Decatur, Georgia, has left a record of the way she knitted socks, the item most in demand among the soldiers. She made one a day—which sometimes required here to work at night by firelight—and packaged each pair separately, enclosing other items of clothing, gloves and handkerchiefs, and a note of encouragement such as 'Never saw I the righteous forsaken.' These were mailed in groups of 12 to an officer of a unit for distribution to his men. Women also formed societies, sometimes involving more than one community, to make clothing for soldiers.

When a son came home on leave, the family killed the fatted calf, sometimes their last, to entertain him and always sent him back to the front with new clothing of some sort, usually home-made underwear of scarce flannel or other warm material. As they have in all wars, soldiers brought their comrades to share in the comforts of home.

Communities made an effort to amuse or comfort units stationed nearby. During lulls in the fighting, soldiers were entertained at picnics, parties, dances, band concerts, and even weddings. In 1863, an epidemic of some sort broke out in Third Maryland Artillery while it was billeted near Decatur, Georgia. The good ladies of Decatur took the sick 'whose faith in the justice of our cause was so strong' into their homes to treat them. In border areas, the arrival of Confederate troops in a sympathetic town was an occasion for celebration.

The roles of women began changing in other than material ways as soon as the war broke out, however, and the change accelerated as the war called more and more men to the front. Women worked in war industries, garment plants, and textile mills and entered government service. The ladies of Richmond produced thousands of sandbags for the

Mary Tippee was a sutler with the 114th Pennsylvania, the Collis Zouaves.

defenses at Yorktown and elsewhere. They did hazardous work at times, too, and always at lower rates of pay than men received. A number died in a powder mill explosion in Richmond.

When the great landowners departed for war, the women managed the plantations. This meant they had to organize the work and direct the slaves. Many of them had had comfortable, sheltered girlhoods and knew little about the work. They had to learn quickly about planting, cultivating, and harvesting as well as how to measure, weigh, treat, and store food and materials. They learned about looking after livestock, raising, slaughtering and curing hogs, cutting wood, and dozens of other functions.

Women virtually ran the hospitals of the South, taking over successfully as both administrators and nurses. A section of Chimborazo Hospital in Richmond providing care for Alabama wounded was sustained by $200,000 in donations from an Alabama woman. A young Jewish widow, Mrs. Phoebue Yates Pember, was for more than two years the chief matron of one of the divisions of Chimborazo, which may have been the largest hospital in the world at that time. The Sisters of Charity were widely praised for their healing work at the infirmaries of St. Joseph's and St. Francis de Sales.

THE STAUNCHEST REBELS

A more subtle change occurred, too; the on-a-pedestal image of Southern women was altered by the new contribution they were making in society. Women had such a primary role in the history of the Confederacy that they have been described by one author as the 'staunchest Rebels.' They climbed to the roofs of Charleston to watch the bombardment of Fort Sumter. They wore miniature Confederate flags, sang patriotic songs, and urged their men to join the military. The letters they wrote to the men in arms usually were psychological shots in the arm. Popular heroes were showered with feminine attention, especially General Beauregard. When he re-

turned to South Carolina, he was the toast of Charleston.

Although some women were secret Union sympathizers, most despised the invaders and sought to avoid contact with them. When confronted, they were not averse to spitting in the face of a Yankee officer.

A few women were not content to play a passive role and wanted to participate directly in the war. Some actually saw action. Nancy Hart, renowned as a Confederate spy, led an attack on Summerfield, West Virginia, which captured the Union garrison. She also helped Jackson in his famous Shenandoah Valley campaign and escaped arrest in 1862 after killing a Federal guard.

A few women cut their hair, disguised their identities and followed their men into the ranks until they were discovered. Mrs. L.M. Blalock and Mrs. Amy Clarke may have been beside their husbands during several battles. The women of Bascom, Georgia, formed a female military company to protect the home front while the men were away.

Women made the best spies. Belle Boyd of Martinsburg, West Virginia was only 17 when the war broke out. She became incensed by Yankee action and thereafter was an ardent Confederate. She was twice imprisoned and finally released to go to England. Rose O'Neal Greenhow gave vital information to the Confederates at First Manassas, spent a term in prison, and was drowned while running the Union blockade with money she had raised in Europe. Mrs. Mary E. Surratt was one of those hanged for conspiring to assassinate Lincoln.

FEEDING THE MILITARY

Civilian shortages were aggravated by efforts to feed the military. In the spring of 1863, when commissary agents began impressing food in Richmond markets and seizing foodstuffs being hauled into the city, the reaction was predictable: farmers stopped bringing food to the city.

On April 2, wives of workers at the Tredegar Iron Works sought redress from Governor John Letcher. The march to the governor's

Three of the South's more picturesque spies: Nancy Hart (top left), Rose O'Neal Greenbow (top right), and the flamboyant Belle Boyd (right).

CIVIL WAR WOMEN: STAUNCH AND COMPASSIONATE

Women were an important strategic asset to both sides, but particular to the Confederacy. They were among the staunchest rebels, despite privation caused by the war. In the absence of men, they quickly learned to perform many of tasks unfamiliar to them. They managed plantations, worked in the war factories, sewed uniforms, staffed hospitals, donated their gold wedding rings and even collected urine so the salt could be extracted for use in munitions. A few followed their husbands to war and, until discovered, fought at their sides.

Sally L. Thompkins received a captain's commission from Jefferson Davis after organizing her own hospital in Richmond to care for soldiers wounded at the Battle of the First Manassas (Bull Run). During the war, her hospital treated 1,300 soldiers.

The efforts of other Southern ladies on behalf of the wounded was just as gallant. Chimborazo Hospital in Richmond, managed mostly by women, was chronically crowded, but treated more than 76,000 men during the war. An Arkansas widow, Ella King Newsom, supervised hospitals in several cities. Mrs. Arthur Francis Hopkins of Alabama walked with a limp after twice being wounded assisting casualties during the fighting at Seven Pines near Richmond. On occasion, when hospitals were crowded or not available, Southern women treated wounded and sick soldiers in their homes.

In Richmond, Virginia, the capital of the Confederacy, citizens did not have to depend on the ringing of bells to know that something was going on, but could rely on the activity around them. The fewer men engaged in normal pursuits and more soldiers moving through the streets, the more obvious something important was going on nearby.

As more and more men marched of to war, the female presence came to dominate many aspects of life. Sallie A. Putnam of Richmond, Virginia, who later wrote a book about her wartime experiences, noted the shortage of males in church services at the time of the Battle of First Manassas too (Bull Run); even fewer men would be present as the war progressed. Women worked in government, stores, offices and munitions factories. They worked at home, as well, sewing, and knitting socks, badly needed by the soldiers. It did not matter that these home-made items were of imperfect size; the shoes the soldiers wore were imperfect in size, too.

Northern women were especially useful in alleviating the poverty of families whose men were away at war. They organized and held numerous charity events, some of enormous size, which raised large sums for the wives and widows of soldiers. Many women were not content to remain at home; they took field positions with the United States Christian Commission and United States Sanitary Commission, civilian agencies which attempted to oversee military health conditions, and even operated sutler's stores.

Women made major contributions to the care and treatment of injured soldiers. Clara Barton, a Patent Office clerk who followed General George B. McClellan's army from Washington to Antietam to tend the wounded, provided a critical service by bringing medical supplies and food during the early hours of the fighting, before the regular army supplies

arrived. Antietam, where men died at night because doctors did not have light to tend them and too few doctors were available anyway to care for the thousands who fell during the day, made an indelible impression on Clara Barton. She convinced the chief quartermaster in Washington to provide wagons and supplies for a number of later battles and became superintendent of nurses of the Army of the James in 1864. In 1877, she founded the American Red Cross on the concept of providing aid and comfort during disaster in war and peace.

Dorothea Lynde Dix, who already had acquired an international reputation as a reformer of hospitals for the insane, volunteered for duty as soon as firing broke out and was appointed superintendent of women nurses by the surgeon general.

An Illinois widow, Mary Ann 'Mother'

Bickerdyke, was even more famous as a front-line nurse, overcoming the hostility of army surgeons and commanders to care for the soldiers in the Union Army of the Tennessee. She even earned the admiration of General William Tecumseh Sherman, and was one of the few civilians the general allowed to travel with his army.

In many other instances, women took the initiative in rendering assistance. Women from several States gathered in Gettysburg after the battle to care of the sick and wounded.

More than 3,000 women served as nurses in Union hospitals, partly as a result of an order issued in 1862 by the surgeon general that at least one-third of the nurses in the army general hospitals had to be women. The only woman appointed as a surgeon in the Union army, Mary Walker, was captured in Georgia by Confederates.

In this small farmstead outside Richmond, the corpses of Confederate soldiers lie in eerie counterpoint to a slain horse. Note too the damage wrought by cannon fire on the farmhouse.

mansion attracted supporters, who numbered several hundred by the time the governor appeared in an attempt to calm them. When he provided no tangible answers, the group became a mob and headed for the commercial district, where they broke into bread and other food shops in a 10-block area. The mob ignored the pleas of Letcher and Richmond's mayor, Joseph Mayo, but soon were confronted by President Jefferson Davis himself and a company of reserve troops composed of workers in the Confederate armory. Davis mounted a wagon, tossed all the money in his pockets to the mob, and shouted: 'We do not desire to injure anyone, but this lawlessness must stop. I will give you five minutes to disperse, otherwise you will be fired upon.'

'Load!' shouted the captain in charge of the reserve company, and his troops obeyed.

Davis won the test of wills and the crowd began to disperse before the real test came – of whether the soldiers would have fired on their friends and neighbors.

Similar 'bread riots' occurred in Atlanta, Macon, Columbus and Augusta, Georgia; Salisbury and High Point, North Carolina; and Mobile, Alabama. Efforts were made to alleviate food shortages. Farmers were ordered to turn from growing cotton and tobacco to food crops, and municipal agents redoubled their efforts to find food supplies. But success depended on the skills of the agents. While Richmonders rioted, representatives of nearby Petersburg were successful in obtaining adequate supplies from as far away as Alabama.

BUSINESS AS USUAL

Confederates observed the normal holidays, and a few communities even continued to mark the Fourth of July. Yet holidays were a bleak time, even early in the war, despite efforts to celebrate them in the best manner possible. Families made special efforts to send Christmas packages and greetings to men in the armed forces. When manufactured toys became unavailable, children had to be satisfied with corn-shuck and rag dolls placed

in home-made stockings. Adults often had to go without alcohol.

Confederate postal service was irregular, but it maintained a link between soldiers and their families and enabled business to continue functioning. Couriers were used both for military and civilian communications, and notices were printed in newspapers citing the departure of long-distance courier runs – say from Shreveport, Louisiana, to Mobile and Richmond. The 'champion courier' was Major A.J. Rose, who operated between several trans-Mississippi towns and Richmond.

Civilians continued to use rail transportation, but trains were crowded, fares expensive, accidents were frequent, and schedules uncertain. The rail system consisted of numerous small lines, which usually had separate stations in towns where they met.

Mrs. Mary Boykin Chestnut, on a ride from South Carolina to Richmond, spent the night waiting in a crowded station in North Carolina. Her boxes were badly damaged and had to be patched together to hold their contents. An officer from Louisiana cleared a place for her near the fire beside an old lady and two children. The group talked all night about the progress of the war, while station personnel worked to prepare for the train's arrival.

When the train ride resumed, one woman complained bitterly that men crowding the aisles would not make room for her and later shook her fist in the face of a soldier who sat down beside her, saying he had done so 'for no good purpose.' In Petersburg, Mrs. Chestnut met a widow who began by telling a sad story about the loss of her husband in the fighting near Richmond, then took the first open seat beside a man so she could flirt with him.

Travel near the war zone was always risky. A Richmond woman returning home from a visit with friends in King and Queen County was forced to detour south of the York River, where she received assistance from men running contraband supplies and was arrested on the final leg, a train ride. She was released only when a Confederate officer on the train recognized her and vouched for her.

Below Black laborers lounge on a James River wharf in Virginia while awaiting work assignments.

SLAVES AND BLACK LABOR

About 3,500,000 slaves and 135,000 free blacks lived in the Confederate States at the outbreak of war. The changes in the lives of the blacks mirrored those of the whites. As the diets of their masters changed, so did those of the slaves—only worse. Slaves continued to work on plantations under the direction of the mistress of the household or hired overseers, some of whom were black. They engaged in tanning, boiling sea water to obtain salt, making soap, spinning, weaving, and other essential chores. A few accompanied their masters to war as body servants, and generally remained loyal to them although ownership of body servants became less and less practical as the war wore on. Stories of slaves bringing their wounded masters in for medical treatment were common. At Sharpsburg, one got a horse to bring his master in—then remounted and rode to the Union lines.

Black labor made a significant contribution to the Confederate cause. Although many

Above George Washington Carver, agronomist and educator, was born a slave in Diamond, Missouri, and he drew this sketch of his plantation birthplace from memory.

Above The reality was little better than the memory, as this more accurate sketch of the Carver birthplace shows. Carver was to devote his life to bettering the lot of black agricultural workers.

plantation owners resisted the use of their slaves, Negroes were hired and impressed to build fortifications, repair railroads, and perform essential public works jobs. They also drove supply wagons and served as cooks for the military on occasion; they did yeoman service as orderlies and nurses in hospitals. In the last year of the war, the Confederacy opened the ranks of the army to blacks, but the decision came so late that few were enrolled. Fair-skinned blacks passing as white may have been in Confederate army, though.

While Southern whites feared insurrection, none occurred. Minor incidents did happen, but were easily quashed. The slaves as a group adopted a passive role and preferred to let the whites fight it out among themselves.

Still, the war altered the institution of slavery in both obvious and subtle ways. The customary relationship changed; whites appeared less like master, blacks less like slaves when the master was away at war and the prospect of liberation was thinkable. Women and elderly overseers, not experienced in management, could neither provide leadership nor cope with malingering the way the master could. Blacks developed a new consciousness of the leverage their labor gave them in a time of crisis. A few instances occurred where they demanded, and received, wages.

Slaves reacted more as individuals than as a group during the war. Many slaves deserted as the Union army came near, while some remained loyal to their masters to the end. Some told Union soldiers where plantation owners had hidden property, and some volunteered intelligence to Union officers. General Grant received from a slave important information that helped him cross the Mississippi River near Vicksburg. But some slaves even hid their masters from Union soldiers.

But the South could not have continued the war without the support of white laborers, who manned the essential industries. On occasion, however, economic conditions made them restive. Skilled workers were in a much

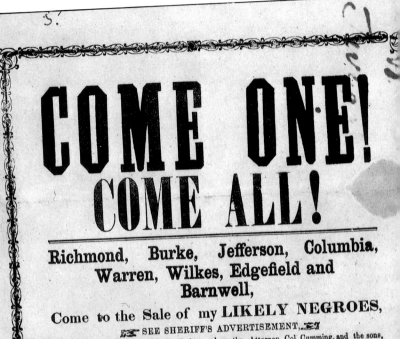

This 1856 broadside, which advertised the sale of slaves in Albany, Georgia, also revealed family feuding over the settlement of an estate.

greater bargaining position than unskilled workers, who could be easily replaced by blacks. A strike by white graveyard workers in Richmond ended with white strikers driving off the blacks and going back to work. Mass meetings were held to support price controls and other measures that would help workers. Unions experimented with political pressure and collective bargaining – without much success. Workers in the Confederacy never considered themselves part of a proletarian movement.

REFUGEE PROBLEM

The war produced the greatest refugee movement in American history. Every State in the Old South was affected to some degree. It started when many Southern citizens went home at the start of the war. The first mass migration, which included the wife of Robert E. Lee, was to Richmond, Virginia, from the environs of Washington, which were occupied by Union forces as soon as the war started. Others later slipped through the lines or were deported by the North.

Union invasion uprooted both whites and blacks. The whites would flee ahead of advances as best they could and the blacks left the farms to follow Union forces or to become vagrants. The trickle of homeless grew to a flood after 1862, as large sections of the South were invaded by Federal troops. Uprooted whites sold their valuables or turned to relatives and friends for help. They utilized any space they could find as living quarters – parlors, libraries, dining rooms, basements, attics, overseer's cottages, slave cabins, stables. More unfortunate ones had to settle for train coaches and boxcars, churches, college and university buildings – any place that put a roof over their heads – and a minority had to be satisfied with outdoor accommodation.

In most cases, refugee status was more permanent than temporary. Those who returned to their homes when immediate danger passed more than likely would be forced to leave again. Many people were driven from their homes several times.

The influx of refugees naturally made life harder for the permanent residents of an area. Living conditions became deplorable because the communities or farms were not equipped to handle such large numbers. These mass movements crowded trains and clogged roads, frequently at a time when the transportation systems were most needed by the military.

As it always does, warfare brought out both the best and the worst in North and South. But the majority of those who served, at the front or at home, did so with high motives and firm resolve. The sad moments of the worst can never diminish the high courage of the best.

BARTERING WITH MINIE BALLS

By the end of the war, consumer goods were so scarce that cold and hunger stalked almost every section of the new nation. Even the few who had saved their money, instead of patriotically putting it back into the war effort, could not purchase the means of livelihood. Where goods existed, merchants were reluctant to accept Confederate money

as defeat became inevitable. Mrs. Gay and a helper, after learning that a store in Atlanta would trade food for lead, collected Minie balls from battlefields to exchange. She informed others in the Atlanta area who needed help and soon women filled the fields like berry pickers in the springtime.

CHAPTER 13

General Ambrose E. Burnside, who resisted command of the Union army in Virginia because he felt unqualified, was more confident about dealing with civilian opposition to the war in the Midwest, which reached a peak in 1862–3. He jailed Clement Vallandigham, an Ohio politician who fearlessly advocated a negotiated peace with the South, and closed the *Chicago Tribune* which attacked the Lincoln administration and the war.

However his defeat in these instances was almost as decisive as his failure before Marye's Heights in the Battle of Fredericksburg. President Lincoln, under whose authority Burnside had acted, altered both actions. Lincoln shipped Vallandigham off to the Confederacy and lifted the ban on the newspaper, which continued to oppose both Lincoln and the war. Vallandigham soon was nominated for Governor by Ohio Democrats and later returned to his home State without interference. Lincoln wisely chose to ignore him rather than make a martyr of him.

Military Rule: Freedom's Folly

Burnside's high-handed tactics were legal under proclamations issued by Lincoln suspending the constitutional right of habeas corpus, which protects citizens against unlawful detention, and making the War Department responsible for internal security. Congress later endorsed these actions, which gave extraordinary powers to commanders of military districts into which the Union was divided.

Military commanders had virtual life-and-death control over the people of their areas, subject to review of major acts by Lincoln. The traditional rights that American citizens take for granted suffered grievously as a result. About 15,000 political prisoners most of whom lived in Border States or the occupied South, were incarcerate for various periods. Among them were editors, clergymen, and public officials whose only offense was criticism of the administration or opposition to the war.

Civilian opponents of the war were tried in military courts without juries which might have sympathized with them. These proceedings did not go unchallenged, but legal vindication was subordinated to wartime necessity. Two years after his conviction, the United States Supreme Court ruled in the case of Lambdin P. Milligan of Indiana that military courts could not try civilians as long as regular courts were functioning. It was 1867, long after the war ended, before the U.S. Supreme Court issued a definitive ruling in McCall v. McDowell: Congress could give the president authority temporarily to suspend writs of habeas corpus without the threat of judicial inquiry, but the president could not suspend the constitutional right on his own initiative. This abrogated the proclamations issued by Lincoln under which thousands had been oppressed.

Officially, newspapers were censored. Under General Order No. 67, approval of the general in command was required before any military information could be published. The order was laxly enforced almost everywhere, however, and newspapers both North and South were read closely by the other side for intelligence purposes. Newspapers were used for 'disinformation', too. An article in St. Louis, Cincinnatti, Chicago, and Louisville newspapers about a major Union offensive in Kentucky was planted by military authorities to mislead the Confederates..

Some Union military commanders used their power to act as virtual dictators, dominating State governments, levying punitive taxes, and expropriating property without normal process of law. In addition, intrusions into the daily lives of citizens took place on and off the battlefields. In some instances, authorities stood by while contesting groups of civilians fought it out or loyalists beat, robbed, and even killed Confederate sympathizers.

One of the foremost Northern opponents of the war, Ohio's Clement L. Vallandingham was arrested but released and deported by Lincoln. He was nominated for Governor of Ohio while under banishment.

Engd by W. G. Jackman, N.Y.

149

Cass County, Missouri, suffered as much as any area. Its Confederate sympathies brought down upon it both official wrath and marauding Unionists. Finally, in an effort to secure the region, almost the entire population of the county was forced to move out. At the end of the war, only 600 remained of the 10,000 people who had resided in the county at the start.

Might often made right. Union General Nathaniel Lyon ignored the pleas of Missouri's elected governor, Claiborne Fox Jackson, to let the State remain neutral and embarked on an active campaign to cement the State to the Union. As commander of the arsenal at St. Louis, he shipped most of the arms store there to Illinois for safekeeping, then marched 7,000 men to Camp Jackson and forced the pro-Confederate State Guard to surrender. During Lyon's triumphal re-entry into St. Louis, citizens hurled stones at the soldiers and a shot was fired; the soldiers opened fire, killing 28 civilians. Next, Lyon captured the State capitol at Jackson as part of a military cam-

Below Military arrests of civilians were common in both North and South. In this period drawing, a 7th U.S. Cavalry unit arrests citizens of Lincoln and Claiborne parishes in occupied Louisiana.

paign to drive Confederate forces, including the State militia, from Missouri. Success at Boonville was followed by defeat and death at the Battle of Wilson's Creek, but Lyon's bold action was a major factor in keeping Missouri in the Union.

MILITARY OCCUPATION OF MARYLAND

Maryland, which held a strategic position astride the vital lifeline to between Washington and the northeast, went through the war virtually under military occupation. While Maryland politicians debated their position on secession, Union troops under General Benjamin Butler occupied Annapolis, the State capital. On May 14, 1861, Butler occupied Baltimore, a hotbed of Confederate sympathizers.

The writ of habeas corpus was suspended first in Maryland, long before other States remaining in the Union. General Nathaniel Banks, who succeeded Butler as military governor, arrested scores of officials he con-

Left Citizens stoned the first Union troops passing through Baltimore on May 19, 1861, en route to the national capital. In this contemporary engraving, Massachusetts soldiers fend off their attackers with bullets and bayonets.

Left Major General Benjamin Butler led the Union troops occupying Baltimore, where opposition to coercion of the seceding States was strong–and sometimes violent.

sidered to be Southern sympathizers. One of them was Severn T. Wallis, the man who had written the State legislature's resolution that it had no authority to pass an ordinance of secession but that Lincoln was to blame for the anti-war riot in Baltimore. Homes of those arrested were searched by soldiers in an attempt to uncover incriminating evidence.. The officials were first jailed at Fort McHenry, where the 'Star Spangled Banner' was written, then moved to Fort Monroe in Virginia and Fort Warren in Boston.

The loud outcries that followed these arrests, included a protest from the Maryland legislature, had little impact. The actions were defended on the grounds of 'military necessity.' Most of the prisoners were finally released after taking loyalty oaths, but Wallis argued he should not be asked to promise not to be 'hostile' toward the Federal government because he had never been hostile in the first place. He was kept in jail for a year, but became such a political embarrassment to

151

Lincoln that he was released.

Whether Maryland would have seceded if given a chance is open to question. The resolutions passed by the legislature were compromises designed to avoid a direct stand on the issue. Whereas the State was badly divided on secession, it continued to support slavery. Confederate sentiment was strong in the eastern part of the States; Unionist sympathies dominated the western portion. Maryland units fought in both armies.

WAR DEPARTMENT ACTIONS

War Department officials in Washington participated in dubious schemes. Despite a warning that he could be 'covered with prosecutions,' Secretary of War Edwin M. Stanton gave Indiana Governor Oliver P. Morton $250 million in Federal funds to keep the State operating without a meeting of the State legislature, which was dominated by Peace Democrats. After the Secret Service was transferred from the State Department to the War Department in 1862, it incarcerated hundreds of people in jails maintained especially for political prisoners. Those detained usually had to wait months to find out what they were accused of and then were subjected to summary proceedings. Objections of lawyers and jurists were ignored; the agency was so powerful that even the most influential men in government feared it.

The conspirators in the Lincoln assassination were tried a military commission, not by a civilian court. The trial was held in a building connected with the Arsenal Penitentiary. Three men and one woman were hanged in the Arsenal courtyard. Four others,

Above **This painting by Jack Clifton depicts Dr. (Lieutenant Colonel) John J. Craven with Jefferson Davis. Craven got the fort commandant to improve the conditions of Davis's imprisonment. Davis was confined for two years in this small cell (inset) in the wall of Fort Monroe at Hampton, Virginia.**

including Dr. Samuel A. Mudd, whose only crime was that he treated the broken leg of John Wilkes Booth, who later proved to be one of the conspirators, were imprisoned at Fort Jefferson off Key West, Florida.

Lincoln often was accused of wanting to establish a dictatorship, but in one instance he turned the accusations to advantage. When he appointed General Joseph 'Fighting Joe'

Hooker to command the Army of the Potomac, he was aware that Hooker had said the country needed a 'dictator.' Lincoln wrote to Hooker: 'Only generals who gain successes can set up dictators. What I now ask of you is military success, and I will risk the dictatorship.'

Confederate President Jefferson Davis was imprisoned without trial for two years after the war, most of the time at Fort Monroe in

After Lincoln's assassination, John Wilkes Booth (near right) died while attempting to escape. Lewis Payne (far right) failed to carry out his part in the plot, and was merely imprisoned. Four conspirators were less lucky and were hanged at Arsenal Prison, (below).

Major General Joseph ('Fighting Joe') Hooker said the Union needed a dictator; Lincoln replied he would risk it if Hooker would win victories on the battlefield.

Virginia. Finally, after enduring hardship and lack of privacy (he was watched at all times, even when he went to the toilet) he was released and spent the last few years of his life writing a book defending his role in the Confederacy. Ironically, Davis's imprisonment helped him regain in the South the prestige he had lost as a result of his direction of the war.

Government agents infiltrated peace societies, which were especially important in the Middle West. The groups were accused of everything from antidraft resistance to conspiracy to revolt and set up a 'Northwest Confederacy.' Vallandigham, the Ohio poli-

tician jailed by Burnside, was the first supreme grand commander of the Sons of Liberty, successor organization to the Knights of the Golden Circle and Order of American Knights.

LIFE IN COMBAT AREAS

In combat areas, military actions dominated life. Cornfields were trampled by marching troops or mowed down by gunfire; animals were killed and buildings were destroyed. Houses were taken over for use as headquarters: the Carter House in Franklin, Tennessee, still bears scars of the battle waged around it, when Union General Jacob D. Cox used it as a command post. Private homes also were used as billets for senior officers, and soldiers were quartered in public and private structures. On numerous occasions, Union armies in the South stripped churches of their pews and houses of their furniture to use as firewood. Horses sometimes were stabled in churches. In the early stages of the war, soldiers brought to Washington to defend the national capital were billeted in the halls of the Capitol building.

Civilians did not always have a chance to leave their property before fighting broke out and, even when they did, some chose to stay. Mrs. Judith Carter Henry refused to leave her home during the Battle of First Manassas (Bull Run) and became the only civilian casualty of the battle.

In 1864, as he prepared for his March to the Sea, General Sherman created the greatest refugee column of the war by ordering all the citizens out of Atlanta and neighboring communities. They were forced to abandon their homes and personal property and move either north or south by whatever means they could contrive. His aim was to clear the roads before moving to the coast in what would go down in history as the 'March to the Sea.' White-haired grandmothers, young mothers still not fully recovered from childbirth, and adolescents were among those 'dumped out upon the cold ground without shelter and without any of the comforts of home, and an autumnal mist or drizzle slowly but surely saturating every

Above A contemporary photograph of Antietam National battlefield.

Right The Henry House near Bull Run was destroyed during the first Battle of Manassas. The owner, Mrs. Judith Carter Henry, was killed by shellfire. The Robinson House shown here was erected on the site.

article of clothing.' Special permission was required to remain in the area.

Mrs. Mary A. H. Gay of Decatur, who wrote about her experiences many years after the war, decided her home, which already had been stripped of most of its valuables by Union soldiers, would have better protection if she remained. After undergoing an interview in which she promised to darn and repair clothing for the soldiers encamped on her property and to allow her maid to wash and iron at reasonable prices, she secured permission to stay from the Federal provost marshal. Mrs. Gay was able to obtain a pass through Union lines to visit relatives in central Georgia. On another occasion, she was given a Union escort to protect her during a time of unrest in the area.

Union soldiers showed compassion, as well. General James B. McPherson wrote out an order stationing a guard at the home of an elderly woman a short time before he died in battle – an order that remained in force until Federal troops left the area.

Property in the path of the fighting was in danger well before and long after the battle. Legal foraging stripped farms of produce and livestock to sustain whatever army happened to be passing by or camping there. While officers were supposed to issue receipts, they did not always do so. Sometimes the requisition orders were uncollectible; some areas were so worked over year after year that nothing could be found to requisition toward the end of the war. Midnight requisition, unauthorized forays by hungry or bored troops, also took a heavy toll at times.

But proximity to the fighting was not all negative. Selection of a home as a headquarters usually saved it from destruction, unless the fighting itself overwhelmed it. Owners came to know principal figures in the war, and sometimes could make a claim for damages through them or with their assistance. The inhabitants of a farmhouse caught in the fighting at least had first-hand knowledge of what went on.

In the last years of the war, the Union adopted a scorched earth policy by which the crops, barns, and even homes was burned. Sherman's March to the Sea through Georgia was emulated–in a slightly more humane way–by General Philip Sheridan in Virginia's breadbasket, the beautiful Shenandoah Valley.

Corruption and malfeasance occurred with regularity. In Louisiana, General Butler's record in requisitioning food and other farm products, including cotton needed in the mills of New England, and the fortune amassed by his brother who acted as agent, came under War Department scrutiny. Butler was suspected of corruption, and recalled because of it, but he was never convicted.

In the western Border States which remained in the Union, a heavy military hand was especially evident. Confederate sympathizers were singled out for harsh treatment, both by their Unionist neighbors and by military forces operating in the area, which

Right These bullet scars on the walls of Fort Mason were caused not by combat, but rather by guards trying to overcome boredom as rumored threat after rumored threat failed to materialize.

Left Although California was far removed from the battlefields, conspiracies among Southern sympathizers and rumours of invasion persisted. Fort Mason was part of the defenses of San Francisco.

considered them fair game for theft, insult, and arson. Nor did these always distinguish between Confederate sympathizers and loyalists. In addition, citizens of all opinions were in danger from marauders.

KENTUCKY EXPERIENCE

Kentucky was a prime example. Popular sentiment was against both secessionists and coercion, and both State and national officials at first walked gingerly. Governor Beriah Magoffin, U.S. Senator John C. Breckinridge, and about half the State legislature accepted the idea of secession as a right, but almost everyone favored neutrality. Nevertheless, many Southern sympathizers went south to serve the Confederacy, and both sides recruited troops – illegally – in the State during that period. However, when the citizens of Kentucky elected a majority of Unionists to Congress in 1861, Lincoln ended the standoff by denouncing neutrality and opening Camp Dick Robinson to recruit soldiers. 'I hope to have God on my side,' Lincoln told a friend, 'but I must have Kentucky.'

The Confederates moved to forestall a Union advantage by occupying the strategic city of Columbus and fortifying it. Federal troops then seized Paducah. Unionist members of the State legislature, taking control of the State away from the governor, called for Federal assistance and endorsed military action against seceding States. Confederate sympathizers held a convention in Logan County and asked to be admitted to the Confederacy.

Kentucky suffered throughout the war. The State was occupied by Union forces, but whole sections cheered when Confederates rode in. Kentuckians were required by Union generals to repeat loyalty oaths frequently. Citizens accused of engaging in disloyal activities, criticizing the war, or displaying Confederate flags or symbols were jailed and their property seized. The army drafted the slaves of Confederate sympathizers as workers, but impressment gangs often ignored the politics of the slave's owners. Teachers and clergy-

men were forced to show fealty and even voters were given a loyalty test before voting.

On battlefields, Kentucky brother fought brother in the armies of the nations. At home, few Kentuckians escaped the internecine warfare that developed between the Home Guard, created to control pro-Confederate elements, and the Partizan units formed by Confederate sympathizers in self-defense. Both forces engaged, without concern for flag, as much in plunder as in defending a helpless public.

In western Kentucky, Union General E.A. Paine achieved a reputation that rivaled Butler's during a 51-day reign of terror against civilians that included arbitrary arrests, confiscation, plunder, and pillage. He levied taxes on the whole areas—$300,000 on the Purchase area and $85,000 on the citizens of McCracken County—and on individuals. When citizens could not pay, their land was confiscated. He imposed a tax on tobacco shipments by anyone not an 'unconditional' Union supporter and seized the rent of prop-

Wagons continue to roll along Peachtree Street, Atlanta's main thoroughfare, despite the wartime destruction evident at lower right.

erties of suspected pro-Southerners. There was a suspicion that he killed 40 men.

Paine's actions caused such a furore that the United States Senate investigated them. He fled to Illinois, but was returned for trial by courts martial on charges of malfeasance, extortion, oppression, and murder. He was convicted of only one small charge and was let off with a reprimand in official orders.

The 'great hog swindle' in Kentucky, also perpetrated under military orders, was an attempt to counter a sharp rise in the price of processed pork. General Stephen G. Burbridge, the military commander, decreed that hogs could be sold only to army agents, who paid less than the market price. Farmers who tried to sell hogs quietly on the private market were imprisoned and the hogs confiscated. Packing houses not given government contracts closed for lack of meat to process. Public reaction was so strong that the scheme was abandoned, but not before Kentucky farmers had lost $300,000.

Although malfeasance of this type generally was dealt with leniently, official policy never condoned such activities. Furthermore, such deviations must be balanced against the many honorable decisions made by military commanders. General Grant not only rejected the bid of his own father for government contracts, but successfully resisted the efforts of would-be profiteers at Cairo, Illinois, despite intercession by Leonard Sweatt of Chicago, a personal friend of Lincoln and a major stockholder in the Illinois Central Railroad. Grant told Sweatt he would seize the railroad if Sweatt interfered.

Property rights were seldom observed where slaves were concerned. Slaves were frequently taken by the military, first to do manual labor and then to serve in the army. Loyalist owners were given receipts, while Confederate sympathizers received nothing.

The Emancipation Proclamation produced unusual situations. As the Union army moved south, slaves by the thousands left the plantations to migrate northward. Those passing through Kentucky and other States where slavery was still legal sometimes were taken into custody and returned to their owners upon payment of a fee. Slaves not reclaimed could be sold at auction.

The deleterious effect of corruption, a persistent problem during the war, is depicted in this 1861 cartoon castigating a dishonest Union supplier of blankets and uniforms.

SPIES AND GUERRILLAS IN THE BORDER STATES

In the Border areas, military commanders had real problems with spying—professional and amateur. Confederate sympathizers eagerly awaited the return of the Boys in Gray and offered choice intelligence to them when they could. On occasion, they were suspected of doing a bit more for The Cause. General Paine complained to Grant that snipers were picking off Federal guards while they walked their posts at Hinds Point in Missouri. Grant authorized him to remove the citizens within a six-mile circumference, if he could prove civilians were doing the sniping. Anyone who returned would be liable to execution. Aware of Paine's reputation for harsh methods, Grant cautioned that the purpose of the order was not to take political prisoners but 'to cut off a

The Albany Contracters who have "influence" at Washington, and   Their Victim.

"The blankets served from the State of New York were small in size, bad in texture, and almost rotten, so that you could poke your finger through them. They were not one third the width and size of the army blanket. The same sort of swindling was apparent in tents, blankets, clothes, shoes, &c. * * * * * Some of the colonels had been seen riding about on horseback, in dressing-gown and slippers. * * * * They had seen men mount guard without pantaloons, walking about on duty in that condition."—Extracts from Surgical Report on the Condition of the Army.

STOLEN FRUIT THE SWEETEST.

'Stolen Fruit The Sweetest'–hungry troops took what they wanted as they marched through the countryside. This sketch is by Samuel Reader.

dangerous class of spies.'

In trying to prevent guerrilla activity, official or impromptu, Union commanders imposed harsh and arbitrary rules on civilians in Border States and occupied areas of the South.

Military commissions were set up to assess Confederate sympathizers, innocent or not, for the cost of any damage to property of loyal citizens. Anyone aiding guerrillas was subject to the death penalty. Any pro-Confederate found within five miles of a guerrilla raid could be arrested and ejected from the country. Among the numerous ill-conceived orders issued by General John Pope while in command of Union troops on northern Virginia was one ordering the seizure of citizens as hostages against 'bushwhackers' or marauders.

Guerrillas were tried by military courts. Captain Jerome Clarke, who served under Morgan, took up marauding after Morgan's death late in the war. When captured, he was tried in Louisville, Kentucky, by a hastily assembled military court and hanged on March 15, 1865. In 1864, General Burbridge decide that four guerrilla prisoners would be shot for every Union soldier killed, a policy that apparently resulted in the execution of an unspecified number of captured Confederate soldiers as well.

Research tends to reveal more examples of Union misbehavior than Confederate. To a great extent, this results from the war being fought mostly on Southern soil; and to the greater authority given to Union district commanders. However, the South, despite a genuine reluctance to impose controls on citizens except under the direst of circumstances, did not have a record to be proud of in this regard.

SUSPENSION OF HABEAS CORPUS BY THE CONFEDERATES

Unlike Lincoln, Jefferson Davis did not suspend habeas corpus without prior congressional approval, even when conditions were critical. Suspension of habeas corpus rights was vigorously opposed by the public and many officials, but was reluctantly approved by the Confederate Congress on three occasions, primarily to deal with the growing bands of deserters and draft dodgers in the mountains and to strengthen enforcement of the conscription law. The suspensions also were used in areas where fluid fighting rendered normal law and order procedures ineffective.

Sizable areas were affected. General William H. Carroll placed Knoxville, Tennessee, under martial law in 1861, even though he did not have the authority to do so. Norfolk, Portsmouth, Richmond, Petersburg, and 15 counties in Virginia were all placed under military rule when they were threatened, as were Salisbury, North Carolina and vicinity; parts of Texas and South Carolina; East Tennessee; Mobile, Alabama, and New Orleans.

The eagerness of the military to suspend writs was under constant scrutiny by Congress, and several boards investigated the arrests of civilians. A provision of the law requiring reporting of arrests usually was ignored, but each approval of the law narrowed the scope of the authority to suspend habeas corpus and impose martial law. The final bill in 1863 restricted arrests to 13 specified charges; when it expired in October 1864, political opposition was so great there was no hope of extending it, even though the Confederacy was racked by internal dissension, sabotage, and the formation of secret societies.

OPPOSITION TO MILITARY RULE

Public opposition restrained military rule. Generals in the South were much more concerned about public opinion than were those in the North. Local and State officials, backed by popular opinion, interposed their authority; Governor John G. Shorter of Alabama successfully resisted military control on one occasion. District courts which continued to function under martial law were effective in protecting civilian rights. A general in South Carolina faithfully abided by a court ruling which denied confiscation of a piece of land.

Troops in the field often took over whatever shelter was available. The owners were supposed to be compensated, but in fact they often were not.

Still, excesses occurred. Many Union sympathizers were arrested and imprisoned. Unionists were discriminated against by other citizens, refused protection of the law by authorities, and even sometimes beaten. A former United States congressman from Virginia, John Minor Botts, whose only crime was to insist on remaining neutral, was arrested.

When martial law was imposed in Richmond, General John H. Winder, the provost marshal, ordered surrender of all private firearms, banned the sale of whisky (his zealots even confiscated patent medicine and arrested druggists), made railroads and hotels turn in lists of passengers and guests, and instituted a passport system to control the movement in and out of the city. The traffic was so heavy at times, however, that control was virtually impossible. Passport clerks who became suspicious of people and denied them passports often were overruled by superiors.

General Winder used detectives imported from New York, Philadelphia, and Baltimore to ferret out spies and military lawbreakers. their reputation in the local community was evident from their nickname–'plug uglies.'

Legal impressment was used to supply Confederate military needs when they could not be met otherwise. For the construction of a pontoon bridge over the James River at Richmond, General Winder impressed 500 men, black and white, from the saloons and streets of the city. He also obtained boats for pontoons, lumber for planking, and stones for anchors. The bridge was ready in five days.

Soaring prices, hoarding, and profiteering rankled with most senior military officers. Efforts were made to eliminate abuses in impressing supplies for the armies, but excesses abounded. On occasion, officers charged with obtaining supplies for the Confederate army used authority granted by the Secretary of War to seize high-priced materials at cost. Sometimes the payment given by the military was demonstrably below the farmers' actual cost of production. The problem became so grave that the Confederate government had to establish an appeals pro-

William C. Quantrill, who had an almost boyish face, was among the most feared Confederate raiders. His attack on Lawrence, Kansas, ended in murder and robbery.

cedure. Richmond was flooded with complaints that impressment destroyed farmers' means of livelihood by taking work oxen and mules, milk cows, and seed.

All these actions caused controversy, and President Davis tried to discourage them, especially after the beginning of 1863.

Inflation was so detrimental to the war effort that the military advocated a variety of means of controlling it. The most stringent was the recommendation of General T.H. Holmes of the Trans-Mississippi Department that the military authority be used to enforce a system of fair prices. President Davis, believing that army action of that type reduced its stature among civilians, told Holmes to limit army intervention in civilian affairs to the extent possible. No amount of force could restrain prices in the face of severe shortages, Davis wrote the general.

Destruction of private property was normal in the course of battle, but not all that occurred during the War Between the States was unavoidable. Private property was not always safe when units were camped nearby, either. Some units deserved the reputations they got for taking what they wanted, without compensation, from farms near their encampments.

The first Southern incursions into the North were purposely humane. Southern forces thought they were liberating Maryland and expected to be welcomed by the inhabitants— a forlorn hope. Before invading Maryland, General Robert E. Lee issued orders that civilians were not to be bothered, except for necessary foraging. The order was enforced and, as a result, depredations were few. The indulgence of Confederates toward Barbara Fritchie, whose home in Frederick still proudly flies the Stars and Stripes, typifies the forbearance that existed at the time.

Lee continued to control his army during the invasion of Pennsylvania that ended in the Battle of Gettysburg. A Pennsylvania-born clergyman in Lee's army, on passing through his native city of Greencastle, saw few people that he recognized because most people wisely remained in their homes. The few outdoors who recognized him exclaimed in surprise, 'Great God!' An old aunt welcomed him warmly, however, and wished him success.

An English officer in the Confederate army noticed that the women of Chambersburg were surly toward the invaders and made fun of their ragged uniforms at first, but became more docile as the invaders ignored them.

Despite Lee's humane approach, foraging could be quite trying to residents; to the hungry Confederate troops, the well-stocked farms were a virtual cornucopia. Southerners aware of the Union devastation in their home States took particular delight in foraging. A farmer who was about to lose a fresh, prime horse in exchange for an exhausted Confederate mount bought off the officer with gold, only to lose his horse when another unit passed by.

Raids into Northern States later in the war were harsher. In 1864, in retaliation for earlier Union destruction in the Shenandoah Valley, Southern raiders burned two-thirds of Chambersburg, Pennsylvania, when citizens could not produce the demanded ransom— $100,000 in gold or $500,000 in greenbacks. General John Hunt Morgan's raid into Indiana and Ohio took more than two weeks and caused the alarm bells to ring in community after community, including Corydon, before his forces captured at New Lisbon, Ohio. On a later raid into Kentucky, his undisciplined troops looted Mount Sterling and Georgetown and burned part of Cynthiana.

Some guerrillas who operated as Confederates were more interested in murder and plunder than in serving any cause. William Clark Quantrill led a destructive raid on Lawrence, Kansas, in which most of the men in the town were killed in retaliation for the Confederate defeat at Gettysburg and wrongs committed by Unionists. His men also stripped the community of all its valuables.

Barbara Fritchie refused to budge when 'Stonewall' Jackson marched through Frederick, Maryland, on September 10, 1862. She was immortalized in a thrilling episode of John Greenleaf Whittier's poem.

PART THREE

THE WESTERN THEATER

‘It was a mighty mean fowt fight,’ one of the Confederates wrote home after the Battle of Wilson's Creek. That was an understatement, yet Wilson's Creek in 1861 was not even the best example of the intensity of the Civil War clashes in Missouri. Actually, Missouri was ablaze long before the rest of the country dissolved into Civil War. The territory's petition for Statehood precipitated the great national debate on the extension of slavery and the Missouri Compromise, which admitted Missouri to the Union in 1821 as a slave State, was only a temporary solution. The attempt to extend slavery into neighboring Kansas in the 1850s bled both Missouri and Kansas, as slavery and anti-slavery partisans fought openly and in the process devastated good portion of the border region.

The assault on Fort Sumter in 1861 intensified a fight that had been going on sporadically for seven years and added to the carnage. Although newly elected Governor Claiborne Fox Jackson and many other legislators favored secession, both the State legislature and, a

Western Theater: Opening Salvos

General Lyon's death as he rallied his outnumbered men for a charge against the Confederates at Wilson's Creek is depicted in this period Kurz & Allison engraving.

convention called to decide the issue voted against it. Federal troops under a captain-promoted-to-general, Nathaniel Lyon, disarmed the State guard and helped the Unionist faction install a new government at the capital, Jefferson City. At a meeting in Cassville, the Jackson faction approved an ordinance of secession and petitioned for admission to the Confederacy. Callaway County wanted no part of either side; it voted to become the independent Kingdom of Callaway.

Missouri men enrolled in substantial numbers on both sides one estimate is 100,000 in the Union army and 30,000 in the Confederate army. Some served as far away as Virginia. More than 1,100 military activities of all kinds rank the State as one of the greatest battlegrounds of the war, even though only a few of the incidents were large enough to be classified as battles. Union records indicate 13,885 died in blue uniform alone. Although Missouri's loss in Confederate gray would be less, it was substantial.

The Civil War experience in Missouri was divided between guerrilla action and regular warfare, both vicious. Anti-slavery and pro-slavery guerrillas roamed the State, looting, burning and killing. Anti-slavery raiders thought of themselves as 'reborn Puritans and their neighbors as nothing but dirt-hauling,

whisky-soaked illiterates,' according to the commentary at the Wilson Creek battlefield. 'The Southern sympathizers were the rural Jeffersonian idealists defending their property against the wretches pouring out of Eastern and European slums.'

Regular warfare was often just as bitter and Missouri residents had experienced 'total war' before the term was invented. General Lyon, who in the early stages controlled all Federal units in Missouri, was determined to drive the secessionists from the State. He rejected pleas from Governor Jackson to allow the State to remain neutral and began a campaign against Jackson and the State militia before they could unite with Confederate units. Lyon moved his troops by steamboat up the Missouri River to Boonville and, on June 17, 1861, drove the State guard from the town in the first regular battle in Missouri.

A few weeks later, on July 5, 1861, Federal units under Colonel Franz Sigel, a refugee from the German Revolution of 1848, attempted to block Jackson's rendezvous with Confederate forces in southwest Missouri but were defeated at Carthage and hurried back to the safety of Springfield. The Carthage fighting is shown on a mural, in the Jefferson County Courthouse, which depicts the history of the city and is entitled, 'Forged in Fire'. Although the battlefield is not intact, interpretive signs beginning about eight miles north of the city and extending to Carter Park in Carthage trace the events of the battle. The fighting and the damage to Carthage had a curious side effect; a teenage observer named Myra Belle Shirley later became the famous Belle Starr, Confederate spy and eventual outlaw.

BATTLE OF WILSON'S CREEK

The Battle of Wilson's Creek, the largest fought in Missouri, was not long in coming. In southwest Missouri, the State guard under Major General Sterling Price was joined by Confederate troops from Texas, Arkansas, and Louisiana under Brigadier Generals Benjamin McCulloch and N. Bart Pearce, bringing the total to about 12,000 men. Lyon, spoiling for a fight, was encamped 75 miles away at Springfield. The Confederates were eager to trap Lyon and thus regain control of the State; but Lyon, though outnumbered, hoped to surprise the advancing Confederates by attacking first.

Lyon mauled the Confederate vanguard at Dug Springs but was forced to fall back to Springfield in the face of superior numbers. The Confederate army followed and camped on the fields and bluffs overlooking Wilson's Creek, with Price eager to attack and McCulloch hesitant. McCulloch, who had a low opinion of the effectiveness of the Missouri guard, agreed to act only after Price, though superior in rank, offered to place his entire command under McCulloch.

WILSON'S CREEK TODAY

An overlook on the ridge, which is at places 160 feet higher than the creek, is the prominent point of Wilson's Creek National Battlefield on State Route 181 southwest of Springfield. Looking at the tangled brush and trees, ravines and sinkholes of the terrain from the protected overlook, it is easy to understand why the battle was so long and so costly. A map and recorded commentary provided the details of the fierce fighting for control of this commanding feature. A walking trail, just under a mile, follows the crest of the hill, where the decisive action of the battle took place, and passes the spot where Lyon, who already had received two minor wounds, was killed during a counter-attack. The view of the valley and forested farms of the area also is spectacular.

The short self-driving tour from the park's Visitors' Center also passes the route of the main Union advance along the creekbank to Bloody Hill; the site of the Pulaski Arkansas Battery that

'Living history' programs interpret aspects of Civil War **life each summer at Wilson's Creek Battlefield.**

Lyon again decided on a surprise attack, and sent Colonel Sigel on a wide flanking movement against the Southern right. The Confederates, who also had planned a surprise attack on August 9, 1861, but called it off because of rain, did not reset their pickets and were surprised by Lyon's attack at 5 a.m. on the morning of August 10. They immediately lost several key positions, including the crest of a ridge that would become known before the battle was over as Bloody Hill. Arkansas artillery was able to halt the attack and gave Price time to form a new battle line on the south slope of the hill. The fighting on that ridge, much of it at close quarters, raged for five hours the firing was so intense it could be heard in Springfield.

The owner of the Ray House watched the Battle of Wilson's Creek from his porch.

The house still looks much as it did in this 1897 photograph.

halted the initial attack; the Edwards Cabin, which dates from the period and is similar to the one before which Price set up his headquarters in 1861; Sharp's cornfield where Sigel's flanking movement lost momentum and ultimately was thrown back; and the 1852 Ray House, a farmhouse used as a Confederate hospital and as temporary resting place for Lyon's body after it had been abandoned on the field by the retreating Union army. The owner had stood on the porch and watched the battle unfold from the advance through the fields to fighting on Bloody Hill. In fact, the porch was a continuing window on the war; for four years, the Rays watched soldiers and equipment march by on the Old Wire Road. After the war, the house served first as a post office and then as a stop on the Butterfield Overland Stage route. It has been restored to what it looked like in 1861.

In the Visitors' Center, a 13-minute slide presentation and superior seven-minute electric map program, with other displays, place the battle in the context of the contest for control of Missouri. McCulloch's hesitation, when a bold attack might have destroyed Lyon's smaller force and put the Confederates in command of Missouri, resulted at least in part from his lack of confidence in the Missouri guard after the skirmish at Dug Springs. The park brochure identifies another important aspect of the fighting: 'Though this was one of the first battles of the Civil War and many troops had little training, on few other fields was there a greater display of courage and bravery.' Of the Union officers commanding at Wilson's Creek, 30 became generals before their military careers ended, an unusually high number. A few of the youth who served there almost anonymously would become famous after the war, including 'Wild Bill' Hickok, a Union scout and spy, and the James boys, Frank and Jesse, who marched in the Confederate ranks.

Living history programs each summer interpret certain aspects of life during the Civil War, such as music and medicine.

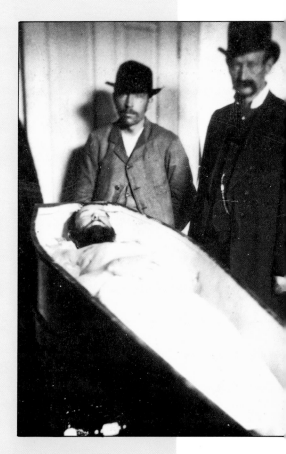

Jesse James, seen in his coffin, was a product of the Civil War.

With its leader, Lyon, dead and ammunition almost exhausted, the Federal army, leaving many of its dead behind, retreated to Springfield and then to Rolla, where it entrained for St. Louis. The victorious Confederate army, though superior in numbers, for some unknown reason did not pursue. Casualties on both sides exceeded 2,500. The bodies of thirty Union soldiers, buried in a sinkhole on the ridge by the Confederates, later were reinterred along with almost 1,600 others from both sides in Springfield National Cemetery.

THE BATTLE OF HEMP BALES

Lexington, Missouri, a busy river port with pro-Southern proclivities, preserves both the battlefield (off U.S. Route 24, not far from Interstate 70) and bitter memories of Federal occupiers, who seized nearly a million dollars from the bank. The battle on September 18–20, 1861, was a leisurely one, even by Civil War standards, as the larger Confederate forces surrounded the Union position before making a major attack, and nearby Union units failed to join their beleaguered comrades due to lack of communications. It is remembered as the Battle of the Hemp Bales, a name derived from the wet bales which

Of the 70,000 buried at Jefferson Barracks Historical Park in St. Louis, Missouri, 11,623 are Civil War soldiers.

Confederates used as movable breastworks when assaulting the Union fortifications. Union cannon set fire to several buildings in the town and chipped a piece from the courthouse column. A farmer, lunch pail in hand, joined Price's besieging forces and industriously shot heads which appeared above the Union defenses until lunchtime, contentedly ate his meal, and then went back to his grisly task. Original earthworks and trenches remain. The Anderson House, constructed in 1853 and used alternately as a hospital by both sides, is preserved as a museum and contains Civil War relics and period furnishings.

The unusual battle was a victory for the Confederates under General Price; the Union surrendered the entire garrison, 1,000 horses, 3,000 muskets, 100 wagons, and five pieces of artillery. One Union officer surrendered his sword to his brother, who served on Price's staff – a good example of why the conflict is sometimes called The Brothers War. Price was chivalrous, allowing the Union officers to keep their guns and horses and permitting the Irish regimental band to parade its colors before stacking arms. The Confederate army remained at Lexington for two weeks before marching south again.

GIBRALTAR OF THE WEST

Columbus, Kentucky, a pro-Southern community occupying a strategic point on the Mississippi River, became involved in the fighting at the outbreak of the war. In September 1861, General Grant was ordered to occupy the city, but Confederates in Tennessee did not wait for him to arrive. They moved in and fortified it so well it became known as the 'Gibraltar of the West.' Columbia-Belmont Battlefield State Park preserves part of the huge chain that Confederates stretched across the river in an attempt to block Union gunboats, restored earthworks, and numerous Civil War relics, some of which are located in the park's museum.

With Columbus in Confederate hands, General Ulysses S. Grant occupied Paducah instead, and turned it into a base from which

he pushed south along the Mississippi River.

BOWLING GREEN

Bowling Green was another Confederate strongpoint early in the war, and is regarded as the capital of the Confederate State of Kentucky from 1861 to mid-1862. It occupied a strategic location on the Louisville and Nashville Railroad, as well as the Barren River. The temporary fortifications built there impressed Union officers, who arrived after the Confederates evacuated the city in 1862. During Old South Week nowadays, the site of Fort Webb-one of four strategic hills included in the defensive system-is often used for ceremonies. Vinegar Hill is now the site of Cherry Hall on the campus of Western Kentucky University.

TENNESSEE: THE FIRST LINE

'Unconditional Surrender,' as both a concept and a play on the real name of General Ulysses S. Grant, began in early 1862 when the North achieved its first major victory with the capture of Forts Henry and Donelson in northwest Tennessee. Far greater battles would follow in the State, one of which could have prolonged the war, but these seizures established the pattern of pressure warfare that would dominate in the Western Theater. This and subsequent events would not only provide the military leadership the North desperately needed, but would establish Grant as perhaps the first modern general.

Forts Henry and Donelson were part of the Southern attempt to defend extensive borders at all points against greatly superior forces

The 1853 Anderson House was used as a hospital during the 1861 Confederate rout of Federals at Lexington, Missouri. It now houses a Civil War museum.

Fort Henry (far left) was the first land target to fall to naval bombardment during the Civil War. The isolated post surrendered to Commodore Andrew H. Foote in 1862 after only a short defense.

and industrial capacity, an effort that dispersed the limited resources of the Confederacy. Neither fort could survive without support, and with Union naval forces in command of the Tennessee and Cumberland Rivers, they were quickly cut off by the superior land forces Grant led down from their base in Cairo, Illinois. In the first use of rivers for a major operation during the war, Fort Henry was attacked and surrendered to the naval commander after most of its guns were disabled. The bulk of the troops at nearby Fort Donelson missed an opportunity to evacuate overland, mainly because of the indecisiveness of the commanders, and thus were trapped.

The strength of the fort was never tested in land combat. Union forces had penetrated only about half of the outer defenses when the isolated Confederates surrendered on February 16, 1862; an attempt to break out had failed largely because Confederate troops, on the verge of victory, were ordered back to their entrenchments. Several thousand Confederates did escape, including about 700 cavalrymen and determined foot soldiers under Colonel Nathan Bedford Forrest, who would soon become a legend in his own time. When surrender became inevitable, the two ranking Confederate generals left with some of their men on ships which arrived with 400 new recruits.

The loss of the forts was a stunning defeat for the Confederacy. With the capture of Forts Henry and Donelson, Grant had seized the initiative, made inevitable the evacuation of heavily fortified Columbus in Kentucky, and, in fact, forced the Confederates out of Kentucky, broken their defense line in northern Tennessee, and permanently changed the strategic situation in the West. The surrender was celebrated throughout the North by the ringing of bells. Union forces had fared badly in other early battles, and this was a refreshing change. Grant's insistence on 'unconditional and immediate' surrender earned him a nickname and gave him a reputation for toughness on the battlefield that attracted the attention of President Lincoln, far away in Washington.

Confederate Brigadier General Simon Bolivar Buckner, to whom command had been passed by his departing superiors, surrendered to Grant at the Dover Hotel which had been his headquarters. The hotel is situated in a detached section of the Fort Donelson National Military Park and is open to visitors. Many Confederate soldiers stacked arms near the hotel and left from the landing for Northern prison camps. The meetings between Grant and Buckner were poignant; the officers had known each other at West Point, and Buckner had helped Grant out of a financial difficulty in New York prior to the war.

The loss of Forts Henry and Donelson subjected Tennessee to a long period of see-saw warfare that devastated the state. Tennessee was the primary battleground of the Western Theater. Federal forces insecurely occupied the northern section of the State, including its capital, Nashville, and the Southerners created a new defensive line in the southern part of the State. A total of 1,462 military activities of all kinds, at least 454 of them significant, took place in Tennessee — more than in any other state except Virginia.

ARKANSAS

Arkansas was in an uncomfortable position in the Civil War. It was not a priority for either side, yet it was a running battleground. More than 770 military events of all kinds occurred there, five of them classified as battles. Military units of both sides criss-crossed the State for

The Water Battery, which punished attacking Union fleets, overlooks the beautiful Cumberland River at Fort Donelson Military Park.

FORT DONELSON TODAY

Fort Donelson National Military Park preserves enough of the fortifications to demonstrate how strong the fort, designed primarily to guard the river, could have been with proper outside support. Remains of the earthworks that enclosed 15 acres on a bluff overlooking the Cumberland River are part of a self-driving tour of the park. In one of the most beautiful areas of the park, the overlook on the site of the original river batteries, are displays of the types of cannon installed at the fort, including a 22-inch Columbiad and eight 22-pounders. In the early stages of the fighting, inexperienced gunners defeated Federal ironclads in a major land-naval battle. Not far away, log huts of the kind which housed the defenders have been reconstructed.

The driving tour also passes remnants of the Confederate outer trenches, a hiking trail to one of the principal artillery positions and the Confederate Monument, a tall marble column erected in 1933 by the Tennessee Division of the United Daughters of the Confederacy. The national cemetery holds the remains of 670 Union soldiers, 512 of them unknown. Uniformed Park Service interpreters conduct musket firing demonstrations and establish a Civil War camp during the warm months. A 15-minute slide presentation at the Visitors' Center interprets the events and their significance.

four years, from isolated Pea Ridge in the northwest to the strategic Arkansas Post in the southeast. The largest and bloodiest battle was not even fought for control of the State, but to determine the fate of neighboring Missouri, and fighting went on after the Union took possession of the Mississippi, cutting Arkansas and other trans-Mississippi states off from the rest of the Confederacy.

Arkansas left the Union reluctantly. Although the State took over the Federal arsenal at Little Rock in February 1861, a convention in March voted against secession–but also against coercing those States that did leave the Union. After the fall of Fort Sumter and President Lincoln's call for troops, another convention reversed that decision and, in May 1861, Arkansas entered the Confederacy. Being on the edge of the frontier, Arkansas was crossed by many trails – the Camden-Pine Bluff Road, the Fayetteville-Huntsville Trail, Mt. Elbe Road, Memphis-Little Rock Road, the Old Military Road, and the Old Army Road among them. The result was numerous skirmishes at places with picturesque names like Buffalo Creek and Chalk Bluff. What has been called the 'most destructive shot of the war' was fired at St. Charles when a shell from a land battery struck the steam pipe of a Union ship and killed 150 soldiers. Remnants of earthen fortifications remain at Morrilton, on the road to Petit John Mountain. Richland, a farming area that lived up to its name, was visited frequently by both sides. Arkansas had its share of bushwhackers, too.

PEA RIDGE

Arkansas' awkward position in the war is evident at Pea Ridge National Military Park on U.S. Route 62, ten miles north of Rogers. Displays in the Visitors' Center museum candidly admit that 'the Federal victory here saved Missouri for the Union.' Just as important, the battle marked the 'beginning of the end for the Confederate hope of retaining control of the Mississippi.' The museum reflects these assessments in its displays on

Above The Visitors' Centre at Arkansas Post National Memorial houses relics of the colorful history of the strategic spot. Some Civil War fortifications remain, although erosion has destroyed the principal Confederate fort.

Below This stone chimney, relocated from nearby Rhea's Mill–which was a Union supply point–is an attractive but unusual memorial to the 2,500 casualties of the Battle of Prairie Grove. Other historic structures from the region are also preserved.

the war in Missouri and friction in the West. It also chronicles another unusual feature of the battle, the participation of 1,000 Cherokee and Creek Indians in conventional combat as part of the Confederate army. That was, according to the park's guide booklet, 'the Civil War's only major battle in which Indian troops were used.'

The Cherokees and Creeks, who came from Indian Territory (now the State of Oklahoma), participated in an attack on a troublesome Union artillery battery. They captured it, but were driven back when their curiosity about the 'wagons that shoot' got the best of them and they stopped to inspect them. Many of them had never seen artillery in action before.

A 12-minute slide program and seven-mile self-guided automobile tour follow the events of March 7–8, 1862, which involved almost 30,000 men. Pea Ridge was one of the few battles in which Union forces emerged victorious without superior numbers. The

death of several Confederate generals at a critical time created confusion in the ranks, and the Rebels ran out of ammunition when supply wagons inexplicably turned away from the battle area. Combined casualties totaled more than 2,000.

Pea Ridge was the end of a successful campaign launched by Union Brigadier General Samuel R. Curtis to drive pro-Confederate forces, principally the State guard under General Price, from Missouri. Price led the guard into Arkansas in February 1862 to join Confederate regulars under Major General Earl Van Dorn. The combined force intended to move north to St. Louis, but was intercepted by Curtis with 10,500 men dug in on the ridge overlooking Little Sugar Creek. Van Dorn sent his men, some without shoes and already weary from three days of marching with little to eat, to Curtis' rear but delays gave Curtis time to reposition his men to meet Van Dorn's two-pronged attack.

Elkhorn Tavern, around which the fighting

Above Observation points provide a clear view of the Pea Ridge battlefield and nearby the hills from which the attack was launched. The battle marked the end of Confederate hopes of holding Missouri.

Inset Elkhorn Tavern was a busy place during the Battle of Pea Ridge, Arkansas. Confederate generals huddled there to plan strategy; later, surgeons worked while soldiers fought all around it.

cavalry sabers among a small collection arranged around a 12-pounder U.S. cannon. A model of the action is complemented by a six-minute slide show about the battle, the last major Confederate effort in the region, and the events leading up to it.

The battlefield park, three and a half square miles, has a multiple personality. It preserves the old Morrow House, first used as a head-on one prong raged, has been reconstructed and is part of the self-guided battlefield tour and is open to the public. At different times during the fighting, the white frame structure was used as a headquarters and hospital by both armies. Not far away, along the strategic old Telegraph Road, are displays which explain the fighting in that area. It was there that the Confederates, after pushing the Union troops back, began to run out of ammunition and were forced to retreat.

Two overlooks give panoramic views of the battle site. From the Pea Ridge East overlook, approximately 60 per cent of the rugged terrain involved in the fighting can be seen. A recorded commentary gives details of the decisive battle. Pea Ridge West overlook provides a good view of Boston Mountain, from which the Confederate attack was launched. A good ground-level view of the battlefield is possible along State Route 94.

Other principal stops on the self-guided tour are the graves marking the site where Leetown stood at the time of the battle—with nearby Round Top it was one of the major points of conflict—and the Little Sugar Creek trenches, which lie in a detached area of the park just off U.S. Route 62 and were part of Curtis' original defense line.

Twenty-five years after the battle, soldiers from both sides came together on the battlefield to raise a monument showing hands clasped in reunion. Appropriately, the ceremony honoring the dead of both sides was held at Winton Spring, where thirsty Union soldiers had refreshed themselves during the fighting. Later, the monument was moved to a site near the tavern.

PRAIRIE GROVE

While Pea Ridge was fought for control of Missouri, the battle of Prairie Grove 43 miles to the south determined the fate of northwest Arkansas. Prairie Grove Battlefield State Park, ten miles southwest of Fayetteville, preserves part of the site and a few of the relics of the inconclusive battle fought on a cold December day in 1862. Of the more than 18,000 soldiers in two armies who took part, 2,500 of them became casualties or were captured or missing before the day was over.

The Visitors' Center museum has an excellent assortment of rifles and muskets and quarters by the Confederate commander, Major General Thomas C. Hindman, and then as a hospital; and the reconstructed Borden House, which was used as a vantage point by Confederate snipers one of whom was Frank James. The stone chimney from nearby Rhea's Mill, used by the Union as a supply point during the fighting, has been relocated to the park as a battle monument dedicated to all the soldiers who fought at Prairie Grove. It is surrounded by a wall composed of stones taken from pioneer homes, mills, schools, churches, post offices, and other historic buildings throughout Washington County. Interpretive programs are conducted by park historians in Civil War costume; guided tours are held hourly from Memorial Day to Labor Day, while maps lead visitors over a ten-mile self-guided driving course. Annual re-enactment of the battle is held on the weekend nearest the anniversary, with more than 150 'soldiers' from historical associations in Arkansas and neighboring states participating. A camp is also set up which shows visitors how Civil War soldiers lived, and demonstrations of infantry and artillery drills are given.

Unrelated, but occupying a major part of the park, is a recreated nineteenth-century Ozark Mountain village, composed of structures brought from various places in the region.

The devotion of old soldiers to this battlefield is one of the major reasons it is preserved. Beginning in 1886, they began returning to reminisce with comrades in arms or to show their families where they had fought. As time went by, these reunions became more and more organized, with rides and programs, and the area became known locally as the Old Reunion Grounds. In 1909, a United Daughters of the Confederacy chapter set aside a parcel of ground as a memorial. The reunions continued until the late 1950s but became smaller and smaller and, in 1957, the State purchased 50 acres for a battlefield memorial foundation. General Hindman's sons left $100,000 in their wills as a memorial and, in 1971, the site was made part of the State park system.

Along the Old Telegraph Road in Pea Ridge National Military Park Confederate attackers began to run out of ammunition and were pushed back.

General Albert Sidney Johnston, the second-highest ranking soldier in the Confederacy, rode along the line of battle-weary soldiers at Shiloh, touching the bayonets on their rifles. 'I will lead you,' he declared, apparently on an impulse. Delays and stubborn resistance by Union soldiers from behind trees had created a critical situation for Southerners trying to break the Union left flank. Inspired by Johnston, they swept forward and drove the Federals from the Peach Orchard and flanking positions before bogging down once again because of heavy casualties. It was another bloody action in one of the bloodiest battles of the Civil War. To one Federal participant, Confederate casualties looked like 'a line of troops laying down to receive our fire.' The most important casualty of the action would die a short time later, bleeding to death while he continued to issue orders. A severed artery in General Johnston's right leg went largely unnoticed because it bled into his boot until he collapsed in the saddle.

Shiloh and Other Pivotal Battles

Johnston was not only courageous, he was an able and determined commander who provided the kind of leadership the South needed to engage superior Union manpower and resources. He was the 'good soldier' who had resigned a western post to join the Confederacy. To Confederate forces in the Western Theater of war, his death was a loss comparable to that of Jackson in the east. 'The West perished with Albert Sidney Johnston and the Southern country followed,' one of his subordinates wrote later.

Shiloh National Military Park, located on State Route 22 seven miles south of Crump, is a complete Civil War battlefield. The cemetery, historical markers, and monuments remember the 25,000 casualties and recall dramatic events, and a stopping place on the self-guided automobile tour at the place where Johnston bled to death dramatizes the extent of heroism and disregard for personal safety shown by both sides on an almost daily basis. The shaded memorial area includes part of the trunk of the tree identified later by the Governor of Tennessee, Isham G. Harris, who was present, as the one under which the Southern commander died. Nearby is a monument made up of a cannon and cannonballs.

The Union commander at Shiloh almost became a casualty in another way. General Ulysses S. Grant considered it the most misunderstood action of war. He would dwell on this battle longer than on any other in which he participated, partly because he resented the criticism of him—evoked due to his heavy casualties—in the Northern press. Aware of the battle's importance, he would later declare that few battles of greater significance had 'taken place in the history of the world.' Grant may be forgiven the exaggeration as he had a personal stake; the battle tarnished his reputation and almost ended his career.

All battles are fateful, some are pivotal. Shiloh was pivotal. The Union push into the interior of the South had followed the Cumberland and Tennessee Rivers, which were easier to capture than the mighty Mississippi and which provided secure and rapid means of reinforcing and resupplying forward forces. At Shiloh, the Confederacy lost a golden opportunity to achieve a major victory in the west, where one was desperately needed. Western Tennessee was effectively lost to the Confederacy, which would spend the next three years trying to get it back. The inability of Confederate forces to clear southern Tennessee left Union armies encamped in the heart of the Confederate west and in control of large chunks of critical territory. Shiloh reduced the Confederacy's ability to control the central Mississippi River. A decisive victory

General Don Carlos Buell's army was engaged at Perryville long before he knew it. Neither side would commit all its troops to the battle.

at Shiloh would have improved the chances of holding Vicksburg.

Still, the results were as much psychological as military. Shiloh solidified thinking in the west the way First Manassas (Bull Run) did in the East: the idea of quick victories and maneuvering were replaced by a realization that armies had to be defeated in head-on confrontation. Union forces found a new determination, and a new confidence; command leadership was developing to augment the Federals' superior grasp of strategy. Yet Shiloh was another of those battles that almost didn't happen, and then was decided by Union units which held their ground tenaciously without being aware of their influence on the outcome.

The Northern push into southern Tennessee in the spring of 1862 threatened the vital railroad hub at Corinth, Mississippi – the Confederacy's only direct rail connection with the East. The object was to cut or to limit the use of that rail line, and for that purpose Grant's forces were to be united with those of General Don Carlos Buell from Nashville to create overwhelming superiority. General P.G.T. Beauregard was the first to see the advantage of striking Grant's camp at Pittsburg Landing before the two armies could unite, but later urged that the plan be abandoned because he thought delays had cost the Confederates the element of surprise. Yet Johnston insisted on attacking even if a 'million' Federals confronted him, and he fell upon the unsuspecting Union army encamped at Pittsburg Landing.

One of the stops on a driving tour of the battlefield is Shiloh Church, where the initial Confederate assault took place on April 6, 1862. Ironically, the church survived the

At Shiloh, the Confederacy lost a golden opportunity to win a major victory in the West, where one was desperately needed. The rebels spent the next three years trying to win it back.

fighting only to be destroyed a short time later; the present brick church was built in 1949. Equally ironic is the meaning of its name: place of peace. A small pond near the church became known as Bloody Pond. It was used by soldiers of both sides to bathe their wounds, but that did not stop other thirsty soldiers drinking from it.

The tour of the battlefield begins with the critical phases of the battle. The first stop identifies the ridge along which Grant formed his final battle line after being driven from most of his original positions. Union defenders at the Hornet's Nest and the Sunken Road, by repulsing four frontal assaults, bought Grant the time he needed to organize his new defensive line to their rear and to man it with fresh troops. Confederates finally captured the Hornet's Nest after Brigadier General Daniel Ruggles bombarded it with sixty-two cannon, the largest concentration of artillery used to that point in the war.

The Peach Orchard comes much later in the tour, but was part of the defensive line buying time for Grant. The firing there was so intense that bullets cutting blooming buds on the trees created the illusion of falling snow.

Another critical point of the first day's fighting was the Union left flank, anchored on the Tennessee River, where troops reinforced by Buell's vanguard repulsed the final Confederate attack of the day. In this area, monuments have been erected by Iowa, Ohio, Wisconsin, and Arkansas. Other monuments on Federal Road were given by Pennsylvania, Indiana, and Illinois. The Missouri monument has the shape of the State.

General Beauregard, who assumed command of Confederate forces upon the death of Johnston, was unaware that Buell's forces had arrived and thought he had Grant 'just where I wanted him and could finish him in the morning.' Concerned about Confederate disarray produced by confused fighting, he ordered a halt to the attacks and a withdrawal to the captured enemy camps. Later, he would be accused, with some justification, of making one of the greatest mistakes of the war. On the second day of fighting, Confederates sought to recapture ground they had voluntarily evacuated the night before, now manned by Buell's fresh troops. The Water Oaks Pond stop on the park tour represents the major phases of that day. By noon, the outnumbered

Confederates were near exhaustion, but Beauregard organized a desperate attempt to break the Federal line at Water Oaks Pond, where heavy see-saw fighting was under way. It was a case of too little, too late, and Beauregard ordered a retreat to Corinth. The Confederate retreat was slow because the troops were exhausted, but Grant's army was in no condition to pursue in earnest.

A Confederate burial trench on the battlefield holding the bodies of 700 men emphasizes the carnage that took place. It is only one of five such trenches at the site. General Johnston's son, Colonel William Preston Johnston, said, 'No Confederate who fought at Shiloh has ever said that he found any point on that bloody field easy to assail.' The National Cemetery, which overlooks the river near the Visitors' Center, holds 3,590 Civil War dead and additional casualties of later wars, including Viet Nam. A monument marks the site where Grant located his field headquar-

Two headstones symbolically frame a siege gun in the national cemetery at Shiloh battlefield. Some 77,000 men fought in the battle; 23,000 were casualties or captured.

ters, while a pair of siege guns backed by gravestones create a corner of appropriate symbolism. Other major battlefield points are Pittsburg Landing, now an overlook with a beautiful view of the river; the site where Federal surgeons established one of the first tent hospitals of the Civil War, an action which no doubt saved numerous lives; and the Confederate Monument.

The Visitors' Center consists of several buildings and metal plaques relating both Federal and Confederate actions during the battle. Displays and a 25-minute visual presentation inside the reception building provide a valuable introduction to the battle-field tour.

Federal occupation of western Tennessee was completed with the capture of Memphis while forces crept toward Corinth to initiate a string of actions in northern Mississippi that would help seal the fate of Vicksburg, the strongest remaining Confederate bastion on the Mississippi.

Grant would be involved in all of them, and ultimately in the victory in the east, but the qualities that would achieve results were only partly revealed at Shiloh. These were princi-pally his determination and his tactical abil-ity. He was almost naive at times; and yet Shiloh contributed to an order of battle that would produce later results. Grant's subse-quent successes ultimately would propel him into the presidency.

Another future president, General James A. Garfield, served in a subordinate command

A view of Lookout Mountain, which dominates the Moccasin Bend of the Tennessee River beyond. A visit to the national park illustrates the Federals' difficulty in clearing Confederates from the slopes.

All kinds of ships, including small steamboats such as these under construction at Chattanooga, were pressed into military service.

at the battle. Perhaps the youngest soldier of the war, 10-year-old Johnny Clem, who was unofficial drummer of the 22nd Michigan, was present at the battle.

Shiloh battlefield also preserves a much older segment of history. Not far from Pittsburg Landing are two types of mounds raised by prehistoric Indians, one a burial mound and the other a foundation for ceremonial houses.

BATTLE OF BRITTON'S LANE

The Battle of Britton's Lane is typical of the raiding that went on in western Tennessee during the war. A six-foot marble monument marks the mass grave of 25 Confederates killed in the struggle between five companies of General Forrest's command and the 20th Illinois Infantry. Federal troops, who organized behind bales of cotton and a wooden fence, were attacked five times during a four-hour period, with the Confederate troops capturing more than 200 prisoners and a quantity of arms. Battlefield markers relate the deaths of 179 Confederates and five Federals, with larger numbers being wounded.

A connected incident demonstrates a common practice among Southerners whose home areas were occupied by Union forces – slipping through the lines for brief visits at home. Two Rebel soldiers from Madison County, home on clandestine leave, were attending services at Denmark Presbyterian Church with their girl friends, who were of course wearing their most stylish dresses. Suddenly Union forces came looking for them. They searched every inch of the church, unsuccessfully, while the congregation sat in stony silence. The Rebels were hiding under their sweethearts' skirts. The men may really have been advance scouts for the Confederates planning the Britton's Lane attack.

PERRYVILLE, KENTUCKY

The Commonwealth of Kentucky held a key position in the Civil War. President Lincoln understood that as early as 1861, when he wrote to a friend: 'I think to lose Kentucky is nearly the same as to lose the whole game. Kentucky gone, we cannot hold Missouri, nor, as I think, Maryland. These all against us, and the job on our hands is too large for us. We would as well consent to separation at once, including the surrender of the capital.' The Confederacy, too, recognized the necessity of winning Kentucky, the ninth most populous State at the time, to its cause.

Like most border states, Kentucky was sharply divided, but the division was not always what might be expected. The Commonwealth had been formed from Virginia as a slave state, and thus maintained cultural and political ties with the South.

Furthermore, the commercial life of Kentucky was oriented toward the Mississippi River and its tributaries. The presidents of both sides during the Civil War were native sons: Abraham Lincoln was born at Sinking Spring Farm near Hodgenville and Jefferson Davis was born at Fairview. Yet, in the election of 1860, Lincoln and the Republican Party were so unpopular that he failed to carry a single county. This tangled political situation induced some big slave owners to defend the Union, while a few anti-slavery partisans fought to defend State's Rights. Although Kentucky officially remained within the Union, many citizens were so dissatisfied with the status that they formed a rival Provisional Government, which was formally admitted to the Confederacy. The 'Kentucky colonel' thus wore blue and gray with equal ease, but would have preferred to remain neutral.

Kentucky was an early and a often-used battleground; 453 military activities of all types occurred in the State, but only two of them qualify as battles. A number of places lay claim to the first armed clash; but the distinction probably has to be shared by several communities, including Columbus and Hickman, where action followed occupation.

The Perryville battlefield, located in farming country about two miles from the town with the same name, is preserved as a State park. Perryville, fought on October 8, 1862, was the largest and bloodiest battle fought in Kentucky, with over 7,500 casualties, and it sealed the State within the Union. It has curiously been neglected by Civil War historians and enthusiasts.

In 1862, Confederate General Braxton Bragg devised a two-pronged plan which would enable his Army of Tennessee to 'free' Kentucky. It started successfully with 12,000 men under General Kirby Smith advancing from Knoxville as far as Lexington. Bragg moved his army from Chattanooga toward Louisville, an important Union base. Capture of Louisville would put Bragg to the rear of the Union Army of Ohio, commanded by Major General Don Carlos Buell, and give the Confederacy control of the State. Bragg would have a defensible river boundary and be in a position to advance to the Great Lakes, cutting the North in two. It was a good plan, but suffered from lack of coordination and was much too ambitious for the resources at Bragg's command. He counted on Kentuckians rallying to his colors, once he was firmly established, and thus providing additional forces. They did not: most of them cautiously waited to see whether he could clear Buell from the State.

The town of Perryville has a large interpretive battle map at the intersection on U.S. Route 150 where the visitor turns onto Kentucky Route 1920 to reach the battlefield. Some of the town's old structures are part of the Civil War experience, including Elmwood

The log cabin in which Abraham Lincoln was born is now housed in this granite memorial building in Kentucky. 'With malice toward none, with charity for all' is engraved above the entrance.

Top **Reactivated units prepare for simulated attack at Perryville, just as their forebears did. Re-enactment of the battle is an annual event.**

Inset **Behind a menacing cannon stands the Confederate monument at Perryville Battlefield in Kentucky.**

Left **Confederate General Braxton Bragg's campaign to 'free' Kentucky from Union forces was just one of his many wartime exploits.**

Inn and the redbrick Crawford House on State Route 68 (Harrodsburg Pike) which Bragg used as his headquarters. The Confederate Cemetery holds nearly 400 bodies collected from the battlefield and buried in mass graves. The Dug Road which, according to legend, Confederate artillerymen cut into the hillside to facilitate movement of their cannon, remains in use as a dirt road.

On the weekend nearest the October 8 anniversary, reconstituted Civil War units re-enact the battle. It began during the pre dawn hours on a hill overlooking Doctor's Creek, but eased off during the morning as 16,000 Confederate troops moved into position for a concerted attack against 22,000 Federals. That movement confused Union commanders, who thought the Rebels were retreating, and the attack that was finally launched about 2 p.m. by men 'yelling like fiends' caught them by surprise. At nightfall, the Confederates held the ridge and thus had the advantage, but Buell had committed only a third of his 61,000 troops, and Bragg believed himself too weak for victory. Thus, at midnight, Bragg began to withdraw from the battlefield and soon retreated from Kentucky; he had won the battle, but he had lost the war to control the State. Bragg's aborted invasion was the last major effort to keep Kentucky in the Confederacy.

Both Buell and Bragg were preoccupied with political matters before the battle began. Buell, who had heen dismissed by the War Department in Washington and then reinstated, was beset by command problems as well. Bragg hoped that by installing the secessionist government in Frankfort, the State capital, he would help rally the State behind both his invasion and the Confederate cause. Neither general consciously picked Perryville as the site of a battle; maneuvering forces met there primarily because the Union army was short of water in a hot, dry October and had been informed that Doctor's Creek was a good source. Neither side would employ all its forces, part of Bragg's army being immobilized

by diversionary action near Frankfort. Most of the Union fighting would fall on Brigadier General Alexander McCook's I Corps, while other units were never engaged.

PERRYVILLE TODAY

Perryville Battlefield State Park is small, but it has a number of interesting objects packed within 100 acres of the northern end of the battle lines, which at one point during the fighting stretched for three miles. Across the road from the Visitors' Center and Museum, where a slide presentation and Civil War relics relate the story of the battle, stands a tall Confederate monument in a shady fenced-in grove fronted by two cannon and United States and Confederate flags. At one outside corner is a painting of the battle, along with plaques bearing a map and commentary on the fighting. A short path leads past a tall white column, authorized by Congress in

The strategic location of beautiful Cumberland Gap, gateway to the West, made it an important Civil War site.

1928 to commemorate Union participation in the battle; memorials to Michigan units that were among the 61,000 Union troops at Perryville, including Battery A of the First Michigan Light Artillery – whose commander, Coldwater Lewis, refused an order to spike his cannon and retreat and thus prevented the Confederates from turning the Union right flank – and memorials to General Buell and Brigadier General James S. Jackson, commanding the 10th Ohio Division, who was killed in the fighting.

A look-out tower on the crest of the ridge provides a splendid view of some of the most important terrain of the battle, as well as the , rolling countryside nearby that muffled the sounds of combat so well that Buell did not realize for several hours a major battle was in progress. A map at the base of the steel-frame tower shows the movement of units.

NEW MEXICO TERRITORY

At the outbreak of the Civil War, the New Mexico Territory (now the states of New Mexico and Arizona) was a sparsely settled, lightly defended area with considerable appeal to the Confederacy. It extended almost to the West Coast, had sizable stocks of weapons and

Below Hardly noticed in the East, the Battle of Glorietta Pass, New Mexico, blocked the Confederate invasion of the southwestern territories. This reenactment is an annual event.

supplies stored at Union forts, and was the gateway to great mineral wealth, both inside and outside its boundaries. Texans invaded the territory soon after the war began and precipitated a showdown that involved maneuver as much as fighting, but which from time to time produced spirited battles between the small forces involved.

At first, Confederates met with success against small Union forces divided among a number of posts. Mesilla was proclaimed capital of the Confederate territory after the surrender of Fort Fillmore.

Union defenders traded land for time and concentration of forces, surrendering forts and towns in the southern part of the territory as 3,700 Confederates advanced northward along the banks of the Rio Grande River.

VALVERDE

The first major conflict occurred on February 21, 1862, at Valverde, about six miles north of Fort Craig and three miles east of the Route 85 100 miles south of Albuquerque, when the invading Confederates threatened the fort's supply lines. Union troops sent to keep the Confederates from crossing the river drove them back, and gradually the forces of both sides were committed piecemeal as the fighting continued. A feature of the battle was 'one of the most gallant and furious charges ... ever witnessed in the annals of battles' by Texas lancers – Confederates on the frontier were armed with whatever weapons were available. They were beaten back with heavy losses. In the end, the battle was decided by a furious Confederate charge against the artillery on

Opposite Colonel 'Kit' Carson invaded the rugged but beautiful Canyon de Chelly in New Mexico, a Navaho stronghold, to keep the Indians from taking advantage of the Civil War.

Fort Union as it appeared in 1860 in a watercolor by William Hays.

one Union flank. Colonel Edward R.S. Canby, who commanded the Union forces, then pulled them back to the fort.

The ratio of casualties to the number of men involved was high on both sides, but the Confederate victory produced sizable stores of small arms and supplies, in addition to the captured cannon. A truce was declared for two days while both armies treated their wounded and buried their dead, after which Colonel Canby again refused to surrender the fort. The Confederate commander, Brigadier General Henry H. Sibley, then bypassed the fort and marched on to capture Albuquerque and Santa Fe. Neither the battlefield nor ruins of the fort are accessible to the public.

PIGEON'S RANCH: WESTERN GETTYSBURG

The most significant Civil War battle in the

New Mexico Territory, at Pigeon's Ranch 19 miles southeast of Santa Fe, is sometimes called the 'Gettysburg of the West.' It is re-enacted each year by history organizations.

Army records list two battles, but the first encounter on March 26, 1862, at Apache Canyon was only a preliminary to the Battle of Glorieta two days later. The site of the latter is preserved, but only partly developed for visitors. The ruins of a three-room adobe ranch structure remain to mark the site where Confederate and Union forces fought a furious hand-to-hand battle over rugged terrain. Although Union forces retreated to their base at the Kozlowski Ranch after the battle, the Confederates could not pursue because their supply train had been destroyed by an isolated cavalry.

Fort Union, the Union's principal bastion

Above Kit Carson (1809-68) led an adventurous life as mountain man, scout, Indian agent and, finally, Civil War soldier.

against the Confederate invasion, was untouched. At Fort Union National Monument, a self-guided 1 and quarter mile trail leads to adobe and brick ruins, while the Visitors' Center highlights the history of the three forts that protecd the region from 1851 to 1891, including undeveloped remains of the Civil War earthen fort. Those who fell in New Mexico battles are buried in the Santa Fe National Cemetery.

The loss of their supplies and ammunition at Glorieta Pass forced the Confederates to retreat to Santa Fe and then to their base at Albuquerque. As further Union reinforcements arrived from Colorado, and the California Column moved from southern California into the southern part of the territory, Sibley abandoned Albuquerque, and, after an indecisive battle at Peralta, retreated to his base at Fort Bliss, Texas.

WARFARE WITH THE INDIANS

The Confederate threat to the territory was effectively over, but the fighting was just beginning for the California and Colorado Volunteers. Warfare with the Indians of the region was frequent and became very savage. Men who lamented having to destroy horses

Above During the Indian Wars that were fought during the Civil War years, Carson was promoted to brigadier general for his skill in fighting the Indians in New Mexico.

they could not take with them willingly killed Indians. Log forts continued to sprout along the established trails in an effort to protect settlers and traders, but the campaigns conducted by Colonel Christopher 'Kit' Carson were more effective in forcing the Indians onto the Bosgue Redondos Reservation.

Carson's campaign against the Apaches in 1862 and the Navahos in 1863-4 were typical. His tactic was to maintain pressure on the Indians by a series of encircling maneuvers that resulted in small engagements and kept the Indians from uniting. Canyon de Chelly National Monument near Gallup, New Mexico, preserves the Navaho stronghold Carson invaded in an effort to break their resistance. Indian guides lead visitors through the rugged, 35-mile-long canyon whose walls rise 1,000 feet in places. An attempt to arrest Cochise and his followers resulted in a substantial fight on July 16, 1862, between the Apaches and a detachment of California Volunteers. It was a Hollywood-style battle, with the Indians attacking and withdrawing, then ambushing the soldiers from the high ground in the pass. The Indians lost, and were permanently denied one of their favorite haunts by the erection of Fort Bowie, which continued active until 1894.

The flag in the plaza at Taos flies 24 hours a day because of an incident that occurred during the Civil War. Carson had the Stars and Stripes nailed to the flagpole and set a guard to prevent it from being taken down. The Kit Carson Museum, a half-block from the plaza, retains numerous momentoes of the famous fighter of the Indians.

INDIAN TERRITORIES

Both North and South were accused of fomenting Indian uprisings, but neither government condoned such action, nor did regular forces in the field encourage Indian violence. However, the sight of whites fighting each other was a psychological stimulant to the Indians, and the Civil War divided many Indian tribes in much the same manner as it split white families and clans in the border

WESTERNMOST BATTLE

Present-day Arizona claims the 'westernmost battle' of the Civil War. On April 15, 1862, units of the California Column encountered a 16-man Rebel raiding detachment at Picacho Pass near the Santa Cruz River, now far from the main highways. Most of the Texans escaped, and presumably returned to the Confederate base at Tucson.

states. Many Indians saw the white division as an opportunity to reverse the invasion of settlers and opportunists, and periodic uprisings troubled both frontier settlers and the contesting armies. Others counseled peace as a means of retaining the economic gains they had made under a sedentary way of life; for example many well-to-do Indians owned slaves. Both the Confederates and the Federals recruited Indian soldiers into their regular forces.

Indian conflict was periodic, but it ranged all the way from Minnesota to the New Mexico Territory and even involved the Five Civilized Tribes in Indian Territory, now the state of Oklahoma. The small, intense battles were only vaguely related to the Civil War and more properly should be regarded as portent of the fitful warring that would persist almost to the end of the century as Indian resistance to continued settlement mounted. A number of them are included in tabulations of Civil War battles, however, although few of the sites have been developed to receive visitors.

THE INSURRECTION OF THE SIOUX

The most destructive Indian uprising during the Civil War, and certainly one of the most publicized in the press, was the insurrection of the Sioux in Minnesota in August of 1862. The tribe had signed away its lands in Eastern Minnesota in 1851 in exchange for annual payments and a guaranteed one million acres reserved for their use, but many of the tribe

Opposite Canyon de Chelly National Monument near Gallup, New Mexico, preserves the Navajo stronghold Carson invaded in an effort to break their resistance.

Buffalo Bill was famed as an army scout during and after the Civil War. He is pictured here with Chief Sitting Bull.

members had heen unhappy with the arrangement and the payments were frequently late. Traders took advantage of the financial naivety of the Indians to keep them in debt, and some debt claims were simply fraudulent. The Indians resented white attempts to Christianize them and turn them into farmers.

The situation was ripe for violence, but it did not actually begin until some young braves taunted another, saying he was afraid of white men. To show his peers that he wasn't, he shot a farmer near Acton, and his taunters followed up by killing four others, including a woman and girl. They fled to the reservation, where their story divided the tribe into two groups, one wanting to surrender the braves and take the consequences and the other willing to take to the warpath. The Indians, apparently following a preconceived plan of driving all whites back across the Mississippi River, attacked some well-defended areas, including Fort Ridgely and New Ulm, where at least a third of the town was destroyed. Some Winnebagos joined the uprising, producing fear of a general Indian insurrection which did not materialize. However, the Sioux rampage was one of the worst massacres in American history, killing at least 800 and driving thousands from their farms and settlements to the safety of St. Paul and Fort Ridgely.

New Ulm preserves a number of relics from the period, including the Frederick W. Kiesling building on North Minnesota Street (now the offices of the Chamber of Commerce); it was filled with hay so it could be burned to provide light for defense if needed. Women and children took refuge in the Frank Erd building (part of the original remains). The Frederick Forster building—which along with the Henry Schalk building was a principal defensive point during the uprising—has been altered but retains original features. The ruins of Wajaru Distillery and displays and paintings in the Brown County Historical Museum, together with the Defenders Monument erected by the State of Minnesota in 1891, also recall the heroic defense of the City by its citizens. Fort Ridgely, about 20 miles from New Ulm, has been partly restored and has an interpretive center.

Although the area north of the Minnesota River was most affected, the side-effects extended beyond the Iowa border and into the Dakota Territory. The uprising was broken by a campaign conducted by Brigadier General Henry Hastings Sibley, a former governor,

who had lived and traded with the Sioux for 28 years and thus knew them well.

THE BATTLE OF WOOD LAKE

The Battle of Wood Lake on September 23, was actually an Indian ambush that was accidentally discovered. It raged for two hours and included close combat. The rout of the 500 braves strengthened the hand of the Indians who opposed the warpath, and the warring faction began to dwindle as Sibley pushed up the Minnesota River Valley. War parties continued to operate under Little Crow, the nominal leader of the uprising, but gradually the Indians returned to the reservation.

Little Crow was soon after killed in the fighting, but 306 of the leaders of the uprising were convicted and given the death penalty. President Lincoln noting that the evidence against most of them was unconvincing, commuted the sentences of all but 38; who were hanged in a mass execution at Mankato on December 26, 1862.

STONE RIVER, TENNESSEE

Such incidents were hardly noticed in Tennessee, where back-and-forth campaigning continued. The armies clashed again in December 1862 at Stone's River near Murfreesboro.

One of the most obvious parts of the Stone's River National Battlefield is the cemetery, located opposite the entrance to the battle-field park. That would be appropriate for any battle in central Tennessee, which, because of their intensity were bloody affairs, but it is particularly appropriate for Stone's River. More than a third of all the soldiers involved, or 23,000 of them, became casualties during the three days of fighting.

The cemetery should be the last stop on a tour of the battlefield (now at the outskirts of Murfreesboro) because the well-tended lawns and fields and the quiet woods of the battle-field are deceptive. The artillery pieces occupying strategic points in the park, as they did when this was farmland in the strange winter battle in 1862, give only a small indication of the decisive role they played in this battle, where Confederate courage could not match the efficiency of Union artillery units. The well-positioned explanatory markers cannot convey the struggles of the foot soldiers as they fought at close range, often in hand-to-hand combat. The battle comes vividly to life at one place on the preserved battlefield: the rock-strewn woods where Michigan troops under General Philip Sheridan made a desperate stand against advancing Confederates. There in the woods, scattered among the rock outcroppings which provided ready-made rifle pits for the Michigan infantry, are the remains of two demolished rifled cannon. To the troops involved, the area would be known thereafter as the Slaughter Pen.

One of the displays in the Visitors' Center,

The stubborn resistance of troops under General Philip Sheridan was an important factor in preventing a Federal rout at the year-end Battle of Stone's River near Murfreesboro, Tennessee.

DIVISIONS AMONG THE INDIANS

In the Indian Territory, three battles indicate the bitterness of the divisions among the Indians. Creeks under Chief Opothleyoholo would not support the Confederacy, as most of their tribesmen did, and began a pilgrimage to Kansas, where they thought they would be safe. Superior Indian and Texas units caught up with them on November 19, 1861, but were repulsed in the confusing Battle of Round

Mounds which took place at night. The next morning, Opothleyoholo and his band were gone, but later they were discovered at Bird Creek by a mixed-blood Indian named Clem Rogers, the father of humorist Will Rogers. This battle ended in a draw, with the pursuing force returning to Fort Gibson. The fleeing band was attacked again at Shoal Creek, however, and broken into smaller units, which were hunted down.

Concentrated artillery fire by Union soldiers, under the command of General William Rosencrans (insert), helped blunt the final Confederate attack in the Battle of Stone's River on January 2, 1863.

OAKLAND PLANTATION

An earlier, less significant battle took place in Murfreesboro on the grounds of Oakland Plantation, the home of a frontier doctor. While Federals were using it as a headquarters in July 1862, Forrest surprised the Union troops and routed them. The wounded commander, Colonel William W. Duffield, surrendered, and the two commanders then sat down to a meal in the main dining room.

In December 1862, Confederate

President Jefferson Davis stayed at Oaklands on a trip to confer with General Bragg. The mansion and 10 acres of the original 1,500-acre estate form a municipal historic park that recalls the graciousness of the nineteenth-century plantation life style. Furnishings vary according to the period in which each particular section of the three-part house was built and include some original to the Massey family, which owned the home at the time of the Civil War. Stately oaks, which gave the estate its name, are planted extensively in the park.

entitled 'Strange Christmas 1862,' is indicative of the mood that preceded the battle. Union General William Rosecrans had marched out of Nashville in winter to crush the Confederate forces under General Braxton Bragg, who was encamped in winter quarters near Murfreesboro, and then move on to Chattanooga. Bragg's cavalry kept him informed of Rosecrans's progress while his troops prepared for Christmas, most of them thinking of home. Corporal Johnny Green of the 9th Kentucky Regiment dreamed of returning home victorious in a letter to his family, hoping 'this joyous season would find us on Kentucky's soil with the invaders ... driven north of the Ohio River.'

The eve of the battle was almost festive as bands in both armies played under starry skies. This soon became a contest to see which band could play the loudest. Then, the homespun westerners in both armies began singing 'Home, Sweet Home.'

Although Bragg held a strong position, he attacked Rosecrans's right wing at dawn on December 31 and drove it back. 'Old Rosy' gave orders to 'contest every inch of ground' while he prepared a new defensive line with his reserves. The costly stand by General Sheridan's forces, along with those commanded by Major General George H. Thomas and the use of cannon at almost point-blank

range, bought him the time. Fighting continued until darkness fell, when a silence settled over the battlefield that would continue through the next day. Bragg was so confident that Rosecrans would withdraw that he wrote to his superiors that 'God has granted us a happy New Year.' His exultation was premature. Rosecrans, with a superior force, stubbornly held his new positions. Bragg ordered a new attack on Januay 2, 1863, which forced Union troops back across Stone's River, but the offensive was halted by concentrated artillery fire at what is now a detached section of the park distinguished by an artillery monument.

Both armies claimed a victory. Bragg won the battle but did not have the resources to force Rosecrans from the field; so he withdrew to Tullahoma, Tennessee. Another rich farming area was lost to the Confederacy, and Rosecrans had acquired the base from which later attacks on Chattanooga could be launched—Fortress Rosecrans, as the Union General modestly named it.

STONE'S RIVER TODAY

The driving tour of the park, starting at the Visitors' Center, follows the progress of the battle. Nearby are the Cedar Forest through which the Confederate attack was launched, and the Chicago Board of Trade Battery (named for the organization which contributed the funds to equip it), which blunted the Confederate attack at that point. A short distance beyond the woods where Sheridan made his stand is the area where Confederates made their deepest penetration, and the place where Rosecrans established his new line. At the only position which Union forces were able to hold throughout the battle–the Round Forest–stands the oldest Civil War monument in the nation; it was erected in 1863 by the survivors of Colonel William B. Hazen's brigade, which held the position.

Other detached sections of the battlefield park identify the sites of buildings, since destroyed, which Bragg and Rosecrans used as headquarters.

The cemetery occupies the hillside where Union artillery stood during part of the battle. Artillery pieces, their muzzles pointed across the 6,100 white headstones identifying Union casualties, are mute testimony to the intensity of the fighting at Stone's River. Handsome monuments to many of the units involved, including the 'last shot' memorial to the 15th, 16th, 18th, and 19th Infantry units and to Battery H. of the 5th U.S. Artillery, provide a different perspective.

ALABAMA

Control of Tennessee put the Union army in a position to invade northern Alabama almost at will; but the lack of strategic targets made it a

The cannon that decorate the national cemetery at Stone's River battlefield are a symbolic recreation of reality. The artillery that occupied this rise caused many casualties.

low priority compared to Mississippi, where the battle for the great river was being fought, and Georgia after the decision had been made to trisect the South. Alabama was subjected to frequent, but relatively minor action. More than 300 military events took place in the State at almost 200 different sites. Alabama enrolled 75,000 men in the Confederate army, and her sons participated in almost every major battle. In addition, a few whites and perhaps 10,000 blacks wore the Union blue.

The Tennessee Valley was occupied from 1862 onward and Athens, Guntersville, and Tuscumbia were among the cities looted, burned, or bombarded. The Old State Bank Building in Decatur, whose 100-ton columns were quarried in the Trinity Mountains and hauled eight miles to the site in 1832, shows the scars of various battles for the city.

Civil War memories are strong at Selma, the home of the Confederate navy yard—which built the Confederate ram Tennessee—and of 50 acres of armories and munitions plants which supplied many of the cannon and much of the ammunition used during the last two years of the war. Monument's identify the sites of the arsenal and other units of the industrial side of the city; they were burned, along with two-thirds of the other buildings, on April 2, 1865. A memorial to those who defended the city stands on remnants of the earthworks on the outskirts of the city. The five blocks of Water Avenue that escaped the torch, including the historic St. James Hotel, comprise one of the few antebellum riverfronts in the South. Sturdivant Hall, constructed in 1853 with a lace ironwork balcony behind Corinthian columns, is a museum furnished in antiques and Civil War relics.

As the capital of Alabama, Montgomery was a natural target of Federal forces and was taken by siege late in the war. It was an emotional target, as well, because Jefferson Davis had taken the oath of office as president of the Confederacy on the steps of the 1847 Capitol Building, which remains one of the city's most impressive stuctures. Northeast of the capital is a tall monument, whose cor-

nerstone was laid by Davis after the war, which commemorates the devotion and sacrifice of Southern women to the cause. Nearby is the so-called First White House of the Confederacy, where Davis lived until the capital was moved to Richmond, Virginia. Although the building has been moved from its original site, it is intact and holds a number of items owned by Davis and other Civil War mementoes. The Military Museum in the Department of Archives and History contains the score of 'Dixie' used at Davis's inauguration and other relics.

The Confederates were first to recognize the potential of the iron ore near Birmingham and use it to produce arms. Although the furnaces were destroyed by Union raids, a course had been set that would make the city the largest iron and steel center in the South. Civil War relics, antique furnishings and a museum of great Alabama women are on view at Arlington House.

Built in 1841, it was used as a headquarters by Union Major General James H. Wilson during his March-April 1865 raid through Selma and into Georgia .

Six major raids, one of them employing more than 13,000 cavalry, harassed the hinterland. Union troops met their match in the dean of Athens College, then a school for girls. When the soldiers approached Founders-Mall, the dean sallied forth to confront them, and they quickly went on their way. Just what she said to them is not known.

Confederate forces in Alabama were not large enough to defeat Union raiding armies, but one Union commander was talked into surrendering. On April 21, 1863, Colonel Abel B. Streight led a force of 2,000 cavalrymen from Eastport across northeast Alabama toward Rome, Georgia. He was hounded by General Nathan Bedford Forrest, whose frequent attacks with a Confederate force of 600 men kept so much pressure on Streight that he thought he was outnumbered and surrendered at Cedar Bluff. It was a rare moment in a struggle that increasingly went against the South.

The crest of Lookout Mountain, now part of the national battlefield park, overlooks Chattanooga. A Union attack on the fortified hill failed, but success elsewhere forced the Confederates to abandon it.

CHAPTER 16

It was a chilling sight. Combat-hardened veterans of the slaughter pens of the Civil War sat on the ground and pinned pieces of papers to the backs of their blue uniforms as they waited for battle. This was not some strange ritual which had infiltrated the Union's army, but recognition that the mighty war machines created by two nations locked in mortal combat had become meat grinders which consumed soldiers in ever increasing numbers. Soldiers in the Civil War, who were not issued identification tags, used various private devices, some more permanent than patches of paper, to retain their identities in the event of death. Events would justify their precaution.

ON THE MARCH

The combat soldier suffered in other ways, too. He was never comfortable and seldom rested. While railroads and troopships were utilized to an extent for long journeys — both sides made effective use of mass transportation systems throughout the war — armies for

Soldiers at War: Endurance and Death

the most part maneuvered and fought on foot.

Units began marches in high spirits, but the long miles of choking dust or ankle-deep mud soon turned the route into a test of endurance. Infantry usually had to march in fields beside the roads, where artillery and wagons labored. In summertime, soldiers' throats ached with thirst, their lungs hurt, and their nostrils became coated and inflamed. Grit collected between their teeth and made their lips and gums sore, infiltrated their ears, and matted their hair. Their eyes, caked with dust, became 'almost useless' as company followed company along the dirt paths. Their wool uniforms clung irritatingly to the sweat of their bodies, while sand seeped into their shoes and penetrated the clothing to grind at the neck, wrists, and ankles. Heavy packs filled with a few necessities and food rubbed their shoulders. Rookies usually started a march loaded down, while veterans traveled light. When it rained, water and mud took the place of dirt as an irritant.

Soldiers received rations enough for several days before starting a march and had to prepare them as best they could during pauses. The Confederate men often chewed on parched corn and raw bacon as they walked. It was said of General Thomas J. 'Stonewall' Jackson's men that they preferred to carry their rations in their stomachs. So did others. Even in the well-supplied Union army, wagons did not always arrive in time to resupply the troops, and men might wait hungrily for as much as three days for the wagons to catch up.

Animals and crops along the route were in dire danger of surreptitious or open requisition. Cornfields and fruit orchards along roads were stripped by the time an army had passed. Officers and enlisted men flocked to farmhouses to buy, beg, or take what they needed. Union soldiers were adept at 'enlisting' chickens and turkeys in their units. Honey from beehives was popular with both armies.

Southern troops often were treated to cheers of welcome and given food and gifts as they moved back into an area which had been occupied by Federal forces.

In winter, the soldiers of both armies marched on slippery, frozen ground or through snow. It was impossible to keep warm or dry, rations and tobacco became wet and sometimes unusable. Furthermore, when they paused en route, the soldiers slept on the icy ground and even welcomed a light snow, which would cover them and help keep them warm. For those standing guard, the trees cracked like rifles under the weight of ice and driving

The Kansas State Militia of the Kansas Brigade prepares to invade Missouri in 1864.

winds. The only solace was the occasional snowball fight during stand downs.

Artillerymen had bumpy rides – when they could ride. They had to push carriages through mud, streams, and snowbanks, and spent endless hours caring for their weapons and horse. Cavalrymen had the best life and frequently could supplement regular fare with chickens and vegetables from farms in their path; but they, too, had fatiguing chores.

Soldiers frequently went into combat in a state of near exhaustion. At Winchester, 'Stonewall' Jackson gave his men, who had marched all night, one hour of rest before attacking Union General N. P. Banks.

Siege operations were a cut above fight-and-maneuver, as far as creature comforts went. The men were relieved of the hazards of the march. Supplies usually were available – General Grant even had ovens built at City Point (now Hopewell) to supply loaves of bread to his troops during the siege of Petersburg–and reached the units on time. The men could obtain replacement clothing, get hot food, and write and receive letters from home. Earth and wood bunkers were warm in winter and usually dry in summer.

COMBAT TACTICS

Combat grew in size and intensity as the war progressed and changed in character as commanders became more skilled and soldiers in the ranks grew wiser. The stand-and-fire tactics employed early in the war were discouraged by improved weaponry. Armies would occupy high ground confronting each other. Cavalry would be sent to harass rear units and supply lines. Artillery fire would soften enemy positions. Then one army would advance toward the other, braving musket and cannon fire the whole way.

The final stretch was always marked by smoke and confusion, shellholes, soldiers throwing hand grenades at each other, and cannon firing point-blank into lines of attacking soldiers. Firing could be so intense at times that it could completely sever the trunks of mature trees.

Attack distances varied from a few hundred yards to perhaps a mile. At Chattanooga, Union troops forced their way up the side of Lookout Mountain. In close combat of that sort, rifle butts were more commonly used than bayonets.

Brutal frontal assaults continued and the casualties mounted; the 1st Maine Heavy Artillery, frequently used in frontal assaults, lost all of its men in a period of 10 months. Experience taught veteran Yankees the futility of direct assault against well-defended Con-

Right The results of a Union ambush: slaughtered horses and a shattered cart lie abandoned outside Fredericksburg, Virginia.

Below A Confederate artillery battery, drawn by oxen, moves slowly toward the First Manassas battlefield in this drawing by an unknown Confederate officer.

A Confederate Bull Battery

federate breastworks. Even Grant, who ordered bloody assault after bloody assault, learned the lesson and settled down to besiege Vicksburg. While recruits might leap to the charge, veterans knew how to use cover and terrain to their advantage. At Stone's River near Murfreesboro, Tennessee, Michigan soldiers made good use of natural rock outcroppings in the woods to beat off Confederate attacks. The battlefields of the Civil War are strewn with hastily dug rifle pits, trenches and forts. Confederates advanced behind hemp bales in their successful attack at Lexington, Missouri.

Amphibious assaults by Union troops against Confederate coastal forts added a new dimension to battle as the soldiers endured

Left Confederate soldiers, including the Boy Soldiers of Virginia Military Institute, storm Union positions in this mural showing the Battle of New Market, Virginia. The Hall of Valor on the well-preserved battlefield honors the youth who fought in all American wars.

"FIRING ON THE HILL!"

All too often soldiers ended up sleeping on the ground (left). Artillerymen sought the high ground, where they could see but could also be seen (above). This sketch, aptly titled 'Chaos', shows the confusion and panic of a disorderly retreat (opposite top). A Union soldier hurls a hand grenade at the enemy (opposite bottom left) and the Union cavalry charges, banners flying (opposite bottom right): both sketches by Samuel Reader.

seasickness, the prospect of drowning or being abandoned on beaches, and the timidity of some commanders. By the end of the war, when General Burnside successfully assaulted Fort Fisher at Cape Fear, North Carolina – once considered too strong to be taken– the army had perfected the technique. On the other hand, the Battle of Sabine Pass in Texas, where 300 Confederates drove off an invasion force of 5,000, revealed how difficult the maneuver could be when conditions were not right.

There were poignant moments, too, as a mutual respect grew, grudgingly at times, between contesting armies. In the early fighting before Petersburg, the 39th Massachusetts won a strategic position after heavy hand-to-hand fighting, but lost its colors when it was forced back. Volunteers who went out to retrieve them were surprised when Confederates, who only minutes before had engaged them in mortal combat, stopped firing and cheered their bravery. On other occasions, Confederate pickets who had fought fiercely during the day, upon seeing a Yankee outlined against the sky on the opposite shore of a stream that night, might call softly to him, 'Git down, Yank!' And many times Union soldiers withheld their fire under similar conditions or called out 'Find a hole, Reb!'

On rare occasions, troops of the two sides mingled socially between battles, the Union troops exchanging coffee, salt, and sugar for souvenirs of the South. Union and Confederate forces camped on opposite sides of the Rappahannock River shared a musical concert by a Union band. Southerners, who listened to Northern martial songs during the early evening, shouted 'Play some of ours.' The Union band responded with 'Dixie' and other tunes familiar to the Rebels. Men from both armies sat along the shores of the river, in full sight of each other, and were entertained by the music.

MILITARY DISCIPLINE

Submission to military regimentation was not easy for young men from the farms and cities

of either the North or South. These youth — often described during the period as 'free, honest Americans' — were accustomed to a less rigid life style; consequently many of them came face to face with the then traditional disciplinary system of the services.

Company punishment was the easiest and might be administered for thievery, being drunk or failure to perform an assigned task. First offenders usually were required to wear boards around their necks citing their minor offences, and even cowardice in battle might result in no more than a drumming out of camp in disgrace. For insolence toward an officer, a soldier would receive harsher treatment, perhaps being forced to stand on the head of

A PRIVATE VIEW OF THE BATTLE AT NEW HOPE CHURCH

Combat was a very personal thing. Private (later lieutenant) Thomas J. 'Thomie' Stokes of the 10th Texas, serving in the Army of Tennessee, took part in the battle at New Hope Church near Atlanta in 1864. His unit was sent forward to prevent Union attackers from turning the right flank. It formed a single line, under heavy enemy fire. Then an Arkansas lieutenant, who had been captured by Union forces and later liberated, told the men that Federal reinforcements had come up. After the battle, Thomie wrote to his family: 'The fighting of our men, to those who admire warfare, was magnificent.'

The fighting broke off about dark but resumed around 11 p.m. that night, when three Confederate regiments charged across ravines and rocks to drive back the enemy. Thomie hurt a leg when he fell down a small rock cliff and found himself in the dark in a field strewn with dead, dying and, wounded men, one of whom, a tall, muscular Federal had his eyes 'riveted on me.' In trying to find his way back to his unit, he captured a soldier from the 15th Wisconsin before he discovered some Mississippians and then his own

regiment. Thomie went back to the battlefield to help the wounded. One man had been shot in the leg. Another, wounded in the head, was crying, 'Oh my God! Oh, my God!' Since he could not be treated at night, he lay on the field until morning.

The next morning, Thomie walked over the battleground, where hundreds of wounded and dead lay 'in every conceivable position; some with contorted features, showing the agony of death, others as if sleeping quietly.' On the bodies were hundreds of photos and letters from mothers, sisters, and friends. 'Though they had been my enemies, my heart bled at the sickening scene,' Thomie wrote to his family.

The opportunities for this form of empathy were numerous and varied. The Civil War was the largest and most deadly ever fought in the Western Hemisphere. Soldiers on both sides were continually frustrated. Victory after victory brought Confederate armies no closer to an end to the war; Northerners saw defeat piled upon defeat, which necessitated new calls for men and supplies.

Grant's two attacks on Vicksburg, one of which is depicted in this contemporary print, were unsuccessful. The city finally was taken by siege.

a barrel or be tied in a sitting position with a pole between knees and arms. Many units kept a black list of offenders, who were assigned the most tedious and odious tasks.

Sleeping on guard duty was punishable by death, but the sentence was not often invoked. Lincoln himself commuted the sentence of one youth thus accused.

Absenteeism and desertion were major problems in both armies, and it was not always easy to distinguish one from the other. As much as a quarter of an army might be missing at any given time, according to some estimates.

Amphibious landings, like this one at Roanoke Island, North Carolina, were large, complex operations. They became better organized and more successful as the war progressed.

Many men in the ranks simply left their units and went home when their families needed them–some more than once–especially in the South, where the protection of the home hearth was uppermost in the minds of most soldiers. Deserters who were caught were sometimes brought back to be executed in front of their regiment. This was more likely to happen if desertion was a problem at the time.

What soldiers feared most was showing the 'white feather' cowardice. But even those who fought bravely might be wounded or captured – a dangerous situation in itself.

MEDICAL FACILITIES

Medical treatment was appalling at the start of the war, and military commanders showed little interest in the problem. In the North, the civilian Sanitary Commission and Christian Commission worked diligently to improve facilities and the care of the wounded by military medical personnel, but with limited success.

In the Union army, each regiment was authorized two surgeons and each corps had a fleet of four-wheel and two-wheel ambulances, but wounded also were carried by stretcher bearers and on mule litters. Illnesses were treated on the spot, and wounded were treated at makeshift hospitals near the battlefield. Generally, forward aid stations were established in tents or under trees close to the fighting and field hospitals were set up in nearby churches, schools, or houses. The Harper farmhouse at Bentonville Battlefield in North Carolina was used as a hospital during the last major attempt to stop Sherman's drive through the South.

Field physicians were mostly country doctors, ill-suited for coping with wounds and epidemics of dysentery, measles, and diptheria. Young doctors were in short supply; older ones had difficulty keeping up with the military pace, and this affected their work. Doctors in the field treated large numbers of wounded, sometimes having to continue operating for days after a battle under terrible conditions – often without anesthetic and in the dim light of lanterns or candles. 'Sawbones' became a common nickname as doctors quickly acquired a reputation for amputating wounded limbs. Complications following amputations were often more serious than wounds. Sometimes these operations were unnecessary. Although most soldiers submitted, a few determined their own fates. A veteran in the 1st Massachusetts Heavy Artillery pointed a gun at a doctor and would not surrender it until the doctor promised not to amputate his leg. The obstinate soldier recovered but was demoted and dismissed from the service.

The fate of a coward. Drumming out of Patrick Cron [Co. 6]

This pencil sketch by an unknown artist (above) shows a deserter from the 25th Massachusetts being drummed out of camp. Punishment for rebellious action was fast and severe: the ringleader of a mutiny by New York Volunteer Engineers at Hilton Head, South Carolina, was given hard labour (left).

Inset A leg wound gets attention in the foreground while other soldiers huddle under a tree at an aid station near Savage Station, Virginia, on June 27, 1862.

Below Soldiers of the New York 57th await inspection on an unknown field in Virginia.

Key wartime figures (top to bottom): Clara Barton, Mary Ann Ball 'Mother' Bickerdyke, Sister Joseph and Poet Walt Whitman all of whom tended the wounded.

Disease and battle were so deadly that undertakers followed the soldiers into the field (top). Wounded soldiers, like these at Chancellorsville, Virginia, in May 1863, often received initial treatment under trees (middle). A U.S. Sanitary Commission team occupied this building in Richmond following capture of the city (bottom).

After initial treatment, seriously wounded men were sent to hospitals in major cities, sometimes traveling by railway hospital car and hospital ship as far as New York and Boston. Soldiers who reached a rear hospital had a good chance of survival, even though conditions there were not always the best. The large numbers of wounded necessitated setting up makeshift hospitals, which often were dirty, poorly ventilated, and ill equipped. In addition, as a result of the need to resort to 'contract doctors,' unqualified men were appointed as physicians in some of these hospitals. By the end of the war, 350 army general hospitals were in operation.

The Confederate army professed a similar organization, but the medical corps, like all sections of the army, was plagued by substantial shortages of personnel and supplies. Local hospital relief and soldiers' aid societies existed in most cities; but sick and wounded soldiers did not get enough food and medicine, especially in the last years of the war, despite efforts which included clandestine trade with the North.

For soldiers in both armies, bullets and artillery shells were not the worst danger. Disease killed at least two soldiers for every one that died of combat wounds. At times, whole units were decimated by measles, diptheria, or malaria; but yet more lethal were the various forms of diarrhea and dysentery that afflicted the soldiers. Even when men did not die, such ailments as bowel complaints put commanders and even whole units out of action temporarily.

Below The first
woman physician in
the United States and
the first woman
medical officer in the
Union Army, Mary
Edwards Walker.

Above Mary Ashton
Rice Livermore was
both an organizer and
a battlefield inspector
for the U.S. Sanitary
Commission.

Below The Christian
Commission was one
of the two most
important agencies
protecting the
personal welfare of
Union soldiers.

PRISONERS OF WAR

The soldier who was captured was not in any better condition. Accepted standards of conduct in warfare sometimes were violated. In the early days of the war, the Union threatened to shoot Confederate officers as traitors, but backed down when the Confederacy had Union prisoners in Richmond draw lots to see who would be executed in retaliation. Late in the war, Union General William Tecumseh Sherman executed James H. Miller, a prisoner of war, in retaliation for continued attacks on his troops in South Carolina.

Prisoners ostensibly received the same fare as soldiers, but in this neither side lived up to its responsibilities. Thousands of Union prisoners were held at Richmond in converted tobacco warehouses. The camp at Andersonville in Georgia, constructed to improve the conditions of prisoners held at Libby Prison in Richmond, instead became in time a symbol of degrading and inhuman treatment. More than 12,000 died during the short history of the camp, some of them killed by fellow prisoners. Thousands of Confederates died at Union P.O.W. camps at Johnsons Island near Sandusky, Ohio; in Rock Island, Illinois; at Fort Delaware; at Point Lookout, Maryland, and elsewhere.

Even officers were treated harshly—even capriciously—at times. Before the bitterness of warfare had reduced human feelings on both sides, Confederate General Simon Bolivar

Top These three Confederates were captured during the fighting at Gettysburg in July 1863.

Inset Confederate prisoners captured in the Shenandoah Valley are guarded by Union troops at a temporary camp.

Above Union prisoners of war play a baseball game at Salisbury, North Carolina.

Above The inside of Andersonville Prison (1864). Note the latrines in the foreground.

Buckner, who surrendered Fort Donelson to Grant, and General Lloyd Tilghman were imprisoned in solitary confinement at Fort Warren in Boston Harbor and not allowed to communicate with their families. Only intercession by Lincoln, at the request of Tilghman's mother (who lived in Pennsylvania), got them better treatment. When Confederate General

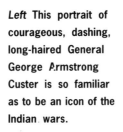

Left This portrait of courageous, dashing, long-haired General George Armstrong Custer is so familiar as to be an icon of the Indian wars.

John Hunt Morgan was captured during his famous raid into Indiana and Ohio, he was treated as a common criminal and sent to prison, from which he escaped after a few months.

There were exchanges of prisoners early in the war, and thousands of soldiers were repatriated. Generals Buckner and Tilghman were exchanged for Union Generals J.F. Reynolds and G.A. McCall. After General Grant was named commander of all Union forces; however, he halted the exchanges to add pressure on the Confederacy. The Union could replace its losses the South could not.

PROBLEM OF GUERRILLAS

Guerrillas or irregular troops posed a different problem. As many as 10,000 men may have acted as guerrillas under Confederate sponsorship. The Union vacillated about their treatment after capture, at first threatening to execute them, then deciding to treat as bona fide prisoners of war those who were acting under official Confederate authority. But the

Above The plight of soldiers in Confederate prison camps was of great concern to citizens in the North.

Sometimes the victors were less than restrained, and prisoners such as this Confederate soldier (above) could suffer serious injury at the hands of their captors.

success of these units caused Union commanders to change their minds again. Although Mosby's Rangers were a recognized Confederate unit, General Grant authorized General Philip Sheridan to 'hang them without trial.' General George A. Custer, one of Sheridan's subordinates, took him at his word and executed seven captured Rangers. Whereupon, Mosby executed an equal number of prisoners from Custer's unit.

ARMED FOR COMBAT

Both sides experimented with new weapons, but for the most part settled for modifications

of tried and true arms, especially in field armies.

The infantry was the most important branch of service, and most of the foot soldiers of both armies were armed with muskets made domestically or imported, principally from Great Britain and Belgium. Union weapons were more standardized than those in the Confederacy, where shortages of machinery and materials made innovation and compromise in styles and standards of production necessary. Confederates, especially, sought to utilize new weapons to overcome the Northern superiority in manpower and productive capacity, but most of the changes had been invented prior to the outbreak of war. However, many weapons which would later enter the organization tables of armies throughout the world got their first test on the battlefields of the Civil War. Although the musket remained the primary infantry weapon throughout the war, more and more were armed with rifles. Breechloaders were used in large numbers for the first time and magazine-using repeating rifles were employed. So were machine guns and weapons with interchangeable parts, neither of which would be used very much until after the war.

Engineers performed prodigious feats, from erecting pontoon bridges to constructing interlocking trenches and earthen forts that, combined with increasing firepower, made frontal assault costly.

The role of cavalry changed perceptibly

A stone dove of peace stands atop the tombstone of one of the Federal soldiers who died at Andersonville, Georgia.

during the war as shoulder-arm rifles virtually eliminated charges against infantry, but the horsemen remained an effective means of cutting supply lines, protecting flanks, and obtaining intelligence. Seven-shot repeating rifles effectively turned dismounted cavalry into emergency infantry trouble-shooters. Both Confederate General Forrest and Union General Sheridan made good use of this method of cavalry fighting.

Improvements also were made in cannon and artillery tactics. The use of rifled cannon increased as the war wore on, but artillerymen continued to favor the smoothbore, 12-pound Napoleon cannon because of its versatility in close support of infantry. Rockets were fired sparingly and breech-loading cannon were proposed but did not see action.

The Battle of Glorietta Pass, near Santa Fe, New Mexico, is re-enacted annually on the 1862 battlefield site (left). The Harper Farmhouse at Bentonville Battlefield in North Carolina still exists, and is used as part of modern re-enactments (above). The entrance to Jefferson Barracks, St Louis, Missouri (right).

227

Malvern Hill, Virginia, near to the James River, was the last of the Seven Days' battles (above). Rows of dead soldiers lie on quiet fields after the momentous Battle of Gettysburg (left).

FIREPOWER RAISES THE ANTE

The Civil War made the infantry 'queen of battle' in fact as well as in name. The simple improvement of rifling the musket barrel extended the effective range of infantry farther than previously thought possible, while quick, one-step reloading greatly increased the firepower of shoulder weapons. Land combat became a contest between manpower and firepower – a concept that still exists in conventional warfare. The war was a testing ground for modern arms, especially crew-operated weapons like machine guns and breech-loaded artillery. The breech-loading rifle, which was later to become standard in armies around the world, came of age.

Weapons and tactics were inextricably linked. Massed formations became obsolete when the firepower, accuracy, and killing distance of the infantryman was increased. Greater accuracy meant infantrymen could

Men of the 39th Illinois Infantry inspect a forerunner of the machine gun, a battery gun designed by Dr. Joseph Requa in 1863.

SECTION OF REQUA BATTERY.
Commanded by Lieutenants WHEELER and KINGSBURY, Thirty-Ninth Illinois.
Morris Island, S. C., 1863.

no longer effectively engage in stand-and-fire tactics. The primary example where this occurred, in the early stage of the Second Manassas (Bull Run), became an object lesson to all who participated. Frontal assaults were deadly; casualties in many battles were so heavy that they demoralized troops.

New infantry tactics stressed mobility, protection, and surprise. Battlefields became deeper and maneuver essential to conservation of force. Armies had to prepare for combat at distances farther apart. Formations were spread out and redesigned. Usually, attack lines were preceded by widely separated skirmishers, who fired at will as they advanced and used whatever cover they could find. Two or more lines with men several feet apart was a popular arrangement. These formations stopped at some point during the assault to fire at the defenders or proceeded in a succession of rushes, hugging the ground between moves.

One formation that is considered an American innovation involved double lines of two close ranks each, with considerable distance between each pair of lines to reduce the

Right The cavalry charge, an effective tactic in the days of smoothbore muskets, was no match for the power of infantry rifles. In this sketch, called 'Rebels Riding into Line of Battle,' horse soldiers begin a head-on charge.

effects of defensive firepower.

The increased firepower of the infantryman practically ended the use of the bayonet, which until then was regarded as the final shock weapon. In close-quarter fighting, soldiers preferred to use their rifles as clubs. Only one per cent of Union battle casualties were bayonet wounds; eighty per cent came from rifle bullets.

Increased infantry firepower gave defense a substantial advantage over offense, especially when combined with makeshift defensive installations. Defenders utilized hastily improvised breastworks and rifle pits or natural terrain features to evade the increased

Left Fortifications were a major preoccupation of the engineers. These wicker baskets filled with earth and rocks were used in the siege of Petersburg.

firepower of the enemy. The longer a unit remained in one place, the more elaborate its defenses became. Even attackers learned quickly to put earth and logs between them and the incoming bullets when pinned down or counter-attacked.

Cavalry charges no longer were decisive when infantry could drop horsemen from 250 yards away and fire two to three times as fast

as previously. Infantry did not even have to mass in close formation, as it did during the Napoleonic Wars, to meet the once-fearsome cavalry charge. A charge by the 1st Pennsylvania Cavalry Battalion to cover the Union retreat at Cedar Mountain, near Culpeper, Virginia, in 1862 was shattered by the fire of advancing Confederate infantry. Only 71 of the 164 men in the unit escaped unharmed.

Artillerymen, previously beyond the range of musket fire, became ready targets of sharpshooters. Only the flanking movement, which became the most decisive tactic of the war, remained unchanged after the advent of rifled barrels.

Some commanders never learned the lesson that battlefield conditions had changed, and their ignorance cost the lives of untold thousands on both sides. The Union Second Corps, which used a massed column formation to attack Confederate defenses at Spottsylvania in 1864, sustained 6,642 casualties in a two-week period. Others, although schooled in tactics that had been developed in the era of musketry, learned to

Above The versatile Napoleon 12-pounder was the most popular artillery weapon. This one helped defend Atlanta in 1864

Right A honeycomb of bombproof shelters protected Union soldiers at Ford Sedgwick, a key position in the Union siege line at Petersburg.

'rewrite the book.' Drillmasters continued to instruct recruits to remain in close order, but the lessons of combat and the irregularity and confusion of battlefields usually moved them farther apart.

The best generals, however adapted quickly. Confederate General Robert E. Lee's early and continued emphasis on breastworks and other temporary defensive structures did not result entirely from his engineering background; he was actually aware of the damage that increased firepower did to his troops. Union General Ulysses S. Grant, despite complaints which persisted throughout his career that he was a 'butcher' unconcerned about the lives of his men, was an early exponent of maneuver. He in effect flanked Fort Donelson by taking Fort Henry first and ravaged the hinterland of Vicksburg before settling down to besiege the city. In his drive to take Richmond, he consistently flanked Lee's smaller army. General William Tecumseh Sherman's favorite maneuver, his famous March to the Sea notwithstanding, was the flanking movement. But both Lee and Grant were capable of ignoring the lesson they had learned when greater considerations were at stake. Grant believed that 'if men make war in slavish observance of the rules, they will fail.'

The effect on United States military doctrine was considerable. The ascendency of the offensive in U.S. Army tactics, while not transmitted in an unbroken line, dates from the Civil War period. The concept of 'unconditional surrender' would surface again in World War II. The objective of 'total war' during the Civil War was to hasten the military victory; the consequences were not considered. That narrow definition of strategy prevailed in the United States until after World War II.

By the end of the Civil War, the foundation stones of modern warfare were in place.

Below **Costumed rangers fire a Napoleon cannon as part of the historical interpretation at Stone's River Battlefield, Murfreesboro, Tennessee.**

Engineers played an increasingly important role in the Civil War. This group (above) were part of the 8th New York State Militia. Flag towers, like this one (left) at Cobb's Hill near New Market, Virginia, in 1864, were used for battlefield communication as early as the Battle of First Manassas.

LINES OF COMMUNICATION

Both sides improved communications. Signal flags were used widely in combat, starting at First Manassas (Bull Run). The Civil War was the first 'telegraph war,' and it saw extensive use of this means of communication, both between major commands and between civilian leaders and military commanders.

The War between the States is often called the 'first railroad war,' too. Although rail lines had been used previously in warfare, nowhere else had they proved their strategic value. The defensive posture of the Confederacy, with internal lines and a smaller number of troops, dictated extensive use. The Confederate victory at Chickamauga probably would not have been possible without the transfer by rail of General James Longstreet's forces from Virginia to reinforce General Braxton Bragg. Conversely, railroads carried adequate supplies and reinforcement for General Sherman's subsequent push on Atlanta.

One of the most important lines in the defense of Virginia was the Richmond, Fredericksburg and Potomac. The Baltimore

Right Wooden blockhouses were used to guard strategic locations; this one protected the Louisville and Nashville Railroad, a favorite target of Confederate raiders. ruined engine house strands locomotives

The instruments and batteries needed to make the wires talk were carried on military telegraph wagons (left). A ruined engine house strands locomotives at Atlanta following fierce fighting for the city (below).

and Ohio probably suffered as much as any railroad, its rails and rolling stock being destroyed at one time or another by both sides.

The war also demonstrated the problems associated with small, unconnected railroads with different gauges. In 1861, the seceding Southern States had 113 separate railroad companies, most of them along the Atlantic seaboard. Even when the lines met in the same city, they had separate terminals – necessitating costly and time-consuming transfers of men and freight. A trip from Mississippi to the Eastern seaboard involved seven separate lines.

Technology moved off of terra firma, too. Professor Thaddeus S.C. Lowe said he was the

Among the innovations tried during the siege of Petersburg was this railroad battery.

first prisoner of war to be taken from a balloon, when a flight begun in Ohio set down in South Carolina. He was arrested and released only after a local citizen identified him as a scientist. Lowe demonstrated his balloons for President Lincoln, but got hung on a tree while trying to reach the battlefield at First Manassas (Bull Run). He made good use of the balloon for observation after the battle. Balloons were used by both sides on other occasions – a Union officer became the first to use one to direct artillery fire – but they never gained great popularity with military officers.

ACCLIMATIZING TO THE MILITARY LIFE

Ordinary soldiers changed, along with tactics and weapons. On the Union side, men who rode in carriages before the war became accomplished cavalrymen. Men who had clerked in stores or worked in offices needed time to adjust to the outdoors, to develop an *esprit de corps*, and to learn combat. There was

no shortage of bravery or perseverance in the ranks, despite being badly led at times. Billy Yanks by the thousands bought their comrades and successors time to learn. Johnny Reb never had enough weapons and equipment; much of what he used at times had 'U.S.' markings that had not been erased after capture.

The Confederate soldier was always hungry, almost always outnumbered, and often short of ammunition. At Second Manassas (Bull Run), 'Stonewall' Jackson's men threw rocks to help repulse one attack. Soldiers equipped with lances were among the Texans who invaded New Mexico. It is indeed remarkable that the Men in Gray accomplished as much as they did.

Soldiers in the ranks, though, no matter how prepared or how brave, seldom were better than their leaders. Failure or triumph depended on the skills and courage of the politicians behind them.

Above General Hermann Haupt, chief of construction of Union military railroads, seen here supervising excavation work on the Orange and Alexandria Railroad.

Opposite Professor Thaddeus Lowe, the war's foremost exponent of balloons, observes the Battle of Fair Oaks in Virginia from aloft.

CHAPTER 17

Lord Palmerston was incensed. 'An Englishman must blush to think such an act had been committed by a man belonging to the Anglo-Saxon race,' he told the Parliament of Great Britain, which had taken time out from the affairs of Empire to listen to the words of a pedestrian American general in far-off New Orleans, Louisiana. The Northern press was just as critical of General Order No. 28, which declared that any woman in the occupied city showing disrespect to a Union officer or soldier 'shall be regarded and held liable to be treated as a women of the town plying her avocation.' In New Orleans, the general was known as 'The Beast' despite his compassionate attitude toward the poor and to other city problems and effective administration of the city's affairs.

Major General Benjamin Franklin Butler's order was an overreaction to a serious problem. New Orleans citizens, who had felt secure behind forts guarding both the Mississippi River and Lake Ponchartrain ap-

New Orleans and Southern Louisiana

proaches to the city, refused to surrender formally, although they submitted to occupation without a fight after the Union navy had bypassed the river forts. Thus, the occupation began on a note of frustration, as well as resentment. Heavy-handed acts of occupation, from hauling down the State flag at gunpoint and requiring the use of Northern textbooks in the schools, to ordering foreign citizens to take an oath of allegiance to the United States, aggravated the situation. Residents resisted the occupation in every imaginable way short of violence. Union soldiers were shunned or treated with disrespect by a diverse population, which was about 40 per cent foreign-born but which was well-integrated into the congenial life and free-wheeling business atmosphere of the community now disrupted by occupation.

General Butler already had acquired an unsavory reputation by the time he issued General Order No. 28. The imperious and erratic politician–turned–soldier already had become a symbol of the arbitrary rule and corruption that followed the Union army into the South and that was late legitimatized by the Reconstruction Era. He brazenly helped his brother accumulate a fortune in Louisiana. He was detested even by his own soldiers, despite military achievements beyond those that could be expected of an untrained commander. Butler was never convicted of corruption, but was censured for suspicion of it; that did not prevent him from achieving his lifelong ambition of becoming governor of Massachusetts after the war.

NEW ORLEANS TODAY

Today's New Orleans would not be totally unfamiliar to her Civil War occupiers. The beautiful hand made iron lace balconies of the French Quarter are as prevalent in Civil War engravings as they are in current photographs. The French Market, which Butler considered too dirty, has improved with time but is still one of the Crescent City's most colorful areas. Jackson Square and historic buildings such as St. Louis Cathedral, Cabildo and Presbytere,

the Pontalba Apartments, and a house named Madame John's Legacy already were landmarks by the mid-nineteenth century. The slogan on the equestrian statue of Andrew Jackson – 'The Union must and shall be preserved' – was carved on order of General Butler. Confederate General Pierre Gustave Toutant Beauregard lived in the Beauregard-Keyes house, built around 1828; the Miro House, built in 1784, represents the traditional Spanish influence. The Hermann-Grima House is furnished to reflect the opulent era in the city which was interrupted by the Civil War. Part of the U.S. Customs House, which was incomplete at the time of the war, was used by Butler as an office, and part was used as a prison for Rebel soldiers. New Orleans' Confederate Museum, the State's oldest, houses an extensive collection of relics, including uniforms, rare battle flags, weapons, medical instruments, and memorabilia of Jefferson Davis. The former Confederate president died in 1889 in a house on First Street in the Garden District, already well established as a prime residential area by the time of the Civil War.

Chalmette National Cemetery, adjacent to the battlefield park commemorating Andrew Jackson's decisive victory over the British during the War of 1812, was started as a resting place for men who died in the numerous Civil War hospitals in the area.

Forts Pike and Macomb, facing the Gulf of Mexico, were built after the War of 1812. Used by both sides during the Civil War, they are maintained as State commemorative areas. At Fort Pike, casemates, with long exit tunnels, retain the original design created by French General Simon Bernard. The citadel's walls have been black since they were burned during the Civil War; the structure now houses historical exhibits. Confederates evacuated the forts, about 20 miles from downtown New Orleans, after the city fell, and the Union used them as bases to raid sites along Lake Ponchartrain and the Gulf of Mexico.

The beautiful plantation houses near New Orleans, many of which have now been re-

BOMBARDMENT OF PORT HUDSON BY ADMIRAL

GUT'S FLEET.

Naval bombardment by Admiral Farragut's fleet was effective at some places on the Western rivers, but not at Port Hudson on the Mississippi. (above) Strong land assaults, such as this one by the Second Louisiana Regiment (composed of black troops) on May 27, 1863, caused heavy casualties but did not breach the Confederate defenses at Port Hudson (below).

stored, became part of the commercial tug-of-war as well as the formal fighting. When skirmishing was not going on around them, Northern speculators or military foragers from both sides extracted food and cotton from their owners. Among the most picturesque are galleried San Francisco, and 1854-6 structure with beautifully painted ceilings; 1787 Destrehan, the State's oldest plantation home; Three Oaks, built in 1840, whose broad galleries with brick columns were fired on by Union gunboats; Whitehall, now a school for the handicapped; Greek Revival-style Oak Alley, built in 1836, whose double rows of live oaks have appeared in motion pictures; and Jefferson College, an 1831 structure used as a barracks by Union forces but now a Jesuit retreat. San Francisco, Destrehan and Oak Alley are open to the public.

BAYOU COMMUNITIES

The names of the bayou communities – Thibodaux, Brashear (now Morgan) City, Raceland and New Iberia among them-

appear frequently in Civil War dispatches and the diaries and letters of soldiers of both sides, who often mentioned the difficulty of terrain and the voraciousness of the mosquitoes. The area was a sort of no man's land where the Union had managed to gain control of enclaves but not the region. Bayou Teche, one of the principal arteries, witnessed much of the pageantry of war in Southern Louisiana, from smuggling and daring ambushes to land attacks on warships struggling against the vagaries of nature.

Both the Confederates and the Federals raised temporary earthen forts at Morgan City in an attempt to control the region. Union troops occupied Morgan City in 1862, destroyed Confederate Forts Chene and Berwick and built two of their own—Forts Brashear (Star) and Buchanan. The New Orleans, Opelousas and Great Western Railway, which at the start of the war had provided free passage to men joining Confederate forces, became a major Union facility. The Union also used Morgan City, the western terminus of the only railroad in Southern Louisiana, as

Fort Morgan, located on Mobile Point, Alabama, is considered one of the finest examples of brick architecture in the U.S. It played a key role in the Battle of Mobile Bay on August 5, 1864.

a major supply center and staging base for army and navy actions on Bayou Teche, against the Confederate salt works on Avery Island and for the Invasion of Texas. On June 22, 1863, a daring attack by 325 Confederates of Brigadier General A.A. Mouton's command retook the city, captured more than 700 Union prisoners and enough stores to sustain Confederate forces into the next year–but held the area for only a few days. Nothing remains of the forts, but the site of Fort Brashear (Star) and the city's wartime experiences are recalled on historical markers.

New Iberia, a steamboat terminus where the paddlewheeler *Teche Queen* carries passengers much as vessels did during the war era, recalls those days principally at its beautiful antebellum mansions–Mintmere, built in 1857; Shadows-on-the-Teche, constructed in 1834 by a wealthy sugar planter and now owned by the National Trust for Historic Preservation; and Justine, started on 1822 and added to in the 1840s and 1890s. A Civil War skirmish was fought on the grounds of Mintmere, which also served as a headquarters for Union Brigadier General Albert Lee.

BATTLES IN LOUISIANA

As the war went on, Union activities in Louisiana were designed as much to obtain cotton for the mills of New England, where unemployed workers were becoming restless, and to enroll slaves as workers and soldiers as they were to engage the Confederates or capture territory. Confederate forces also spent considerable time living off the land and trying to block Union access to farm products. Nevertheless, sizable battles were fought at Baton Rouge, Port Hudson, and elsewhere as Union troops pressed deeper into the State. Ultimately, the Red River campaign into northwest Louisiana resulted in a Confederate victory at the Battle of Mansfield (Sabine Crossroads) which ended the campaign.

The fighting for Baton Rouge, which ultimately would devastate the capital, started with dirty laundry. An officer aboard one of the Federal ships on the Mississippi, while rowing ashore in search of a laundry woman, was attacked and slightly injured by guerrillas. Commodore David G. Farragut thereupon ordered the warships *Hartford* and *Kennebec* to fire upon the city, damaging the Gothic capitol building and the handsome Roman Catholic church and panicking the citizens but causing few casualties. When a small group of citizens rowed to the ships to apologize and explain they could not control the guerrillas, Farragut agreed not to bombard the city again unless attacked. The next day an occupying force was in the city.

The next fighting was much more serious. On August 5, 1862, Confederate troops led by

Powerful Fort Morgan was one of two forts guarding the entrance to Mobile Bay. Farragut ran the gauntlet and defeated the Confederate fleet in the bay.

Major General John C. Breckinridge, a former Vice President of the United States, attacked the camps of the occupying army under cover of morning fog, driving some units in confusion back into the streets of the city. Stiff Federal resistance, and mysterious orders to Confederate units to halt their attacks and fall back, slowed the attack elsewhere. In the river, the Confederate ironclad ram *Arkansas*, which was supposed to support the attack had broken down, and so Union warships were able to supplement Union artillery and provide a sanctuary within the city for defeated units. Breckinridge called off the attack when he learned the *Arkansas* was lost and pulled back to Port Hudson, one of the strongest points on the river.

Breckinridge's attack achieved indirectly what it could not do directly; it caused such concern about a Confederate attack on New Orleans that General Butler evacuated Baton Rouge to concentrate his forces. Departing troops—in contrast to the disciplined manner in which they had conducted the occupation prior to the battle—plundered and defaced the city.

The Battle of Baton Rouge Monument and a smaller marker on the grounds of the Dufroca School commemorate the battle. A 34-storey capitol building has now replaced the turreted structure as the seat of State government. Burned by Union soldiers during their second occupation of the city, the Old Capitol has been restored and operates as a museum and tourist information center. The Old Arsenal, where strong entrenchments were built by Union engineers against the possibility of another attack, also is a museum.

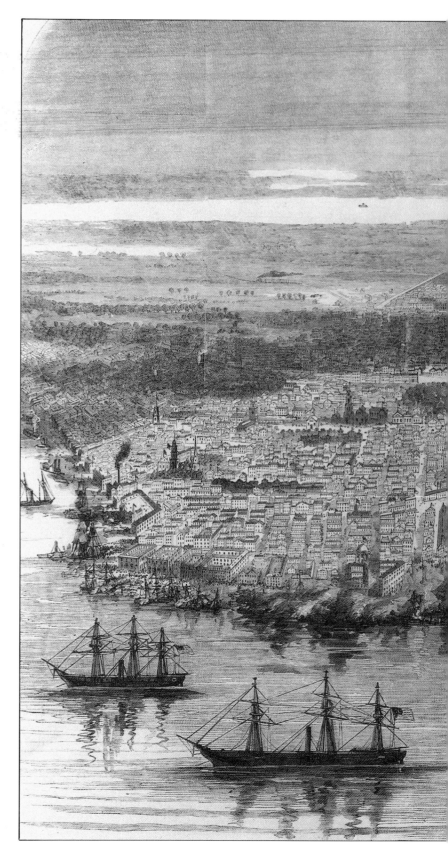

The 'queen city of the South,' New Orleans, was already occupied when this engraving appeared in April of 1862. The Union fleet lies at anchor in the Mississippi River.

CHAPTER 18

Vicksburg National Military Park in Mississippi, populated with handsome memorials, preserved fortifications, and other memories of the decisive siege, is one of the most impressive Civil War battlefields. Vicksburg was the key to control of the Mississippi and, in Union President Abraham Lincoln's view, the war could 'never be brought to a close until that key is in our pocket.' Pocketing the key would require heavy casualties and inflict untold hardship upon besieged and besieger alike – but in reality the fate of Vicksburg was decided before the siege began. Indecisiveness, conflicting orders, an appalling lack of intelligence information, and bad judgment enabled Grant to ravage Vicksburg's natural support areas and invade the town from its vulnerable rear.

The fall of Vicksburg began with a fortress mentality, as Confederate Lieutenant General John C. Pemberton demanded reinforcements but did not appreciate the necessity of an active defense; it was abetted by division of

Closing the Mississippi

forces at a time when concentration might have destroyed Grant's army; and it was confirmed by belated efforts, with inadequate forces, to rectify earlier mistakes.

The first attempts of General Ulysses S. Grant to capture Vicksburg from the north were dismal failures, largely because of impossible terrain. He then spent thousands of man-hours in futile attempts to dig canals through the marshes on the Louisiana side of the Mississippi River in an effort to avoid the well-situated Confederate guns on the heights above the river at Vicksburg. He finally decided to divide his forces and attack the city from the south and east. Confederate General Joseph E. Johnston ordered Pemberton to concentrate his forces and strike at Grant.

'If Grant's army lands on this side of the river, the safety of Mississippi depends on beating it,' Johnston wired Pemberton. 'For that object you should unite your whole forces.' This good advice went unheeded, and Johnston tried again with a similar order, adding, 'success will give you back what you abandoned to win it'. But Pemberton had orders from Jefferson Davis to hold Vicksburg, and he sent inadequate forces to stop Grant.

RAID ON BATON ROUGE

One of the most famous raids of the war, led by Colonel B.H. Grierson from Tennessee through the heart of Mississippi to Baton Rouge, Louisiana, was a spectacular diversion while Grant moved his forces southward on the Louisiana shore of the Mississippi. Grierson's 17-day raid was just as successful as Hollywood later portrayed it, destroying railroads and military targets and evading Confederate pursuers along a 800-mile route.

GRAND GULF

Grand Gulf Military Monument, ten miles northwest of Port Gibson off U.S. Route 61, preserves the site of a successful attempt on April 29, 1863, to stop Grant from crossing to the east side of the river. The Civil War left Grand Gulf a virtual ghost town, and it was not until 1962 that the importance of the strategic

location was recognized by the dedication of the memorial park. Exhibits and relics, including remnants of Fort Coburn and Fort Wade, trace the fighting at Grand Gulf, where the Union suffered heavy losses without dislodging defenders under Brigadier General John S. Bowen. Photographs, maps, scale models, uniforms, muskets, cannonballs, and artifacts recovered in the area are displayed in

Above right **Union General Ulysses S. Grant wore down the Confederacy by persistent attacks and destruction of private resources.**

a museum. Authentic buildings from the region include a frame church and a water mill. Hiking trails and an observation tower, from which miles of the Mississippi River are visible, provide an overview of the battle area.

ATTACK ON PORT GIBSON

Grant responded to the stalwart defense of Grand Gulf by moving farther south and attacking Port Gibson, where an outnumbered brigade could not stop his advance. The Shaffer House near Port Gibson, built about 1840, survived the fighting, but Port Gibson's best-known structure is the 1859 Presbyterian church, whose steeple top is a gilded hand pointing toward heaven. Confederate Major General Earl Van Dorn is buried in Wintergreen Cemetery, facing south, along with both Confederate and Union casualties from the Battle of Port Gibson. Other antebellum structures include St. Joseph's Roman Catholic Church of 1849, the 1860 Methodist Church, 1833 Idlewild mansion, 1811 Miss Phoebe's and the Disharoon House, raised in the 1830s and known for its unusual staircase and chandeliers from the steamboat *Robert E. Lee.* Of the plantation house at Windsor, 12 miles southwest of Port Gibson on Mississippi Route 552, only the handsome columns remain. It was not destroyed in the war, though the plantation house was used as an observation post by the Rebels and as a hospital by the Union; it survived the war only to burn in 1890.

BATTLE OF RAYMOND

The Battle of Raymond, now listed as a stop along the scenic Natchez Trace Parkway that connects many Mississippi Civil War sites, was an example of how Pemberton sent inadequate forces to confront Grant and how effective the Southern philosophy of attack could be. In the smoke and dust that enveloped the battlefield on May 12, a Confederate brigade stymied an entire Union corps for half a day by repeated attacks. In the end, the greater numbers prevailed and the first Federals into Raymond, the 20th Ohio, sat down to a picnic which the ladies of the town had prepared in anticipation of a Confederate victory.

CHAMPION HILL

As Grant marched to destroy Jackson (where the 1857 Manship House, 1846 the Oaks and 1842 Governor's Mansion are among the few buildings to survive), Pemberton missed an opportunity to catch him between two armies and perhaps destroy him. When he finally confronted Grant at Champion Hill and Big Black River, it was a case of too little, too late. Rowen's slashing attack over the rugged terrain at Champion Hill during the May 16 battle, which bent but could not break Grant's line, has left a legacy that includes a gray-clad ghost and an annual re-enactment of the battle at Edwards under the auspices of the Champion Hill Battlefield Foundation. Pemberton held the bridges at the Big Black until it was obvious his rear guard had been cut off, then retreated inside his strong fortifications at Vicksburg.

SURRENDER OF VICKSBURG

Grant at first demanded unconditional surrender of Pemberton, but decided to soften the terms after Pemberton refused to accept such harsh conditions. At 10 a.m. on July 4– Independence Day–Vicksburg was formally

Fort Massachusetts, located on Ship Island in the Gulf of Mexico, remained in Union hands and was a valuable staging area for the invasion of Mobile and other coastal points.

VICKSBURG TODAY

The Vicksburg battlefield park stretches in an irregular arc across the hills around the city of Vicksburg, its northern flank resting —as it did at the time of the Civil War—on the water. The museum in the Visitors' Centre shows both the military and human sides of the siege, the culmination of a year of bloody campaigning by Grant to take the Confederacy's greatest Mississippi River stronghold. A mock-up of the caves where civilians lived to escape the Union bombardment is outfitted with sparse household furnishings. Displays show the meager rations which soldiers and civilians alike received—in the latter stage of the siege a one-day ration consisted of two biscuits, two portions of bacon, a few peas and a spoonful of rice. The defenders of Vicksburg endured these deprivations of 47 days. Among other displays are a mortar and cannonballs, carbines, muskets, swords, and a mock-up of a Confederate hospital room. An audio-visual presentation details both Grant's initial efforts to break the Confederate lines, under the false impression that Pemberton's troop had been demoralized at Champion Hill and the Big Black, and the siege that followed.

A 16-mile drive, starting at the Visitors' Centre, traverses sections of the Union siege line and the Confederate defenses; 1,400 monuments, ranging from a classical domed building to simple marble tablets, can be seen. The roller-coaster road passes through a memorial arch and follows the wooded contours of the hills along the Union siege line and then the Confederate defenses. Artillery batteries are placed at numerous sites , on their original positions, and memorials and statues stand on forts, redans, lunettes, breastworks, and terrain features associated with various units.

The classical lines of the domed white Illinois memorial make it the most beautiful in the park, while the Alabama monument and others have sculptures on the traditional columns. The white frame Shirley House, the only surviving wartime structure in the park, is restored to its 1863 appearance, when it served as a headquarters for the 45th Illinois Infantry. Missouri, whose men fought on both sides, has a monument commemorating both. Fort Hill, which anchored the Confederate left and was so formidable that no Union attack was ever made against it, provides the best view of the countryside and river. Stockade Redan, which guarded one of the roads into Vicksburg, was a focal point of Grant's two attempts —on May 19 and 22 —to storm the fortifications. The second attempt, an all-out attack along a three-mile front, may have been the first use of clockwork to time an attack, but it failed at a cost of 502 Union lives. During the siege, Union forces tried a tactic that would lead to disaster later at Petersburg, Virginia– digging mines under Confederate forts and detonating explosives. At Vicksburg, two unsuccessful attempts were made against the Third Louisiana Redan.

The site where Grant and Pemberton, who had been comrades-in-arms during the Mexican War, met to discuss surrender terms is on Pemberton Avenue. It was the first place to be marked —on July 4, 1863–but souvenir hunters chipped two successive marble monuments so badly they were replaced by a cannon.

The city of Vicksburg preserves its own memories of the war, with downtown memorials and strategically placed cannon overlooking the waterfront—which now is actually the type of canal Grant tried to build in other areas because the fickle river changed its course away from the city after the war. Among the remaining antebellum homes are Cedar Grove, damaged by warship bombardment during the siege; 1835 Balfour House, the site of a Christmas Eve ball interrupted by the arrival of Union gunboats heralding the siege and which was used as a Union headquarters after the surrender of the city; Anchuca, built about 1830 and reportedly a platform from which the Confederate president delivered a speech; six acres of gardens around Great Oaks, built in the 1830s; and the Old Courthouse Museum, whose iron doors and 30-foot columns complement more and 10,000 exhibits.

Confederate General John S. Bowen directed the slashing attack at Champion Hill, Mississippi. This monument is at Vicksburg National Battlefield.

JOHN S. BOWEN
MAJOR GENERAL C.S. ARMY
COMMANDING DIVISION
ARMY OF VICKSBURG

CADET, U.S. MILITARY ACADEMY 1848
2ND LIEUT. U.S. ARMY, JULY 20, 1854
RESIGNED, MAY FIRST 1856
COLONEL C.S. ARMY, JUNE 11, 1861
BRIGADIER GENERAL, MARCH 14, 1862
MAJOR GENERAL, MAY 25, 1863
DIED JULY SIXTEENTH 1863

surrendered by Confederates stacking arms and relinquishing colors. Five days later, when Port Hudson surrendered and the Confederacy was divided, Lincoln could proclaim that 'the Father of Waters again goes unvexed to the sea.'

ROLE OF NAVAL POWER

Lincoln's comment about the importance of control of the Mississippi was justified recognition of the important role of naval power on the rivers in the Western Theater, which has been inadequately covered in memorials because so few relics remain. At long last, that aspect of the war is explored in a museum at Vicksburg national park which includes a partial reconstruction of the gunboat USS *Cairo*, incorporating a 15-ton section of the bow and other artifacts recovered from the bottom of the river. The life of the sailors is shown through personal effects and weapons, such recovered equipment as mess gear and ship fittings, and photographs of Mississippi warships and their crews. Audio-visual presentations relate the sinking of the USS *Cairo* in 12 minutes—without loss of a single life—and the modern tale of how the parts were located and recovered.

The river war was an important adjunct of the land war. 'Tinclads,' or lightly armored shallow-draft ships, were the backbone of the Union navy's campaign to control the Mississippi River. They were especially important in bypassing Vicksburg, as well as other fortified river cities. These 'turtles' also operated on small rivers. By far the greatest number of warships was engaged in this unglamorous but necessary work.

SIEGE OF PORT HUDSON

'To hold both Vicksburg and Port Hudson is necessary to a connection with Trans-Mississippi,' Jefferson Davis had said. As Grant closed in on Vicksburg, General Nathaniel Banks edged northward from New Orleans toward Port Hudson. After a 48-day siege and bloody assaults by 30,000 Union troops against 6,800 Confederate defenders, Port Hudson

A 15-ton section of the bow of Mississippi Warship USS *Cairo*, before reconstruction: now part of a museum at Vicksburg.

became the last Southern stronghold on the Mississippi River to surrender, its defenders reduced to eating mules, horses, and rats. It raised a white flag only after receiving word that Vicksburg had fallen, making further sacrifice meaningless. The Union paid the heavy price of 4,363 casualties. While Confederate losses were about a sixth of that number.

TEXAS AND THE RED RIVER

Louisiana was the cornerstone of Federal action along the Gulf Coast, as well as an important factor in clearing the Mississippi River. The Gulf Coast of the Confederacy was the third front, where land action was light but the navy strained to blockade the ports of Mississippi, Alabama, Texas and Florida. It was an area of daring games, whether played by blockade runners trying to outwit Federal warships or amphibious units trying to destroy Confederate installations and confidence.

Texas escaped heavy fighting during the Civil War largely because of geography, but the State was a major contributor to the Confederate cause. Until the Mississippi was closed by Federal troops and gunboats, Texas was a major source of supplies and manpower. Texans fought on all fronts, from Virginia to Arizona, and saved many a battle by their stalwartness. Colonel Taylor, from his base at Mesilla, redrew the map of the New Mexico Territory as a Confederate territory, with Arizona as a separate jurisdiction. General Sibley's grueling invasion of New Mexico along the Rio Grande moved from his base in San Antonio through El Paso.

At home, Indians were a greater problem than Federal forces. Texas units occupied Forts Washita, Cobb, and Arbuckle in an unsuccessful attempt to secure the northern part of the State against Indian attacks. Home Guard units were entrusted with internal protection and succeeded in keeping the Indians relatively quiet until 1865.

Federal attacks on Texas were concentrated on the coast. Galveston was captured by the Union late in 1862, but was retaken on

PORT HUDSON STATE COMMEMORATIVE AREA

Along six miles of trails at the Port Hudson State Commemorative Area are well-preserved remnants of the 4 and a half miles of breastworks and redoubts, whose actions included the first major fight between white and black troops during the war. The earthworks at Fort Desperate, a Confederate strongpoint which won its name during some of the fiercest fighting, are original, but are neater than the littered area of raw earth shown in photographs of the site taken shortly after the surrender. During the second attack, many wounded Union soldiers died because their commander, General Banks, would not request a truce to tend to them; the stench of decaying bodies eventually became so great that a flag of truce was arranged by the

Confederates so they could be removed. The loss of Union officers was particularly heavy. A Massachusetts soldier called the fate of the wounded 'martyrdom' and said the scene at a field hospital – 'here a pile of booted legs, there a pile of arms'– was more trying than the horrors of the battlefield.

Other significant points on the trails are the Bull Pen, a triangle-shaped low area where Union attackers were caught in a crossfire; Fort Babcock, the most advanced position seized and held by Union forces, who pushed siege lines forward behind shields of cotton bales; Commissary Hill, a strategic artillery location during the first attack that takes its name from its proximity to the Confederate granary and grist mill;

and redoubts held by Mississippi, Alabama, and Arkansas units.

An interpretive center just off U.S. Highway 61, 14 miles north of Baton Rouge provides an introduction to the park, with a museum, a breastworks replica, and an observation tower for viewing the battlefield.

Two nearby State commemorative areas hold the graves of Southerners who died at Port Hudson and in other battles in southeast Louisiana. At least two war hospitals were operated at Clinton, which also for a time was headquarters of mounted Confederate units harassing Banks's rear, and more than half the 150 soldiers buried at the Clinton Confederate State Commemorative Area fell at Port Hudson. In Jackson Cemetery are the unmarked graves of Confederate who died at the battle of Thompson's Creek. The cemetery at Locust Grove, with 27 plots, is all that remains of the plantation owned by the family of Jefferson Davis's sister. Therein, in 1835, Davis's wife of only three months contracted malaria and died.

Fighting in Mississippi did not begin or end with the destruction of Jackson and the fall of Vicksburg. Ship Island, now part of the Gulf Coast National Seashore, was occupied in 1862 by Union troops, who used Fort Massachusetts, restored to its Civil War appearance, as a base to invade Mobile, Alabama, and other coastal areas.

Beauvoir mansion, near Biloxi, is preserved as a shrine to the memory of Jefferson Davis, who lived there for ten years after being released from Union prison. It was there he wrote The Rise and Fall of the Confederate Government. The Tomb of the Unknown Soldier of the Confederate States is located in the cemetery on the grounds. Holly Springs, where more than 100 historic homes are preserved, changed hands 60 times during the war, and was the scene of a successful Confederate raid on Grant's supplies.

Many of the superb antebellum homes of Natchez survived the war, including Rosalie which was used for a time as a Union headquarters, and Dunleith, a stately Greek Revival home with colonnaded galleries, completed around 1856. The city of Columbus claims the first Memorial Day was observed there in 1886, when the ladies of the city placed flowers on the graves of 1,500 Confederate and Union soldiers who died at Shiloh.

Camp Moore, an assembly point and training site for Confederate recruits, stood in Louisiana on a wooded site on the Tangipahoa River and the New Orleans, Jackson and Great Northern Railroad not far from the Arkansas border. It was a tent city throughout its existence, and a Union raid in late 1864 scattered the remaining Confederates, so no traces of the camp or training facilities remain.

The site on State Route 51 north of Amite, however, is preserved as a State commemorative area whose museum relates a lively history: as many as 6,000 men at a time trained there. The cemetery, watched over by a tall monument erected in 1907, testifies that disease killed more men than bullets during the war. Just three months after the camp opened, an epidemic of measles killed 600 to 700 recruits who, according to one of the survivors, 'yielding up their patriotic young lives without having once faced the enemies of their beloved South.'

Numerous Engravings....12½ cts.

Mexican Treacheries and Cruelties.

INCIDENTS AND SUFFERINGS

IN THE

MEXICAN WAR;

WITH

Accounts of Hardships endured; Treacheries of the Mexicans; Battles Fought, and Success of American Arms;

The "Heroine of Fort Brown."

Also, an Account of Valiant Soldiers Fallen,

AND THE PARTICULARS OF THE

Death and Funeral Services in honor of Capt. George Lincoln, of Worcester.

BY A VOLUNTEER RETURNED FROM THE WAR.

BOSTON AND NEW YORK:
1847.

Entered according to Act of Congress, in the year 1847, by Lieut. G. N. Allen.

Dealers supplied at HALL'S, 66 Cornhill, Boston.

Mrs. Sarah Borginnis ('The Great Western') was known far and wide as a warm-hearted camp follower in both the Mexican and Civil Wars.

January 1, 1863, by Confederate General John B. Magruder. Galveston's subsequent bouts with hurricanes have left few relics of its Civil War history, but the city retains the flavor of the economic freebooting that began when the pirate Jean Lafitte made it his headquarters. It cherishes its historic buildings—especially the Williams Home and Ashton Villa which date from before the war—and its Gulf Coast personality protected by its long massive seawall.

BATTLE AT SABINE PASS

The only sizable battle between Confederate and Union regulars in Texas was un unqualified success for the Confederates. On September 8, 1863, a combined army and naval force assembled by General Nathaniel P. Banks and Admiral David G. Farragut launched an invasion of the State at Sabine Pass. Nowadays, a pretty State park overlooking the pass preserves the site of the battlefield where several hundred Confederates under Lieutenant Richard Dowling drove the 4,000-man invasion force back to their ships. Naturally, Dowling became a great hero to the Texans.

CAPTURE OF BROWNSVILLE

Two months later, General Banks invaded the Rio Grande Valley and captured Brownsville and nearby points, then pushed up the coast to occupy Mustang Island, off Corpus Christi, and Fort Esperanza on Matagorda Island. The following summer, the Confederates liberated Brownsville, but were unable to reopen the Rio Grande to traffic. Historic buildings of Fort Brown—better remembered for its use in the Mexican War—are incorporated into a junior college. The port, through which goods from abroad reached the Confederacy until 1863, now harbors a large fishing fleet and is an outlet for the citrus products of the river valley.

RAVAGES OF WAR

Intemperate acts occurred in Texas, as they did elsewhere because of the passions that divided the people. German settlers, who where outspoken in their opposition to slavery and firm in allegiance to the Union, were attacked on August 10, 1862, by a Confederate ranger force. Casualties in the Battle of Neuces, as the engagement is called, were not large, but the numbers grew as clashes between Confederates and Unionists continued.

Gainesville in Gillespie County, not far from the Oklahoma border, was the setting of the 'Great Hanging' in which a Texas ranger,

Captain James Duff, hanged about 50 men and killed a number of others.

In Austin, the State capital, the Daughters of the Confederacy and Daughters of the Republic of Texas jointly maintained an historical museum. Placita Santa Fe, El Paso's Old Town, retains the adobe and stone buildings which were standard when General Henry H. Sibley and his troops passed through. Hillsboro's Confederate Research Center and Audie Murphy Gun Museum has a sizable collection of Civil War relics, including photographs and weapons. The Fort Bend County Museum at Richmond displays local Civil War mementoes. Prisoner of war camps were located at Camp Groce on the Brazos River near Hempstead and at Camp Ford near Tyler.

Central and northern Louisiana escaped most of the ravages of the war, except for foraging and raids. However, pressed as much for political as military reasons, General Banks twice invaded the Red River Valley to confiscate sugar, cotton, and other farm products and slaves and to extend Union control in Louisiana.

RED RIVER VALLEY CAMPAIGNS

The campaigns of General Banks would leave deep scars at Alexandria and Pineville, strategic centers on Red River, and culminated with Banks' defeat in the Battle of Mansfield, south of Shreveport.

The first, a combined land and naval operation, stopped at Alexandria, A Confederate headquarters and supply base as well as a commercial packing center. Confederates retreated after only perfunctory defense of the city but the shallowness of the water prevented Union gunboats from going farther. Banks, who disapproved of campaigns in the Red River Valley, destroyed military targets at Alexandria and Pineville, recruited slaves as soldiers, and returned to his base. The second expedition in 1864 met brief resistance at Marksville, better known now for relics of an Indian culture which existed 1,000 years before America was discovered

A Confederate unit breaks camp during a re-enactment of the Battle of Mansfield, also known as the Battle of Sabine Crossroads.

by Europeans. This time the gunboats were able to cross the rapids at Alexandria and move toward Shreveport, the temporary State capital. Occupation of Shreveport would give the Union effective control of Louisiana.

Banks' army of 20,000 men had been strengthened by 10,000 veterans of the fighting at Vicksburg, but Confederate Major General Richard Taylor chose well the place to make his stand. He stopped the campaign in the Battles of Mansfield and Pleasant Hill.

CAMPAIGNS REMEMBERED

A portion of the battlefield is preserved as a State commemorative area three miles from Mansfield, with a Visitors' Center and quarter-mile trail through the woods, named after General Mouton, one of the Confederate commanders. Along the trail, a reconstructed rail fence recreates one of the features along which the Union defenses were organized. markers identify various phases of the April 8 battle, in which the impatience of General Taylor played in important part. Taylor tired of waiting for Banks to attack and sent his troops against both Union flanks before they could be reinforced. The Union line crumbled and retreated five miles to Pleasant Hill, where a stand by the Union XIX Corps ended the battle.

The Visitors' Centre houses a collection of memorabilia, including a sizable collection of rifles and pistols, a Confederate six-pounder cannon cast in 1861 at Nashville, and good displays on the role of 60 river warships committed to the Red River Campaign. Included are models of the ironclad USS *Corondolet* and the ironclad Confederate ram *Arkansas* and photographs of the riverboats during the campaign.

Monuments at the entrance to the park and elsewhere commemorate the victory and memorialize the officers who were killed in the battle, General Mouton among them. Union losses of 3,000 were about three times those of the Confederates, and Banks retreated first to Alexandria and then to Baton Rouge. His retreat added to the unusual collection of Civil War relics at the cross-river cities of Alexandria and Pineville. Shallow water trapped the Union gunboats above the falls until an ingenious dam enabled them to escape .

The sites of Confederate Forts Buhlow and Randolph, built to protect against further Federal incursions that never came, are preserved. Mount Olivet Chapel, built in 1850, was used as a barracks by Union troops. Kent House, built in 1796 and the oldest remaining structure in central Louisiana, includes separate kitchen, slaves quarters, and milk house. The Rosalie Sugar Mill represents a commodity involved in much of the foraging in Louisiana during the war. Lloyd Hall, and 1810 plantation home at Lecompte whose owner was hanged as a spy by the Federals, was used by armies of both sides.

Alexandria has close prewar and postwar associations with two famous Union generals— Major General William T. Sherman and Major General George Armstrong Custer, respectively. Sherman established the forerunner of Louisiana State University at Pineville and resigned as its president to accept a Union commission. Custer, sent to Alexandria in 1865 to direct the 'reconstruction,' faced one of his most trying challenges—the mutiny of the Third Michigan Cavalry.

The story is told locally this way. As a joke, after having been commended for its soldierly appearance, the 90-man unit turned out with hats on backward, jackets turned inside out, swords on the wrong side, and otherwise in a sloppy condition. Custer, who did not think it funny, court martialed the unit and sentenced a sergeant accused of being the ring leader to be shot. When Custer would not yield to a petition from the men, talk of mutiny began to circulate. Custer, aware of it, faced down the prospective mutineers on the morning of the execution of the sergeant and of another man, convicted of desertion. The guns of the firing squad roared and both men dropped—the deserter dead and the sergeant fainting. Custer had ordered that he be placed just outside the line of fire. The site of the event is now occupied by St. Francis Xavier Cathedral.

Robert E. Lee was among the patrons of the Stabler-Leadbetter Apothecary in Alexandria, Virginia. Today, hundreds of old bottles are the major attraction.

Tyrone House, built around 1840, was spared the torch because its owner was a friend of Sherman's prior to the war. Winter Quarters, a State commemorative site at Newellton, was spared on order of General Ulysses S. Grant while most homes in the region were burned. It was a trade-off: The wife of the owner, a Union sympathizer, offered to feed and quarter Union troops during the siege of Vicksburg. The house, built in sections starting in 1805, demonstrates two architectural styles and houses mementoes of the war and examples of the research on cotton farming done by the plantation owner.

CHAPTER 19

The high seas and coastline of the Confederacy were one of the decisive battlegrounds. As a result, maritime exploits matched those on land in intensity and importance, but not in size. The navies of both countries remained small, but they helped determine the fates of soldiers fighting in the fields and civilians supporting the war at home.

The importance of the slow-developing naval conflict cannot be overrated. It affected the lifestyle of both nations as much as the land war. It assured Northerners of continued plenty; it helped devastate the South.

UNION NAVY

At the start, the Union possessed a small navy of 90 vessels, about half of them in operating condition. Twenty-eight were on foreign station, some as far away as China. However, most of the shipbuilding facilities, including seven of the nine naval yards, were located in the North. Naval yards at New York, Boston,

The War at Sea: Cat and Mouse

Philadelphia, Washington, Portsmouth, New Hampshire, Sackett's Harbor, Maine, and Mare Island, California and numerous private yards immediately began a crash program to build vessels and convert peacetime ships to wartime use. Captured Confederate craft were put back into service, sometimes after alteration.

A total of 626 vessels were constructed and purchased by the Union during the war. Even after losses, the Union navy reported 671 ships on duty at the end of 1864, including ironclads of various designs.

The Northeast had a far stronger seafaring tradition than the South and thus possessed a much larger pool of skilled manpower. Furthermore, the North had control of virtually the entire naval force of about 8,900 men, including about 1,300 officers, and the U.S. Naval Academy at Annapolis. The Union navy reached a peak of about 52,000 during the war, at least a third of whom had been born abroad.

CONFEDERATE NAVY

About a third of the officers in the U.S. Navy – 322 – resigned their commissions to enter Confederate service or return to their homes in Southern States. This created a temporary surplus of officers in the Confederacy since the new nation had few ships. The reverse was true of enlisted seamen; since it takes up to three years to produce skilled mariners, the Confederacy struggled throughout its existence with a shortage of capable seamen. At its peak, the Confederate navy had about 5,200 officers and men. Only the use of foreign mercenaries, principally English and Scandinavians, enabled the Confederate navy to man its newly constructed cruisers. Members of the crew of the CSS *Alabama*, for example, were mostly Englishmen.

The Confederacy's greatest naval asset was the existence of a few bold and imaginative leaders. Secretary of Navy Stephen R. Mallory was an energetic chieftain with imagination to encourage development of new designs and weapons, and a facility for overcoming endemic

shortages. Matthew Fontaine Maury, already famous as the 'Pathfinder of the Seas,' added innovative design and use of mines (called torpedoes at the time) to his many laurels. More than 40 Union vessels were sunk or heavily damaged by mines; many naval historians regard this as the Confederacy's most effective naval defense. Commanders of raiders, including Captain Raphael Semmes of the *Alabama*, were experienced and courageous sailors who captured and sank more than 1,000 vessels – 295 steamers, 44 large sailing vessels and 683 schooners. A naval academy was created from scratch in 1863

Stephen R. Mallory, Confederate Secretary of the Navy, was the only member of the Confderate Cabinet to hold the same post throughout the war.

aboard the steamer *Patrick Henry*, anchored near Richmond.

The Confederacy had virtually no combat vessels at the start of the war. The Confederate government issued letters of marque to privateers, authorizing the seizure of Union vessels, as soon as war broke out. It took control of ships in Southern ports, including a warship which sailed into New Orleans shortly after the war began, and captured others during the war. However, most of the deepwater Confederate navy was acquired abroad. Sleek and speedy warships like the CSS *Alabama* and CSS *Florida* were constructed or purchased abroad, often using subterfuge to evade neutrality laws. States also procured

and operated naval fleets and turned them over to the Confederate navy.

The Confederacy captured the naval yards at Norfolk, Virginia, and Pensacola, Florida, and had small facilities at a few other sites. For the most part, however, the Confederacy had to build new shipyards to provide the vessels to protect its vulnerable rivers and coastline. The Norfolk naval yard remained in Confederate hands only long enough to raise the burned USS *Merrimack* and reconstruct it as the ironclad CSS *Virginia*. Further Federal encroachment on the coastline and along the rivers took away other facilities. Despite a shortage of skilled labor, the Confederacy continued to produce vessels to the

RUNNING THE BLOCKADES

When Lincoln declared an unprecedented blockade of the 3,500-mile Southern coast with nearly 200 inlets on April 27, 1861, he had few warships and resorted to such tactics as sinking old vessels loaded with rocks and concrete at the entrance to harbors. As a result, the early blockade was more psychological that real. However, it had the effect of deterring European acceptance of the South as a separate nation.

As the Union navy grew in size, the blockade intercepted much of the Confederate foreign commerce. More than 1,500 vessels were captured or destroyed trying to run the blockade. At the same time, Union forces occupied enclaves along the Confederate coast to provide provisioning stations for blockading vessels and to attack Confederate ports and coastal forts. One by one, the Federals captured the principal ports of the South. Wilmington, North Carolina, was the last to fall, in 1865.

Confederate blockade runners were

important in supplying munitions to the army and everyday necessities, from medicine to pins, to the civilian population of the South. Blockade runners sailed many kinds of ships and used all sorts of subterfuge. They listed fictitious destinations, used the flags of neutral nations, burned anthracite coal to reduce smoke, painted their hulls in dull colors to escape detection, and slipped through the blockade line on high tide at night. Speed and surprise were their greatest advantages.

Blockade running was a lucrative business, with profits starting at 100 to 200 per cent and reaching 1,500 to 2,000 per cent late in the war. Greed led to hauling luxury items instead of essential goods until the Confederate government began regulating cargoes. One captured vessel even carried caricatures of despised Union General 'Beast' Butler.

Crews were paid what amounted to small fortunes for the period – from $5,000 for a captain to $250 for an ordinary seamen per trip. In contrast, the Union Navy paid a captain at sea only $3,500 a year.

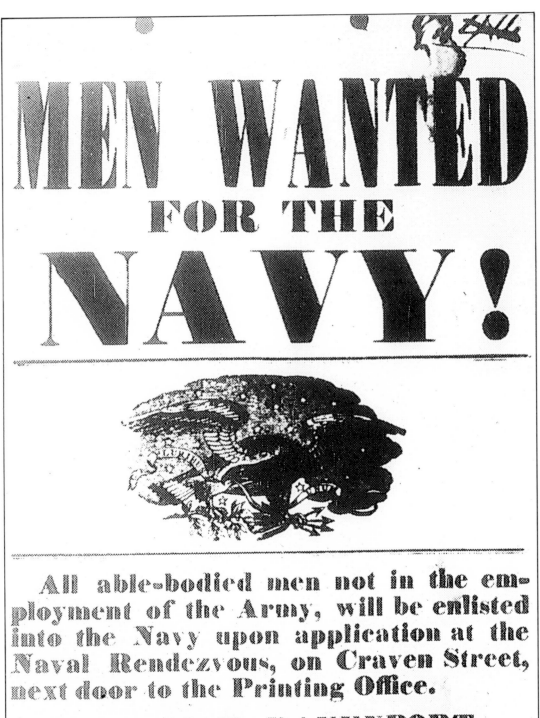

MEN WANTED FOR THE NAVY!

All able-bodied men not in the employment of the Army, will be enlisted into the Navy upon application at the Naval Rendezvous, on Craven Street, next door to the Printing Office.

H. K. DAVENPORT,
Com'r. & Senior Naval Officer.

New Berne, N. C.,
Nov. 3d, 1863.

This recruiting poster for the Federal Navy was displayed in occupied New Bern, North Carolina, in 1863.

The css *Alabama* constructed in Great Britain, was the most famous of the Confederate high seas raiders. It was sunk in a battle with the uss *Kearsarge*.

end, including components in places as remote from water as Charlotte, North Carolina.

The Confederacy attempted to counter the Union's superiority in numbers, many of them wooden ships, constructing ironclads – and thus advanced the science of marine engineering. Overall the records of the ironclads was patchy; they were too unseaworthy to break the Union blockade, one of the main Confederate objectives, and too unwieldy to engage effectively in combat in confined coastal waters. Ironclads were more suited to the Union objective of obtaining command of the Mississippi River because they could run past Confederate shore batteries.

The battle between the css *Virginia* and the uss *Monitor* in Hampton Roads on March 9, 1862, changed the course of naval warfare. The first battle between ironclads was a draw; neither ship was badly damaged, but they did not meet again. The css *Arkansas* impeded Union control of the Mississippi for a while, the css *Albermarle* hindered Union forces around North Carolina's Albermarle Sound, and the css *Tennessee* resisted Admiral David G. Farragut's incursion into Mobile Bay.

The Confederacy led in experimentation with submarines. The most successful was the HL *Huntley*, named after its inventor who was killed in a test dive. The *Huntley* sank the

Right Captain Raphael
Semmes commanded
the css *Alabama*. This
photograph was taken
in Kingston, Jamaica,
in 1863.

Above Officers of the
uss *Kearsarge*,
included Captain John
A. Winslow (third
from left), gather for
a victory photograph
after sinking the css
Alabama.

Above The battle between the *Monitor* (sometimes derisively called a 'cheesebox on a raft') and the *Virginia* continued for four hours but ended inconclusively.

Right A sidewheel steamer gunboat, the uss *General Grant*, plies the Tennessee River in 1864. Exposed sidewheels gave way to screw propulsion during the war.

Left Gun drill was a recurring activity aboard warships, where life during inactive periods was dull and repetitive.

Left Religious services aboard the monitor uss *Passaic* in 1864 draw a crowd to one end of the flat deck.

Union warship *Housatonic* at Charleston, but unfortunately was dragged down by its victim. Confederate officials cancelled further submarine research.

A SAILOR'S LIFE

Sailors who served during the Civil War spent almost all of their enlistments aboard crowded ships, with no organized recreation and little time ashore. The sailor of the period ate unpalatable food, learned his craft on the job, stood watch and performed repetitious tasks at other times. Photos taken during the period show sailors lounging on packed decks, scraping and painting, hauling ropes, polishing weapons and doing other tiresome chores. On long voyages abroad, all of the hardships of shipboard life were aggravated by the problem of scurvy. Sailors on blockading duty or manning warships in rivers and coastal waters at least had an occasional opportunity to obtain fresh vegetables, meat and soft bread.

Battles were noisy and confused affairs as ships closed to point-blank range or tried to outmaneuver each other in waters spiked with mines. Exploding and solid shells ripped sails and sent masts crashing down, blasted holes in hulls and left decks coated with blood. Gun decks were hot, smoky, smelly and slippery; parched throats, smoke and putrid air made the gunners gasp for precious air. Self-induced fire was almost as dangerous as enemy cannon and combat always carried the possibility of drowning. Battles might be brief or lengthy, intense or cat-and-mouse but they left the sailors exhausted and bleeding and their vessels sinking or badly damaged.

Sometimes fire from shore could be deadly; the first naval officer killed in the war, Commander James H. Ward, was shot aboard his ship by a Confederate sniper firing from the banks of the Potomac River.

On the other hand, sailors had certain advantages over soldiers. They seldom had to walk into combat and they had a permanent, indoor home. Personal effects of sailors aboard the USS *Cairo* recovered from the Mississippi River—watches, polished eating and cooking utensils, untattered uniforms and photos in frames—reveal a more settled life than that of soldiers on land.

Right 'The Gunboat Quilt' was made by Panthea Coleman Bullock of Green County, Alabama during the war. It was raffled many times over to raise money for a battleship.

Below The USS *St. Louis* was the first of seven shallow-draft ironclad gunboats built by James B. Eads.

ADVENTURES ON THE HIGH SEAS

The adventures of warships spread across the Atlantic and Pacific Oceans were more romantic. A deadly cat-and-mouse game was played on the high seas, with Confederate cruisers searching for Union merchant vessels to capture, and Union warships trying to locate and engage the Confederate raiders.

The Confederacy constructed and purchased most of its seagoing fleet, which create hope in the Confederacy and fostered a saga of heroism and effectiveness seldom matched, in Great Britain, France and Portugal. Seven cruisers were among the raiders put into Confederate service, including the CSS *Shenandoah*, which took 36 prizes during the war; CSS *Georgia*, and iron-hulled vessel; and most famous of all, the CSS *Alabama*

The construction of the CSS *Florida* demonstrates the method frequently used to evade the British Foreign Enlistment Act, which established British neutrality. The vessel, built ostensibly as a merchant vessel under the name *Oreto*, sailed from Liverpool for Nassau under a British captain. A British vessel transferred two seven-inch rifles and six smoothbores to the *Oreto* in Nassau. De-

Above The navy yard at Norfolk, Virginia, lies in ruins in 1864, but Confederates held it long enough to complete important construction.

spite a protest from the United States consul, the vessel was allowed to depart and was commissioned CSS *Florida* at Green Cay. It picked up additional crew in Havana, and then flew a British flag to reach Mobile unmolested. The vessel slipped back through the Union blockade and, after taking three prizes, returned to Nassau without disguise to land the crews of the prizes.

The *Florida* ultimately went to the South Atlantic and was shadowed into port at Bahia, Brazil, by the USS *Wachusett*, which had been searching for it. Both the captain of the *Florida*, Lieutenant Charles M. Morris, and the United States consul assured Brazilian authorities that the ships would not engage in hostilities in the harbor, but Commander Napoleon Collins of the *Wachusetts* rammed and fired on the *Florida* while most of its crew was ashore and captured it. It was taken to Hampton Roads under a prize crew.

The CSS *Alabama* was designed for speed and was lightly armed. Constructed in Britain, it sailed prematurely to the Azores to prevent impoundment by British authorities. There, the vessel was armed and officers were brought on board to begin a career which in less than four months included the capture of 21 prizes. Captain Semmes then sailed into the Gulf of Mexico to assist beleaguered Galveston and sink the USS *Hatteras*. Later, when trapped in the harbor at Cherbourg, France, he boldly sailed out to engage the USS *Kearsarge*; the *Alabama* was sunk.

The Cruiser *Shenandoah*, attacking Union whaling ships in the Pacific, was the last Southern unit to fly the Confederate flag. When the ship's commander, Lieutenant James I. Waddell, learned of the end of the war from newspapers obtained from a British vessel, he stowed his guns in the hold and sailed 122 days without stop to intern his vessel in Britain on November 6, 1865. The war had been over for more than six months.

Right The double-turreted monitor uss *Onondaga* rides on the James River in Virginia in 1864.

Below The Confederate torpedo boat David was one of the semi-submersibles constructed for the Confederate navy.

CONFEDERATE NAVAL NAIVETY AND NERVE

Quite a few Confederate vessels were destroyed while under construction or repaid as the Union pushed ever deeper into the South. However, Southern inexperience in naval operations caused many vessels to be mishandled or run aground in combat and a large number to be abandoned, scuttled or burned to prevent capture. On February 25, 1863, Confederates abandoned efforts to salvage the Union ironclad *Indianola* because of a ruse directed by Rear Admiral David Dixon Porter. The Union 'warship' which frightened off the Confederates was simply a barge with dummy stacks, superstructure and guns.

Nevertheless, Confederates loved their naval heroes, whose exploits were examples of personal honor and bravery. One of the boldest was Lieutenant Charles W. 'Savez' Read, who sailed the captured Union schooner *Archer* into the harbor of Portland, Maine, and sailed out with the Revenue Cutter *Caleb Cushing*. Read wasn't able to escape with the vessel, but his exploit caused consternation along the coast of New England. Confederates also operated on the Great Lakes. In September 1864, a naval unit operating from Canada burned the steamers *Philo Parsons* and *Island Queen*. A Confederate army-navy team hijacked the steamer *St. Nicholas* on its regular run between Baltimore and Washington and used it to capture several prizes in Chesapeake Bay.

NORTHERN HERO

The North's greatest naval hero was Admiral David G. Farragut, who commanded the West Gulf Squadron. Farragut boldly sailed his ships past forts protecting the entrance to the Mississippi River and captured New Orleans. Subsequently, his fleet operated effectively on the Mississippi, primarily in support of land operations. Farragut's lasting fame rests on the Battle of Mobile Bay.

Below The *Hartford*, Admiral David G. Farragut's flagship in the Battle of Mobile Bay, Alabama, on August 5, 1864.

Opposite Admiral David G. Farragut led the Union naval assaults along the lower Mississippi River and on the Gulf Coast.

T hanks to Margaret Mitchell, whose novel *Gone with the Wind* became a popular motion picture, Georgia's role in the Civil War is perceived to be much greater than it was. Of course, the battles fought at Chickamauga and Kennesaw Mountain were of epic proportions and the burning of Atlanta was spectacular, but the period of death and destruction in the South's richest and most populous State was brief compared to that of the front-line States of Virginia and Tennessee and the annex war along the Mississippi.

The Northern Union strategies of dividing the Confederacy at the Mississippi and of conquering the Confederate capital at Richmond, even the effort to strangle the South by blockading all its ports, including those in Georgia, existed almost from the beginning of the war. The decision to trisect the South came later, after the early effort at holding the border States and occupying Tennessee had succeeded. The battle at Chickamauga, which

Chickamauga, Mobile and Sherman's Final Push

is barely inside the Georgia boundary, did not occur until September 1863 and the State escaped major destruction until 1864.

Georgia's late arrival in the demolition derby meant that it felt the full force of a battle-hardened Federal army and a war-weary Union, ready to accept wanton destruction and the excesses and improprieties committed by individual soldiers in exchange for an earlier end to the fighting. Furthermore, Federal officers throughout the war demonstrated little talent for maintaining discipline among their soldiers in conquered territory. Thus, the accumulated force of the war fell particularly hard on Georgia, and General Williams Tecumseh Sherman's March to the Sea has become a symbol of destructiveness. It was also a forerunner of modern concept of 'total war.'

Historians at the battlefields try to demonstrate both the heroics of combat and the futility of war, but this is difficult in the serenity of park settings where visitors from both North and South come as much to recreate as to experience vicariously the deeds of their ancestors. However, the difficult terrain of northwest Georgia, where the two largest and most decisive battles were fought, combine with cherished memorials and the stark reality of large graveyards at Andersonville and Marietta to create a balanced perspective.

BATTLE OF CHICKAMAUGA

Some historians contend the South almost won the war at the Battle of Chickamauga. A decisive victory for the Confederacy after a string of defeats and retreats in the Western Theater, it could have had far-reaching consequences if General Braxton Bragg had aggressively pursued the demoralized and retreating Union army under General William Rosecrans. But Bragg was cautious by nature and rejected the pleas of his subordinates that quick and forceful action might make Rosecrans abandon all of Tennessee and fan anti-war sentiment in the North. When Bragg finally followed—four days later—Rosecrans was entrenched in Chattanooga, with rein-

forcements on the way and General Ulysses S. Grant soon to take charge. While it is doubtful the South could have overcome Northern superiority in manpower and industrial capacity under any circumstances, a successful follow-up after Chickamauga would have changed the strategic situation in the West so much it could have lengthened the war.

The battlefield at Chickamauga possesses a balance of beauty and solemnity. Memorials and historic places along the seven-mile, self-guided driving tour are unobtrusively spotted in sylvan settings. This is appropriate because most of the battle was fought in forests. The long-silent cannon, are visual reminders of the 'thunder of cannon' that erupted along the quiet lanes on a September day in 1863. One historical marker totals the

'Old Rosy'–Union General William Rosecrans–dug in at Chattanooga after losing the Battle of Chickamauga. It took the combined efforts of Generals Grant, Sherman and Thomas to extricate him.

34,000 casualties of the two-day 'sluggish river of death,' as Confederate Major General William Bale described the Chickamauga battle. The 22nd Alabama lost 55 per cent of its men.

Buildings on the battlefield, even the white columned Visitors' Center, contribute to a relaxed atmosphere. The audio-visual presentation is a 20-minute capsule of the overall strategy of the war, including the Chickamauga and Chattanooga battles. The largest section of the museum, an excellent collection of Civil War and earlier rifles, covers the innovations made in firearms during the war.

The Lee and Gordon's Mill stood on Chickamauga Creek on one flank of the Union line. Confederate troops tried but failed to turn the Federal flank here on September 18, 1863.

The Brotherton House, past which the Confederate attack rolled in 1863 to rupture a Union center thrown off balance by the relocation of units, is as much a curiosity of life style as a battlefield relic. The log cabin stands as it did then, except that marble monuments and historical markers have replaced cattle in the yard and fields. The interior of the cabin reflects the crude conditions and spartan furnishings that were typical of the area during this period.

The cabin on Snodgrass Hill, whose site dominates the slope where thousands of Confederates fell trying to break the Union flank, has a bloodier history. Here, the stubborn stand earned Union General George H. Thomas and sobriquet 'Rock of Chickamauga;' but the memorials remembered the sacrifices of his troops, especially the 87th Indiana, 2nd Minnesota, and 9th Ohio Infantry Regiments. Thomas typified one kind of Union Soldier; a Virginian by birth, he had elected to remain with the Union. He was a bold and imaginative leader who was even more aggressive than

Grant –his troops pushed past their objective to capture Missionary Ridge at Chattanooga while Grant muttered threats of retribution if the action failed– and whose distinguished record led to command of the Army of the Cumberland.

The 1847 Gordon-Lee House, not far from the battlefield park, was used by the Union first as a headquarters and then as a hospital. Behind its Doric columns, rooms where generals huddled over maps and surgeons sawed off shattered arms and legs are decorated with period furniture, Oriental floor coverings, and brass chandeliers.

Chickamauga would prove to be the last Confederate chance to stop the Union invasion.

Lookout Mountain is part of the Chattanooga and Chickamauga National Military Park that stretches across the Tennessee-Georgia border and commemorates two battles and includes a number of separate sites. The oldest and largest noncontiguous national battlefield in the nation includes Point Park on Lookout Mountain, Missionary

DEVELOPMENTS IN FIREARMS

Great Britain sold more weapons to both sides during the Civil War than any other country. Whereas the musket was the principal shoulder weapon of the war, more varieties of guns were used– partly out of necessity–than in any other conflict. Breechloaders were employed in combat for the first time and, as the war went on, more and more muzzleloaders were converted to breechloaders. The magazine repeating rifles that succeeded them became ancestors of the modern infantry rifle. Confederate armories, confronted with shortages of metals, machines, and craftsmen, made innovative use of substitutes but turned out some weapons with crudities.

The Minieball, which is still being

uncovered by Civil War buffs equipped with metal detectors, was adopted by the U.S. Army before the Civil War. It was an improved version of the bullet invented by Captain Minie of France, which made loading a rifle as quick as loading a smoothbore. Self-contained cartridges, which would soon become standard, were invented during the war.

After the war, the United States Army adopted a breechloading, single-shot, cartridge rifle as its standard weapon. The Hall rifle, the first breechloader adopted as a standard weapon by any nation, was also the first gun made in the United States to have fully interchangeable parts, an advantage that in time became a military necessity. The Hall carbine was the 'first official U.S. gun manufactured as a percussion weapon.'

Union General George Thomas earned the nickname 'Rock of Chickamauga' by holding fast against Confederate onslaughts in the vicinity of the Snodgrass Cabin.

Ridge, Signal Point on Signal Mountain, Orchard Knob in Chattanooga, and Chickamauga battlefield in Georgia, where a Confederate victory began the series of events commemorated by the park.

BATTLE OF CHATTANOOGA

The slowness of General Bragg after his victory at Chickamauga gave Federals time to reorganize and fortify the key railroad center of Chattanooga. On the other hand, Bragg's delay created such dissension among his subordinates that President Jefferson Davis made a trip from Richmond to mediate. Bragg's solution was to send General Longstreet and other dissenters to besiege Knoxville, weakening his forces around Chattanooga at a time when Union forces were being strengthened for the effort to break out. Although the Federals were forced on to quarter rations before an adequate supply line could be established, Confederate chances of a successful siege were not good because they could not isolate the city. In November 1863, Union forces under Grant took the offensive.

Confederate units held the high ground around three sides of the city, which also gave them control of the river. The first Union countermove against Lookout Valley, designed to open a better supply route, was successful largely because Bragg would not believe it was occurring until he was taken to Lookout Mountain to witness the masses of Union soldiers below. This critical mistake was compounded by poor planning, engineering, and leadership and by overconfidence as the Union plan to break Bragg's flanks on Lookout Mountain and Missionary Ridge unfolded. Confederate defenders on Orchard Knob were tricked and overrun, providing the forward position from which Missionary Ridge could be assaulted.

The site of Grant's headquarters for the battle, which diverged so much from the way he had planned it that he once threatened to wreak the vengeance on those responsible if

EAST TENNESSEE

Conflict of East Tennessee, which went on intermittently throughout the war, was seldom coordinated with action in the more strategic middle and western areas of the State, yet the fate of the mountainous region was usually determined by events elsewhere, and in particular the battle for Chattanooga. If the Confederates had taken Chattanooga, Union forces in east Tennessee commanded by General Ambrose Burnside would have been outflanked and exposed; and the meager Confederate forces operating there might have prevailed, even though the residents of the region were predominately Unionist in sympathy and enrolled perhaps as many as 30,000 men in the Union army.

East Tennessee was also the home of Abraham Lincoln's second-term vice president, Andrew Johnson, who became president when Lincoln was assassinated and survived impeachment in the tug-of-war over treatment of the defeated South.

Battles in East Tennessee were usually small and sometimes confused encounters, and few of the battlegrounds have been preserved. However, a number of relics stretched westward from Cumberland Gap, which was the major objective of much of the fighting.

Cumberland Gap National Historical Park lies over the major route through the mountains by which early settlers reached the West. Its strategic value during the Civil War is acknowledged with a display of Civil War weapons at the Visitors' Center and a few preserved artillery sites and rifle pits. Knoxville, occupied by the Union much of the war, recalls the era at Confederate Memorial Hall and the antebellum Bleak House,

which General Longstreet used as his headquarters during his unsuccessful 1863 attempt to evict Burnside. The Armstrong-Lockett House dates from 1834. Of the 2,109 Union casualties buried in Knoxville National Cemetery, 1,046 are unknown.

Hale Springs Inn, erected in 1834 on a major stagecoach route, serves as a reminder of the shifting fortunes of Rogersville. Trap doors probably were installed by owners to provide a quick means of hiding silverware and other valuables every time the city changed hands. The inn was headquarters when Union forces were in town; Confederates preferred the Kyle House across the street when they were in control.

Lincoln Memorial University in Harrogate, established after the war by Union Major General O. O. Howard, who had been impressed by the patriotism of the people of the region, has a sizable collection of Civil War memorabilia among items related to its namesake.

Dandridge, thirty miles east of Knoxville, was saved for the Confederacy by a mistake of the U.S. Army Corps of Engineers. A Union Army foraging in the area and a Confederate force wintering at Russellville engaged in inconclusive skirmishing along the French Broad River in January 1864. Union forces completed what they thought was a bridge across the river and sent cavalry charging across — only to discover that the bridge ended on an island in the stream. Embarrassed, the Union troopers withdrew the next day.

Memories of Andrew Johnson, the only American president to be impeached, are strong in Greenville, his home town from the age of 17. Three separate areas—his home, the tailor shop *which he operated, and his grave in the National Cemetery–make up the Andrew Johnson National Historic Site. The one-room tailor shop remains in its original location, but is enclosed in a brick building which also houses other relics. The two-storey brick home where Johnson lived after 1851 while not in Washington holds many mementoes of his political career as congressman, senator, vice president, and President, and as military governor of Tennessee during the war. The 26-foot-high monument at his gravesite incorporates an American eagle poised for flight and a scroll depicting the Constitution of the United States. His epitaph is: 'His faith in the people never wavered.'*

it did not succeed, it preserved as part of the national park.

The flanking attack under General Sherman was an utter failure; but it produced an 18-year-old winner of the Congressional Medal of Honor, Arthur McArthur. He later became a famous general but his son, Douglas, was destined to become even more famous as commander in the Pacific during World War II and the Korean conflict.

The assault on Lookout Mountain directed by General Joseph Hooker was successful, but it was the frontal assault against Missionary Ridge, intended as a diversion, that swept uncontrolled beyond its limited objective to capture the ridge and drive the Confederates from the field.

Park sites along the scenic drive on Missionary Ridge included the place where Confederates repulsed Sherman's repeated attacks, and other critical points now identified by plaques and period cannon. Many of the 5,824 Union casualties in the battle lie in the city's National Cemetery on Bailey Avenue. Confederate losses totaled 6,667, including 4,146 missing.

A Confederate charge, led by General Longstreet, past the Brotherton House and across the farmland to strike the Union center, was the decisive action at Chickamauga.

Lookout Mountain, which dominates the Moccasin Bend of the Tennessee River, is a hodgepodge of tourist attractions, including Ruby Falls and Rock City, with Point Park and the Cravens House at the end of a scenic drive up the steep slopes. Both the drive and visits to the park and house provide an insight into the difficulty of the Federals task of clearing Confederates from the slopes.

From Point Park on the crest, three batteries of Napoleon and Parrott cannon point toward the city and valley. The tall New York Peace Memorial is topped by soldiers of both sides shaking hands, under one flag, and the Ochs Museum and Overlook relate, through pictures and exhibits, the story and significance of the fighting for Chattanooga. The white two-storey frame Cravens House, used as a Confederate headquarters, was badly damaged by some of the fiercest fighting on the slopes but

Major General Joseph 'Fighting Joe' Hooker succeeded Burnside as commander of the Union's 130,000-man Army of the Potomac.

has been restored to depict the life style of the period, with hostesses in costume to complete the picture. Park rangers demonstrate weapons and equipment during the warm months. A number of hiking trails extend from the principal Bluff Trail, which descends the mountain from the Ochs overlook.

The three Union divisions attacking Lookout Mountain greatly outnumbered the Confederates. Artillerymen on the heights could not see through the morning fog–later, the event became known as the Battle above the Clouds–but Union forces could not dislodge the Southerners. However, after darkness, the Confederates withdrew from this exposed position.

Exhibits on two acres of Signal Mountain, which gets its name from its use as a Civil War signalling station, explain other aspects of the fighting. Additional monuments stand along the highways of the region, including those leading to Chickamauga in Georgia. The 'Confederama' on Lookout Mountain uses more than 5,000 miniature soldiers and weapons, combined with flashing lights, battle sounds, and smoke, to recreate the four principal battles which occurred in the Chattanooga area; the attraction is billed as the world's largest battlefield display, covering 480 square feet.

BATTLES AT KOLB'S FARM AND KENNESAW MOUNTAIN

When Grant was made commander of all Union armies in 1864, Sherman was put in charge of major military operations in the West. He sent three armies–some 100,000 men–south from Chattanooga with the objective of crushing the Confederate army of 50,000 under General Johnston and capturing Atlanta, a key rail hub and the 'workhouse and warehouse of the South.'

Bloody fighting–'Hell has broke loose in Georgia sure enough,' said one Confederate– would result at Kolb's Farm and Kennesaw Mountain, both of which are preserved in the Kennesaw Mountain National Battlefield Park; but the superior numbers of the Union army

The Gordon-Lee House, which sheltered Union generals preparing for the Battle of Chickamauga, was built in 1847 by a Scottish immigrant who amassed a fortune in milling.

Right Hastily dug Union fortifications frame the lowlands of Kennesaw Mountain, Georgia, in 1864. Sherman decided to outflank the Confederate fortifications there after a costly attempt to take them.

permitted Sherman to outflank Johnston on a number of occasions.

Kolb's Farm, six miles south of Big Kennesaw Mountain and thus at one end of the battlefield park, was the first major clash of the two armies. The farmhouse, which Union General Hooker used as a headquarters, has been restored to its mid-nineteenth century appearance. The story of the June 22 attacks by Confederate General John B. Hood's corps is recounted there, where it happened, by a recorded message and exhibition on the trail leading away from the house. The fighting was inconclusive; the Rebels withdrew when night fell to their main line.

Five days later, Sherman launched a pair

of coordinated attacks on Johnston's defenses. Trails and roads leading from the battlefield Visitors' Center to both Big Kennesaw Mountain and Cheatham's Hill cover the battle area, preserved earthworks, trenches, rifle pits, cannon, and exhibits explaining progress of the fighting, where it was 'only necessary to expose a hand to procure a furlough.' The best example of earthworks is at the top of Cheatham Hill, where 8,000 Union attackers suffered 1,580 casualties but could not dislodge the Confederates. Remains of the trenches they dug with bayonets and mess kits on hard-earned slopes may be seen below the Dead Angle, a Confederate salient where the bloodiest fighting of the battle took

Overleaf Stone
Mountain near
Atlanta, is the world's
largest granite
monolith.
A city-block–sized
sculpture (inset) on
the face of the 825-
foot-high mountain
features equestrian
statues of Lee,
Jackson and Davis.

place. General Thomas, in command of the
assault on the Confederate center, declared
'one or two more such assaults will use up this
army.' Unable to defeat Johnston by assault,
Sherman resumed his flanking movement
and Johnston had to withdraw.

The 10-minute slide presentation and exhibits at the Visitors' Center place the
Kennesaw Mountain battle in the context of
the struggle for Atlanta and the political cli-
mate in the North, where Lincoln's opponent
in his run from a second term in the presidency
was General George B. McClellan, the still-
popular former commander of all the Union
armies. Among the exhibits are paintings of
the fighting and displays clarifying the func-

Right General William
T. Sherman was given
command in the
Western Theater after
Grant became Union
general-in-chief.

tions of the various military branches, including the infantry —'the queen of battle'— which was so important at Kennesaw Mountain.

ATLANTA AND ENVIRONS

Marietta and Roswell, north of Atlanta, were spared the destruction that occurred in many places in Georgia. As a result, about 80 prewar buildings in Marietta, and substantial numbers in Roswell and Madison reflect the traditions of the period. Among them are the 1855 Kennesaw House Hotel in Marietta. which Sherman used as a headquarters, captors of the *General* used as a conspiratorial meeting place, and which is now a restaurant; and in Roswell the Presbyterian church, which was pressed into service as a Federal hospital, and Barrington Hall. Lovejoy Plantation, built in 1838, was the inspiration for Twelve Oaks in *Gone with the Wind.*

Confederate officials, dissatisfied with Johnston's retrogression before Sherman's flanking movements, turned the defense of Atlanta over to General Hood, who launched savage attacks at Peachtree Creek, East Atlanta (the action is now known as the Battle of Atlanta), and Ezra Church within a period of eight days which did not prevent the occupation of Atlanta. The city became a burned-out hulk, and Sherman left to devastate a 60-mile-wide swath to the sea.

Atlanta today has a unique combination of postwar recreations and genuine relics that escaped the fire. Grant Park —named after the donor of the land and not the Union general— concentrates many of Atlanta's Civil War memories in a package convenient for the visitor. Remains of the city's fortifications, including Old Fort Walker and breastworks armed with period cannon, are complemented by the three-dimensional Cyclorama of the Battle of Atlanta. Narration, sound, and lighting effects recreate the July 22, 1864, battle on a painting 50 feet high and 400 feet in circumference completed in 1891. German and Polish artists oriented it to established landmarks and went out into the field to sketch the battle areas, so that the setting would be authentic down to the wooden bridges over dry washes and the raw earth of torn-up railroad tracks. Atlanta Municipal park stands on part of the site of the Battle of Peachtree Creek, while Mozley Park preserves a small segment of the site of the Battle of Ezra Church.

The Confederate Memorial Carving at the Stone Mountain historical and entertainment complex a few miles east of Atlanta imposes huge equestrian figures of Jefferson Davis, General Robert E. Lee and General 'Stonewall' Jackson on the sheer northern face of an 825-foot-high granite dome measuring five miles around. The carving , which covers an area the size of a city block, is visible from most areas of the park and can be seen close at hand

GREAT RAILROAD CHASE

The General, *the most famous locomotive in a war that demonstrated the strategic importance of railroads, is preserved at the Big Shanty Museum, a few miles from Kennesaw Mountain battlefield. The great locomotive chase – in this century the subject of a Walt Disney movie – started only a hundred yards from where the engine stands in the museum complex. Audio-visuals and exhibits recreate the thrilling chase which began when 22 Union soldiers in civilian clothes, led by James Andrews, stole the engine while the passengers and crew ate breakfast in the station at Kennesaw. The conductor, Captain William A. Fuller, and the crew doggedly pursued by foot, handcar, and commandeered engines, catching the raiders five miles from Chattanooga, their goal. Andrews and seven of his men were executed as spies.*

on a cable-car ride to the top of the rock. A feature of the 'War in Georgia' exhibit at Confederate Hall is a relief map with lights, sound, and narration. Elsewhere in the park are a recreated antebellum plantation; a scenic railroad with replicas of the three steam engines used in the great railroad chase; a display about industries of the Old South; and statues, including one of a mother holding a baby, with the inscription 'The country comes before me,' and another, of a soldier raising a broken sword, which bears the legend, 'Men who saw night coming down on them could somehow act as if they stood on the edge of dawn.'

MOBILE BAY, ALABAMA

While Sherman fought for Atlanta, the navy created history of its own at Mobile Bay in Alabama.

'Damn the torpedoes! Full speed ahead!' has become such an integral part of American military symbolism —it was even used during World War II to stir up patriotic fervor— that it often is believed to derive from a foreign war. In fact, this example of grit and determination was inspired by a critical moment during the Battle of Mobile Bay in the Civil War.

The attack on the outer defenses of the port city of Mobile on August 5, 1864, followed in general the plan for the capture of New Orleans. The entrance to Mobile Bay was protected by the formidable Fort Gaines and Morgan on opposite sides of the bay. Lesser forts protected the city proper. Admiral David C. Farragut was just as successful in running his armada past these forts as he had been in bypassing the delta forts south of New Orleans; he lost only one ship when a torpedo tore a gaping hole in the monitor *Tecumseh*, which sank head first in less than 30 seconds with her full crew aboard.

Farragut's famous words were uttered after his lead ship, the *Brooklyn*, stopped when

A period photo of Fort Morgan, one of two forts which protected the mouth of Morgan Bay. Farragut dodged intensive cannon fire from this colossus before recording a victorious battle with the Rebels.

Destruction of the railroad tracks near Atlanta was only a sample of the devastation that followed. General Hood's wrecked ammunition train is shown below here.

confronted by the danger of underwater explosive devices–today what we call mines–which the Confederates used extensively throughout the war. The action of the *Brooklyn* at first puzzled the veteran fleet commander.

'What's the matter with the *Brooklyn*? She must have plenty of water there,' he said, and moved the *Hartford*, his flagship, to the head of the line. Told there were torpedoes in the water ahead as he passed the *Brooklyn*, a subordinate later recalled, he shouted back: 'Damn the torpedoes! Full speed ahead, Dayton! Hard astarboard; ring four bells! Eight bells! Sixteen bells!'

The mines and heavy fire from Fort Morgan were not the only hazards confronting the fleet. As the ships passed the fort, the Confederate ironclad ram *Tennessee* challenged the *Hartford* but could not keep up with her, and then engaged several other vessels as she moved down the Union line. Confederate gunboats also harassed the fleet but could not stop it. The presence of the Union fleet in

Mobile Bay achieved one objective – closing the port to blockade runners. Defeat of the forts would take longer.

Gunports of the battle-scarred brick walls of the huge, star-shaped Fort Morgan, still show the muzzles of Civil War cannon, while the bloodstains of a victim of the 19-day siege that followed the naval victory mark granite steps. Graceful arches, dark casemates, and a now-dry moat reveal both the care that went into construction and the utilitarian beauty of a nineteenth-century fort that withstood terrific bombardment before surrender on August 23. From Mobile Point, the parapet overlooks the bay and the Gulf Shores peninsula now devoted to recreation.

Fort Gaines on Dauphin Island, a five-sided brick structure with a bastion that now houses a Civil War museum filled with guns, cannonballs, and military equipment, was seized by the Confederacy at the outbreak of war. Its guns could barely reach Farragut's ships and had little influence on the Battle of

Mobile Bay. It was, however, kept busy by the land forces available to Farragut – a 2,400-man contingent under Brigadier General Robert S. Granger – and surrendered on August 7 after a naval bombardment, despite orders to hold out. Now the anchor and chain from Farragut's flagship are located at the entrance to the fort.

When the news of the fall of the forts reached Washington on September 3, President Abraham Lincoln ordered a 100-gun salute to honor 'the recent brilliant achievement of the fleet and land forces.' More serious firing and much larger land forces would be required to subdue the city, which was defended by a series of forts on both the eastern and western approaches. A pincers movement by 32,000 Federal soldiers, sup-ported by naval vessels, took Spanish Fort and Fort Blakeley, after a 12-day battle in which the Confederates were outnumbered 8 to 1. The loss of naval vessels to Confederate mines, including two ironclads and a tinclad during the shelling of Spanish Fort, continued after Mobile was taken. Some of the Confederate fortifications and Union earthworks remain at Spanish Fort, and historical markers describe the ordeal. The Blakeley site and Blakeley Cemetery also are marked.

Union troops occupied Mobile on April 12–three days after Lee had surrendered at Appomattox. The attack of the city apparently had been made only because it could be done. General Sherman's forces already had left Savannah for the Carolinas and control of Mobile Bay closed the port to the Confederacy.

Peachtree Street, Atlanta's main thoroughfare, was not impressive as shown here in 1864, but the city was an industrial center as well as a railroad hub.

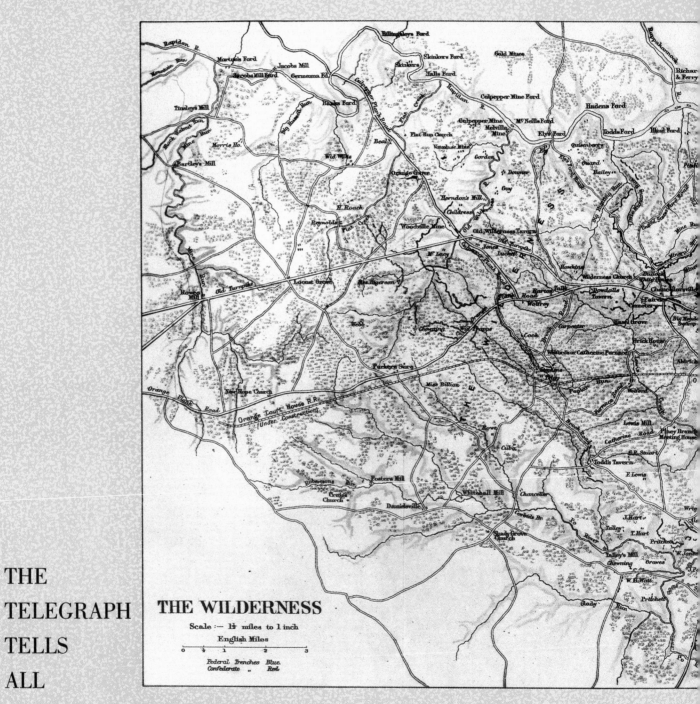

THE WILDERNESS

Scale :— 1½ miles to 1 inch

English Miles

Federal Trenches Blue.
Confederate „ Red.

THE
TELEGRAPH
TELLS
ALL

The telegraph helped transform warfare. It enabled field commanders to remain in constant touch with their bases, to learn quickly of changing developments and to rectify shortages of men and materials as they occurred. More importantly, it enabled commanders of armies divided by thousands of miles to coordinate their activities.

For the first time, governmental leaders had direct contact with commanders in the field. Both President Abraham Lincoln and Confederate President Jefferson Davis corresponded with their commanders, almost on a daily basis. And both visited field commanders on a number of occasions. Naturally, this network, used also by scores of reporters

ran along railway roadbeds. The system was essentially privately owned and operated by civilians and the work of operators was highly prized by both sides. The Union considered telegraphers so important they were exempted from the draft.

For a short period, the Union Signal Corps operated a 'flying' telegraph, designed to facilitate battlefield communications during inclement periods. Colonel Albert J. Meyer, the first Union signal officer, designed and supervised the construction of train cars outfitted as transmitting centers. Most of the time he used a short-range telegraph instrument invented by George W. Beardslee of New York and operated by hand-generated electricity.

The trains were operated successfully as early as General George B. McClellan's Peninsular Campaign. During the Battle of Fredericksburg, when the battlefield was enveloped in smoke, three rail cars kept Union General Ambrose Burnside in contact with the wings of his attacking army. The range limitation of this instrument proved to be an obstacle at Chancellorsville, however, and battlefield telegraph communications were turned over to the civilian companies.

Thereafter, civilian operators played an integral role in the operation of field armies, striking their tents and putting their wagons into line when armies moved. In laying and maintaining wires at army and corps headquarters, they faced many of the hazards of combat. These civilians strung about 15,000 miles of wire and transmitted and received an estimated 3,000 messages a day during the war.

Telegraph lines also were used to eavesdrop on and mislead opponents. Confederate General John Hunt Morgan took a soldier-telegrapher, George Ellsworth, on raids into Kentucky. Ellsworth skillfully tapped into telegraph lines to intercept orders sending Union units in pursuit of Morgan and to send misleading information on the whereabouts of Morgan's raiders.

This contemporary map shows key positions in Virginia, with Federal and Confederate trenches marked.

from newspapers and magazines kept the public informed about action in the field.

The Confederacy was first to establish the signal corps as a separate army service unit on April 19, 1862, and the Union took similar action a year later. These units were involved in battlefield signalling by flag, as well as use of the telegraph. Telegraph wires generally

General Grant, who ordered the attack, said later he had wanted to take Mobile for two years and admitted that the action came too late to have any influence on the war.

Mobile has several historic districts, including that around Oakleigh (which was built in the 1830s) and Church Street East. Other antebellum structures include 1860 Richards-DAR House, the 1835 Cathedral of the Immaculate Conception, Carten House Museum (and 1840 Creole cottage), and the 1820s Conde-Charlotte House. The Museum of the City of Mobile displays Confederate artifacts. Bellingrath Gardens came later, but are one of the city's most famous current attractions. Spring Hill, six miles from Mobile and once a resort city, retains many nineteenth-century buildings.

While these decisive events were unfolding, farther west the fighting was reaching a similar climax.

BATTLE OF WESTPORT

The October 21-23, 1864 Battle of Westport, Missouri, was a two-part fight which covered most of Jackson County and involved about 29,000 men on both sides. The Little Blue Creek was the Union's first defensive line, but it was easily breached on a cold, misty morning. it took the Confederates four hours of street

Opposite **James Henry Lane led antislavery partisans in Kansas; here he is shown at Pappan's Ferry in 1856.**

Kansas City's Wornall House recalls the decisive battle of Westport. The battlefield is now a residential area, but significant locations are identified by historical markers.

fighting to clear Independence, however. The area of the main fighting along Big Blue Creek is now a residential section in Kansas City, Missouri, but is identified on a self-guided auto tour by 23 historical markers and the Wornall House, a handsome 1858 home which was used by both armies as a field hospital. The house has been restored by the Jackson County Historical Society to interpret the daily lives of frontier farm families. Civil War encampments are interspersed with fireplace cooking demonstrations, Christmas tours, craft classes and herb sales.

At the Big Blue, Price's forces were situated between two Federal armies, but he planned to hold off one at a strong defensive position while striking the other, and then turn on the first. The failure of his defensive group almost resulted in his entire force being trapped, and the unanticipated fighting efficiency of the Kansas militia, brought into Missouri against their will, put him at a numerical disadvantage. 'Old Pap' Price, who had used only part of his 9,000 men in the battle, escaped the trap and began to retreat.

BATTLE OF MINE CREEK

Union troops followed Price in hot pursuit. On October 25, 1864, Confederate troops paused and hastily formed defensive positions. In the Battle of Mine Creek, the Union attack drove many into the nearby creek bottom, where they were captured after heavy hand-to-hand combat; but the Union pursuit was stopped and General Price was able to continue his retreat. Over 25,000 men were involved in the battle, more than in any other engagement on Kansas soil. A rest stop on U.S. Route 69 south of Pleasanton marks the site of the largest formal battle in Kansas. Although 228

The only major battle fought in Kansas, at Mine Creek. Confederates halted there to blunt pursuit after losing the Battle of Westport in Missouri.

Right Beecher Bible and Rifle Church in Kansas got its name from crates marked 'Bibles,' which actually contained weapons for antislavery forces.

Above Preacher and orator, Henry Ward Beecher used his influence to oppose slavery and to work for women's rights.

DEPOTS AND SUPPLIES

Fort Scott (still well-preserved today) served as a Union supply depot near the Missouri-Kansas border. It may well have been a target of Confederate units retreating after the Battle of Westport until Union forces caught up with them at Mine Creek, north of the town. Fort Leavenworth was a Union stronghold, too, and the museum on the still-active military post owns the carriage that President Lincoln used *on a visit to the fort and exhibits a good collection of military uniforms up through World War II. The audio-visual slide show telling the history of the fort is shown on a regular schedule. At Manhattan, the Beecher Bible and Rifle Church recalls the practice of using crates marked 'Bibles' to import arms bought with money donated by Henry Ward Beecher's congregation in Brooklyn, New York.*

Right James H. Lane, a puzzling politician and Union raider, survived the destruction of Lawrence by hiding out.

acres of the battlefield are preserved, the site is largely undeveloped. Points of interest are marked on two self-guided trails and an historical marker at the highway turnout relates the highlights of the battle.

The final leg of Price's retreat, which took him through the rugged and inhospitable Indian Territory, was harder on his army than the Battle of Mine Creek, but his exhausted forces finally reached their base in Arkansas.

BLOODY FIGHTING IN MISSOURI

The formal fighting in Kansas was just a climax to a bloody, irregular struggle that had been going on since before the Civil War started. The Brown family of Kansas was notorious—or famous depending on the point of view—as abolitionists long before John went east to capture the arsenal at Harper's Ferry. In 1856, after the Browns and their followers had attacked the homes of pro-slavery farmers and killed several of them, pro-slavery supporters retaliated with a raid which became known as the Battle of Osawatomie.

Irregular fighting of this kind was intensified by the outbreak of the Civil War, and devastated Kansas throughout the war. Union attempts to halt the attacks even extended to the point of arresting the female relatives of Confederate irregulars and jailing them at Kansas City. The deaths of some of them in an accident contributed to one of the most famous raids of the war, the destruction of Lawrence, and an anti-slavery stronghold, in 1863.

While William Clark Quantrill promoted the raid as a way to redress the Confederate defeat at Gettysburg, some of his lieutenants were persuaded to go because of the accident in Kansas City. The 450 raiders were in no

Right Kansas' most feared raider, William C. Quantrill, sacked Lawrence to redress the Confederate defeat at Gettysburg.

299

mood to be lenient, and Quantrill had given orders to kill all the men and burn every house. This order was systematically carried out in a house-to-house search for valuables and horses. No women were harmed, according to the Bushwhackers code, and few men survived by hiding out in various ways. Among them was James Henry Lane, a puzzling politician who was himself a proficient leader of Union raids. In 1861, he had taken delight in destroying Missouri towns that had welcomed the Confederate units victorious at Lexington. His cavalry fired indiscriminately on a charge through Osceola, then set fire to almost all the buildings after finding a cache of lead, powder, and cartridge paper. His men had a more personally satisfying way of destroying barrels of brandy, 3,000 sacks of flour, 500 pounds of sugar and molasses, 50 sacks of coffee, and a quantity of bacon.

Lawrence is more famous today for a role that had been selected before the Civil War — as the site of the University of Kansas. A number of historic buildings remain in the downtown area and the Old West Lawrence Historic District.

General James G. Blunt with his staff (left). Tents on the parade ground at Fort Scott, Kansas (bottom left). Fort Gaines on Dauphin Island played a crucial role in the historic Battle of Mobile Bay (bottom right).

21

After the fall of Atlanta, General Hood moved northward into Tennessee in a bold but futile attempt to draw Sherman after him – or reach the Ohio River, where he could turn eastward to join Lee. After a bloody battle at Franklin, he reached Nashville, where his army was virtually destroyed.

BATTLE OF FRANKLIN

Franklin today is a model Civil War historical community. The centerpiece of its main square – named Public Square – is a tall Confederate Monument. The city has numerous historic buildings, including two that have intimate associations with the war; a map just off U.S. Route 31 south of the city depicts the Battle of Franklin. The principal relics of the battle are Carnton Mansion, built in 1826 and now gradually being restored to its appearance at the time of the battle on November 30, 1864, and the Confederate Cemetery on the grounds of the estate.

Final Acts: Hood Moves North, Sherman Drives East

The Battle of Franklin was one of the war's bloodiest, with more than 8,500 casualties, among whom were five Confederate generals. In the aftermath, John McTavock, the owner of Carnton, collected 1,496 bodies left on the battlefield and buried them. When the wounded gathered that night in his orchard for protection against the sleet and cold, more than 200 were taken into the mansion, where they lay on the wooden floors. The stains caused by surgeons amputating limbs still darken the floorboards. Later, Carnton's owner retrieved other Confederate bodies from temporary graves and reinterred them in his neat, tree-shaded cemetery.

The Carter House in Franklin, a brick structure with simple lines built in 1830, is maintained by the State as a Civil War shrine. The main rooms of the house are decorated with period furniture and appointments, including a quilt on which Mrs. Jefferson Davis and Mrs. Robert E. Lee worked. A museum in the three-room basement, where 22 civilians huddled while the fighting raged outside, displays relics, documents, and maps of the battle. Used as a command post by Union General Jacob D. Cox during the battle, Carter House and its dependencies were struck by a number of bullets and cannonballs, some of which are still visible. Other antebellum structures in Franklin include the 1831 St. Paul's Episcopal Church and the 1825 Masonic Hall.

FALL OF COLUMBUS

While Sherman marched toward the sea at Savannah, a Federal cavalry force moved from Alabama into central Georgia. Columbus fell; but an earthen fort at West Point held out all day on April 16, 1865. A water reservoir has been constructed on the site of the fort, but cemeteries off U.S. Route 29 and in LaGrange hold the bodies of nearly 400 Confederate and Union soldiers. The Griggs House, from which Northern sharpshooters fired into the fort, retains much of its 1865 appearance; it is a private residence.

Columbus, an inland port on the

Confederate General John Bell Hood conducted an aggressive defense of Atlanta, but was badly outnumbered.

Chattahoochee River, is the home of the Confederate Naval Museum, where the salvaged remains of the gunboat CSS *Chattahoochee* and ironclad ram CSS *Jackson* can be seen. The Infantry Museum at nearby Fort Benning has a Medal of Honor Room and Civil War mementoes among its collection. Fitzgerald's Civil War connection is unique among Georgian cities: it was founded as a colony of Union soldiers who remained behind after the war. The last session of the Confederate Congress was held in Macon's City Hall, which had been built as a bank in 1835 but was acquired by the State during the war. Among other antebellum structures in the city is one known as the Old Cannonball House because it was struck during a Federal attack on Macon in 1864. Bibb County casualties are remembered by the Confederate Monument. At the 1855 Bellevue mansion in LaGrange, the owner and other members of the Confederate Cabinet stepped forward to surrender in April 1865.

The 220 defenders of Fort MacAllister finally succumbed to an attack by an entire division of Sherman's army in December 1864, making the fall of Savannah inevitable. This engraving depicts the Unionists' triumphant capture of the town on December 21.

The owner of Carnton, a plantation near Franklin, buried hundreds of Confederate dead in this neat, orderly cemetery (top left) after the battle. Carnton mansion is not far away. Confederate monuments exist in many Southern cities, but none is more attractive than the one in Franklin, Tennessee (top right). Franklin was also an important battleground. The Carter House (left) in Franklin, both a command post and refuge during the battle, still bears some scars. It is furnished in the style of the period and preserves relics of the battle.

AUGUSTA

The 176-foot-high brick chimney, all that remains of the South's principal gunpowder factory, and the Arsenal, now part of a college, recall Augusta's primary role in the Civil War. The First Presbyterian Church was used for a time as a hospital and temporary detention camp. Lieutenant General Leonidas K. Polk, nicknamed 'the fighting bishop of the Confederacy,' is entombed in a crypt beneath the altar of St. Paul's Episcopal Church. Augusta was spared Sherman's prolific torch, so the story goes because he had once fallen in love with an Augustan girl, the sister of his West Point roommate.

SURRENDER OF SAVANNAH

Sherman's famous March to the Sea ended at Savannah, which surrendered to avoid destruction and thus retains much of its original

Crowded conditions made the prison camp at Andersonville, Georgia, officially known as Camp Sumter, a hell-hole for Union prisoners of war. They also suffered from inadequate housing, food, and medical attention in the last days of the war, when supplies were scarce in the Confederacy. The prisoners built wooden huts called 'shebangs,' for shelter.

appearance. This includes the orderly squares mapped out by General James Edward Oglethorpe in 1730s and numerous early-nineteenth-century houses that witnessed the Civil War. Factor's Walk (restored) particularly reflects the lively commercial life of the Confederate port and navy yard.

Savannah's martial side is its four forts. Fort Pulaski, described as being 'as strong as the Rocky Mountains' when completed in 1847, still bears the scars of a 30-hour Federal bombardment on April 10-12, 1864, which demonstrated to the world the destructive power of the new rifled cannon. When the Confederates were forced to surrender, the era of brick citadels was over.

Artillery for the attack was hauled ashore at Tybee Island, where the museum now occupying one of the gun batteries of post-Civil War Fort Screven has a Civil War room emphasizing documents, artifacts, and

Right Prisoners who died at Andersonville were buried in long trenches, as this 1864 photo shows. Wooden headboards (below), used initially to identify the more than 12,000 prisoners who died at Andersonville, have been replaced by permanent markers and small flags.

ANDERSONVILLE

A prisoner-of-war camp, named Fort Sumter by the Confederacy but better known by the name of Andersonville, the railroad stop where the prisoners arrived, is ten miles northeast of Americus on Georgia Route 49. It recalls one of the greatest tragedies of the war. Constructed to provide better conditions for Union prisoners, it became instead a hell-hole for those who were sent there because of overcrowding, inadequate facilities and supplies, and the preying of some prisoners on others.

Andersonville National Historic site preserves some of the features, including the spring that became so polluted that freshness caused by rain inspired the prisoners to name it Providence Spring; earthworks and rifle pits that were part of the fortifications; and holes dug as escape tunnels and in attempts to find water. Memorials honor the soldiers who died there, individuals, and the Women's Relief Corps, auxiliary of the Grand Army of the Republic, that operated the site until it was turned over to U.S. government in 1910. The more than 12,000 men who died there are buried in the national cemetery. Among them are six 'Andersonville raiders' ringleaders of the group of prisoners who preyed on fellow prisoners of war until caught and executed on July 11, 1864. The commandant of the camp, Captain Henry Wirz, was tried by a Federal military tribunal after the war and hanged in Washington, D.C.

The town of Andersonville has a welcome center and museum, as well as a country farm in a five-acre park.

memorabilia of Sherman's arrival at Savannah. Museum displays and living history demonstrations at Fort Jackson, built in the early 1800s but substantially altered after the Civil War, relive the fort's history, including the Civil War period when it was headquarters of the batteries defending the river approaches to Savannah. Part of the earthworks and battery site erected at Wormsloe Plantation, whose 1744 tabby house stands about eight miles southeast of the city, are still visible.

Fort MacAllister, an earthworks fort ten miles east of Richmond Hill on U.S. Route 17, successfully resisted attacks by monitor-type Union warships, demonstrating once again that earthen fortifications could survive the heaviest naval bombardment possible at the time. Its 220 defenders finally succumbed to an attack by an entire division of Sherman's army in December of 1864, making the fall of Savannah inevitable.

INTO THE CAROLINAS

General Sherman remained at Savannah only a short time. In February 1865, he led a 60,000-man army northward into the Carolina.

Except for Fort Sumter, South Carolina was removed from the main battlefields and thus escaped much of the fighting. But Sherman's invasion visited swift retribution. Northern feelings against South Carolina, the first State to secede, were particularly strong and Sherman swept through like an avenging angel. No major battles were fought, but skirmishes and destruction are noted in monuments at a number of places. Beaufort Arsenal has graves of 12,000 Union soldiers and a few Confederates, and the John Mark Verdier House, built about 1790, was used as a Union headquarters. Another war cemetery is at Florence. Brigadier General Barnard E. Bee, who nicknamed 'Stonewall' Jackson, is buried in the cemetery of St. Paul's Episcopal Church at Pendleton, far from the Manassas battlefield where he died. Five Forks Cemetery in Pageland holds the grave of James H. Miller, a prisoner of war executed as a deterrent to attacks on Union foragers during Sherman's

advance. He was chosen as the victim by his fellow prisoners who were forced to draw lots. Miller's headstone reads, 'Murdered in retaliation.' Sweetwater Cemetery has the grave of the first South Carolinian killed in the war, Private Sidney Weeks.

Rivers Bridge State Park, seven miles west of Ehrhardt off State Route 64 near the Salkehatchie Swamp, preserves breastworks, relics, and Confederate graves where the commander of the 32nd Georgia promised to hold 'until next Christmas if you can keep them off my flanks.' But the flanks could not be protected and Confederates continued to retreat before Sherman's advance. Elsewhere, memorial plaques identify various incidents, including the battle on the main street of Aiken in February 1865, when Union troops tried to destroy Graniteville Mills. Museums in Lancaster and Mayfield house war relics.

Confederate coastal defenses outside Charleston drew Union attention throughout the war. The occupation of Port Royal Sound and Hilton Head Island was an early achievement of Union arms. Remnants of Confederate Fort Walker, which succumbed to Union naval fire because it was improperly constructed and armed, exist on the posh resort island, which gives little indication of the isolation and harsh conditions there during the War between the States. Hilton Head was headquarters of Union Army Department of the South, commanded by Brigadier General Thomas W. Sherman (also known as 'The Other' Sherman), and thus a major staging base for the coastal operations in South Carolina, Georgia, and Florida. The ruins of Confederate Fort White, defended successfully against several Federal attacks, are one of the attractions at Belle Island Gardens near Georgetown. During one attack on this fort, the Union flagship, *Harvest Moon*, was sunk by Confederate mines.

Although North Carolina was late in joining the Confederacy, and even had a rump group meet to try to cancel secession, the State was a major source of supplies and manpower throughout the Civil War. The first Confeder-

Fort Pulaski was part of the ring of fortifications defending Savannah. Union use of rifled cannon, the effects of which still show on some of the brick walls (inset), forever changed the way forts are built.

311

Bennett Place State Historical Park near Durham, North Carolina, preserves the farmhouse where the Confederacy's last major field army surrendered. A Unity Monument stands in front of the house.

ate to die, in the little-known Battle of Big Bethel in Hampton, Virginia, was Private Henry Lawson Wyatt, and North Carolina appropriately remembers him with a statue on the lawn of the Old Capitol Building in Raleigh. North Carolina's sons fought and died in every single battle in the East and some in the West.

North Carolina remained relatively free of fighting until late in the war. In the early stages, Union efforts were aimed at controlling the coastline as part of the blockade policy. Fighting on North Carolina soil thus began on the coast, as the Union sought to close the Confederate coastline by blockading ports and capturing strongpoints.

FORT FISHER

War arrived elsewhere in North Carolina in earnest in 1865, as the Confederacy was dying. Wilmington was the last major port in the eastern Confederacy to remain open. That was thanks to Fort Fisher, a large earthworks fort at the entrance to Cape Fear River. The surviving grassy mounds that once formed gun emplacements and protected men and powder are now part of a State historical park, which also includes a small commemorative monument and a museum with a range of exhibits from a 10-pounder Parrott cannon to a pair of naval anchors.

Shortly before Christmas in 1864, the largest U.S. fleet assembled in the war stood off the fort with 6,500 troops under General Butler. Among the 55 warships were an ironclad screw steamer and four monitors. The type of combined bombardment and amphibious operation that had succeeded elsewhere was supplemented by detonating a ship laden with explosives near the fort, in the

A group of Federal gunners with their 3in Parrott gun. Note the characteristic reinforcing hoop around the breech.

NATHAN BEDFORD FORREST'S 'NAVY'

A raid on Johnsonville in the autumn of 1864, whose modest purpose was to disrupt the flow of supplies to Union General William Tecumseh Sherman's army in southern Tennessee, became a monument to the creativity of the Confederate General Nathan Bedford Forrest and his troopers. One of the most interesting features was the use of captured Union vessels to form their own temporary navy.

On October 16, Forrest left Corinth, Mississippi, with two 20-pounder Parrotts and lesser cannon. His mission was to interdict the flow of supplies from Johnsonville by occupying Fort Heiman, an abandoned former Confederate fort on the west bank of the Tennessee River, and shelling Union troop and cargo ships. The guns were supplemented by snipers instructed to fire at officers in control centers of passing vessels.

Their first victim was the transport *Mazeppa*, loaded with flour, hardtack, blankets, footwear, and other *matériel*, which drifted ashore on the opposite bank and was abandoned by her crew. Confederate soldiers under the command of Brigadier General Abraham Buford swam the river and

moved the vessel to Fort Heiman, where she was unloaded before being set on fire.

The idea of forming an impromptu Confederate flotilla occurred the next morning when the Union 'tinclad' gunboat *Undine*, armed with eight 24-pounders, transport *Venus* were captured by boarders. A former riverboat pilot, Captain Frank Gracey of the 3rd Kentucky, took charge of the *Undine* and gave a crew of cavalrymen a crash course in manning the vessels. Forrest then mounted a combined sea-land attack against Johnsonville; although the *Venus* was quickly recaptured, the *Undine* distracted the Union flotilla while Forrest placed his artillery on a bluff across the river from the supply center and opened fire. Ships, rail shops, store-rooms, and warehouses were set on fire by the fierce cannonading, aided by burning whisky which helped to spread flames through the depot.

So complete was the destruction that the Union abandoned Johnsonville as a supply base. Forrest lost his 'navy'; *Undine* fought valiantly against nine Union ships mounting 100 guns until Gracey, running low on coal, sent his cavalrymen crew ashore and scuttled her.

Below Brunswick Town State Historic Site in North Carolina primarily recreates a Revolutionary War community, but preserves these Confederate earthworks, too.

belief that this would damage the fortifications enough to let the assault be a walk-in. Neither the exploded vessel nor the bombardment had the desired effect, and Butler called off the attack on Christmas Day after landing 2,000 men under cover of the naval guns.

A second expedition against Fort Fisher the next month was the largest sea-land contest of the war, with the Union utilizing 60 warships and 8,500 troops under Brigadier General Alfred H. Terry. A diversionary attack by 2,000 Navy men and Marines was repulsed with heavy losses, but Terry's attack from the rear captured the last Confederate coastal

stronghold and closed the North Carolina coast completely. Confederate casualties numbered 500, and 2,083 were taken prisoner while Union losses came to 691. Nearby Fort Anderson held out for another 30 days, but was abandoned after undergoing heavy bombardment during a three-day siege. Confederate Vice President Alexander Stephens described the loss as 'one of the greatest disasters which has befallen our Cause.'

WILMINGTON AND BENTONVILLE

Confederate earthworks are clearly visible at Fort Anderson in the Brunswick Town State Historic Site, which primarily depicts an earlier conflict – a town abandoned by the citizens in the Revolutionary War for fear of attack by British soldiers. The tragedy is told in excavated foundations and explanatory displays throughout the town and by means of a slide show and displays at the Visitors' Center. Civil War relics at the New Hanover County Museum in Wilmington included a model of the Wilmington waterfront during the 1860s

Grand Army of the Republic organizations and official ceremonies brought Union veterans together long after the war ended. This parade of veterans ocurred about 1880 in Ortonville, Minnesota.

and dioramas and ship models depicting the cat-and-mouse game of blockade running.

Sherman brought his scorched-earth policy into North Carolina after applying it liberally elsewhere along his route.

Confederate General Joseph E. Johnston tried to block his path on March 15-16 at Averasboro and on March 19-21 at Bentonville, on the road between Wilmington and Raleigh. The Bentonville Battlefield on State Route 1008 off Interstate 95 preserves the rustic simplicity that existed on many Civil War battlefields. Interpretive signs and Union earthworks in quiet, mostly open countryside serve to back up the displays and maps in the Visitors' Center of the State historical park.

The Harper House, restored to the appearance it had when it served as a hospital during the fighting, is the centerpiece of the park. The first floor depicts the building's use as a field hospital, with furniture pushed back against the walls, straw pallets spread around, medical instruments on display, and even patches of artificial blood on the floor. Other decorations are faithful to the mid-nineteenth-century life style of John and Amy Harper, owners of the house at the time of the battle.

This view of the east face of Fort Macon shows the moat and some gunports. Built before the Civil War, the fort has been partly restored. It is an excellent example of a typical fort of the period.

Only 360 men are buried in a common grave in the small Confederate cemetery near the Visitors' Center. They are only a small portion of the fallen: 1,527 Federal and 2,606 Confederate soldiers died.

Bentonville was little more than the dying gasp of a lost cause, but it was the largest land battle fought in North Carolina, and the first major attempt to stop Sherman after the loss of Atlanta. The battle ended in a draw, and Sherman continued his march to Goldsboro.

Raleigh, the State capital, surrendered a short time later.

BENNETT PLACE SURRENDER

The Confederacy virtually came to an end 30 days later at a country crossroads farm near Durham when Johnston surrendered his remaining force to General Sherman. The generals negotiated in the living-room of the farmhouse, and settled on terms that Washington officials considered too generous. They had subsequently to return for a second meeting to amend them.

The Bennett farmhouse where the two momentous meetings occurred burned in 1921 but has been restored around the stone chimney, which survived the fire. The furnishings in the living-room differ somewhat from those depicted in contemporary drawings by artists not present at the talks, but the rooms and simple furniture are as authentic as possible. Two downstairs bedrooms are au-

Harper House, the centrepiece of the North Carolina State historical park, served as a hospital during the fighting.

Johnston surrendered
his remaining force to
General Sherman at the
Bennett Farmhouse,
virtually bringing the
Confederacy to an end.

A second meeting had
to be convened,
however, as Washington
officials considered the
terms of the agreement
too generous.

WEST POINT.
CHICKAHOMINY.
CHARLES CITY CROSS ROADS.
ES MILLS.
SOUTH MOUNTAIN.
ANTIETAM
U S
FREDERICKSBURG.
GETTYSBURG.
MARYE'S HEIGHTS.
CULPEPPER
SALEM CHURCH.
RACCOON FORD.
JACK'S SHOP.

This processional flag commemorates some of the key engagements of the Civil War.

thentically furnished, too; one of them has a bed with rope slatting.

The detached log-cabin kitchen, where Lucy Bennett and her children may have waited while the generals used her home, is dominated by a large stone fireplace and equipment, including pots and pans, buckets, a spinning wheel, pottery and porcelain crockery, and a log kitchen table with chairs and one high-chair.

Exhibits in the Visitors' Center relate the Bennett Place surrender to the earlier Confederate surrender at Appomattox, and include a copy of the surrender terms and Johnston's order to his army to dispand after 'every hope of success by war' was gone. Photographs and displays illustrate the destruction the war caused in the South.

On a slight mound in front of the farm house stands the Unity Monument. Its two columns, joined by a cap, are symbolic of the reuniting to the two countries which fought the Civil War.

FINAL SURRENDER

Confederate armies remained in the field elsewhere, but soon all had laid down their arms. Texas was the last holdout as the Civil War wound down, and the final battle of the 'cruel war' was fought at Palmito Ranch, east of Brownsville, on May 12, 1865, a month after Lee surrendered at Appomattox.

Although Lee's decision was soundly denounced in Texas, the inevitability of surrender brought political leaders of Texas, Arkansas, Louisiana, and Missouri to a meeting with General E. Kirby Smith in Marshall, Texas, to draft a capitulation agreement. When a few of Smith's officers threatened to arrest him unless he continued the war, he turned command over to Lieutenant General Simon Bolivar Buckner, who went to New Orleans and surrendered his command on paper.

Some of his officers complied, and some did not. General Stand Watie, an Indian, was probably the last Confederate formally to surrender his forces, on June 23, 1865.

The black funeral cortege that carried the body of President Abraham Lincoln through the streets of Washington to begin the long train ride to Illinois for final burial boded ill for the future. A new pall was descending on a nation which already had been torn asunder by four bitter years of Civil War.

The end of the war brought great rejoicing in the North. Bells rang from Maine to California, not in alarm as might have been the case during the war but in happiness. If many doubted the wisdom of certain wartime acts—the denial of constitutional rights or the emancipation of the slaves—at least the Union had been saved. Husbands and sons returned home in triumph, their test of strength and courage behind them.

A different situation existed in the South. Once magnificent cities were now burned-out shells; the great plantations that had been the region's major source of wealth stood in a state of devastation or decay; the infrastructure, like the railroads and bridges, was in ruins;

Aftermath: A Hush Descends on Dixie

and the specter of poverty and starvation stalked the land. Tens of thousands of half-starved soldiers and civilian refugees had to make their way home as best they could, nourished by what little food generous people along the route could give them. Defeated Southerners remained defiant, but at least gave a sigh of relief that the fighting was over.

The socio-economic structure was in a shambles, too. White manpower had been depleted by the casualty lists of war, and emancipation had eliminated the slave labor which had underpinned the Old South. Economic chaos ruled vast areas of the South as soldiers returned home to a nonfunctioning economy and freed blacks congregated in groups or wandered aimlessly. Wartime labor shortages had taught many blacks the (hitherto neglected) value of their services, but not how to benefit from the knowledge.

RECONSTRUCTION ERA

The immediate postwar attitude was reminiscent of the naivety that had existed in 1861.

Neither side understood that reuniting the nation would be as great a tribulation as the war itself had been.

The Reconstruction era was not a happy one. The North was rent by a new debate on the status of the freed slaves and by the economic recession that followed the war. The Democrats wanted reconstruction left to individual States; the Radical Republicans wanted to destroy the South's ruling class and replace it with a cadre of their own choosing. A majority of the citizens probably sided with the martyred Lincoln in wanting to temper retribution with compassion.

Republican regulars exerted a moderating influence on events during the emotional release that immediately followed the collapse of the Confederacy, but they lost control after the 1866 election increased the strength of the Radical Republicans. Their disillusionment with the leadership of President Andrew Johnson was also a factor. A Tennessee

The surrender of the Confederate Army of Northern Virginia occupied most of the front page of the New York Times on April 10th, 1865. The claim to 'Victory' was correct, but 'Peace!' awaited the capitulation of other armies.

Left The interior of the box where Lincoln sat at the time of his assassination is a highlight of Ford's Theatre and Lincoln Museum

Below left President Lincoln was sitting in this box in Ford's Theatre when he was assassinated in 1865.

Democrat, Johnson despised the Southern planters because of their wealth and power, not because of slavery. He shared Lincoln's opinion that the war had been a rebellion rather than a war between separate nations, and that the States thus remained part of the national union.

President Johnson undertook to direct the Reconstruction by executive order. His first proclamation offered amnesty and restitution of property to Southerners who would take an oath of allegiance, with the exception of former Confederate government officials, senior army and naval officers, anyone arrested for military crimes, men who had resigned Federal positions at the start of the war, and people whose worth exceeded $20,000. Other proclamations recognized the governments in Tennessee, Arkansas, and Louisiana and appointed provisional governors of six Southern States with authority to call elections —in which only whites who had taken the oath of allegiance could vote— to select delegates to a convention to draft new State constitutions nullifying secession, repudiating debts in-

Above This ruined area of Charleston, South Carolina, includes the

Mills House on Market Street, famous hotel both then and now.

Left The front page of the *New York Herald*, announcing the death of Lincoln, reproduced an earlier, unbearded likeness of the president.

curred during the war, and abolishing slavery.

This did not satisfy the Radical Republicans. They suspected Johnson was trying to create a new coalition of Northern Democrats, Southern Unionists, and conservative Republicans that would end their own domination of national affairs. They immediately counter-attacked with a campaign for universal male suffrage. Senator Thaddeus Stephens of Pennsylvania urged that land owned by wealthy ex-Confederates be confiscated and given to freed slaves. General Oliver O. Howard, head of the Freedmen's Bureau, disobeyed a presidential directive and refused to return land and property to pardoned Confederates.

Johnson was stern on one matter, accommodating on the other. He ordered return of property to their owners but sought to defuse the voting issue with suggestions to governors and delegates that they enfranchise literate

Above left The heavy
Union losses at Cold
Harbor required
temporary burial. After
the war, these black
soldiers were sent to
retrieve bodies for
reinterment.

blacks and those who owned property worth
$250. None of the new State constitutions
provided black suffrage, but that was not as
unusual as it sounds. At the same period,
voters in three New England States where
only a few blacks lived rejected proposals to
give them the vote.

Congress gradually took the initiative away
from the President. Vindictive Northern
radicals grasped the reins of power and, ignoring Lincoln's expressed wish to avoid
malice, wreaked vengeance on the South. In
the process, they completed the economic
impoverishment that four years of Civil War
had begun. The Reconstruction era, as much
as the war, embittered the South to such an
extent that it would not forget for at least
seventy years.

In 1866, Congress passed over presidential veto a law which established special
courts to function as military tribunals, in lieu
of State courts, until the ex-Confederate States
were admitted back into the union. Although
many Freedmen's Bureau commissioners did
not enforce this law, it nevertheless became a
symbol of despotism to many Southerners, as
did the suppression of laws that were designed
to segregate the races.

The status of the conquered States separated
the President and Congress. The Republican
majority in Congress refused to admit the

Haxall's Mills (above
right) was destroyed
by fire when
Richmond was
evacuated in 1865.
Charleston, South
Carolina (near right)
was badly battered
too. After losing the
Battle of First
Manassas the Federal
troops retreated
across the Stone
Bridge then destroyed
it (above far right).
By the time the Union
troops occupied
Columbia, in 1865,
the town had been
wrecked (far right).

Left This portrait of Andrew Johnson, the former tailor who became President after Lincoln's assassination, hangs in the National Portrait Gallery in Washington, D.C.

Right Andrew Johnson's home in Grenville, Tennessee, part of a national historical park honoring the seventeenth president.

The vital role of railroads in the war led to massive destruction of lines and equipment. In this photo, Union soldiers rip up tracks near Atlanta.

representatives chosen under the new State constitutions enacted pursuant to Johnson's proclamations. They enacted laws defining the rights of freed blacks and giving Federal courts jurisdiction over civil rights cases. These laws were twice vetoed by Johnson on the ground that representatives of the Southern States were being denied seats in Congress and that the court provision discriminated against whites. Congressional leaders took their case to the States in the 14th Amendment, which established blacks as citizens, reduced the congressional representation of any State that denied the vote to a portion of its adult male population, prohibited States from denying any person equal protection of the law, and disqualified from holding public office anyone who, having once taken an oath to defend the national Constitution, had broken that oath. While the proposed amendment gave constitutional recognition to blacks it also reduced Southern representation and disenfranchised senior Confederate military officers and government officials.

Southern States which ratified the amendment were to be readmitted. Tennessee was the first to do so, and its representatives were seated in Congress in 1866, even though the ratification process was far from complete. Such generosity was short-lived. Congress delayed the return of other Southern States by requiring new constitutional conventions, with delegates elected by male suffrage, and approval voting by blacks.

Over Johnson's veto, Congress divided the ten remaining ex-Confederate States into five military districts and subjected all civil authorities to military supervision.

OCCUPATION OF THE CONFEDERATE STATES

Military occupation of the Confederate States was a mixture of benevolence and harshness. The 200,000-man occupying army was, for a time after the fighting stopped, the only source of food and medical assistance for displaced whites and freed blacks. The military also enforced laws through military courts, not always with wisdom and justice. The purpose

Above left Andrew Johnson, who served as military governor of Tennessee, was Lincoln's choice as vice president in his second term.

Above right Radical Republican Thaddeus Stevens of Pennsylvania viewed the Southern States as 'conquered provinces' after the war.

of the Freedmen's Bureau was to assist blacks, but it also aided a few needy whites. About a third of the rations issued in 1865 went to poor whites.

At the same time, the South was inundated by agents of the Federal government who used their unusual powers to oppress or plunder. These men were called 'carpetbaggers' because many of them arrived in the South carrying cheap suitcases made of a thick, rough cloth like old rugs. Southerners who worked with them, principally Unionists, were called 'scalawags.'

Many began with a legitimate purpose. The Federal government laid claim to the cotton that had been purchased by the Confederate government and sent agents to identify it and ship it North. The agents did not restrict themselves to legitimate prizes, though. Pri-

vately owned cotton was seized and sold by the agents on the open market, or owners were forced to pay bribes to keep their property. The number of honest agents may well have exceeded the number of dishonest; but under the conditions that existed, the blatant excesses of the latter colored the minds of the people of the South.

Farms and land were taken from owners through a variety of devices, including claims that taxes paid during the lifetime of the Confederacy were invalid and that back taxes had to be paid – in Union dollars. The Freemen's Bureau leased to free blacks nearly a million acres of land whose owners had fled during the war or which had been confiscated. In some instances, the bureau was also able to provide ploughs and mules, financed by the proceeds of crops.

Most Southerners submitted to the whims and vagaries of the Union soldiers and civilians on the scene and the politicians in Washington, but some remained unreconstructed. They resented the loss of the war and the subsequent occupation, and they showed their distaste for Northerners in various ways, even in outbreaks of violence. It was during this period that the Ku-Klux-Klan came into existence.

CONGRESSIONAL DISTRUST

Congress showed its distrust of Johnson by limiting his authority to remove officials whose appointments were confirmed by Congress – the Tenure of Office Act – and requiring that all Presidential orders to military commanders be issued through General Grant.

Another act of Congress required generals in command of the districts to register voters and initiate procedures leading to constitutional conventions. The disenfranchisement of former Confederate soldiers and the enfranchisement of blacks was a blatant attempt to establish political and economic control of the Southern States. When registration of Southern voters was completed in 1867, blacks outnumbered whites – 735,000 to 635,000, respectively – and represented a majority in five States. Three-quarters of the constitutional convention delegates elected were Republicans and, of these, 45 per cent were Southern whites who were Unionist in sympathy, 25 per cent were Northern whites who had gone South after the war (many of them former Union army officers or Freedmen's Bureau commissioners) and 30 per cent were blacks.

The constitutions they drafted conformed

Above left Edwin Stanton, Secretary of War, sided with Congress in its dispute with President Johnson over postwar policy.

Above right Major General John B. Gordon had the unpleasant task of surrendering the Army of Northern Virginia at Appomattox Court House, Virginia.

to the wishes of Congress, but Congress imposed a new requirement. Afraid the 15th Amendment, prohibiting State denial of voting rights on grounds of race, color, or previous condition, would not receive the required approval in Northern States, Congress insisted the last four Southern States readmitted also had to ratify the amendment. It was not until 1870 that the last Southern State was allowed to take its seats in Congress.

In the meantime, congressional imposition of taxes on cotton, designed to make Southerners pay for the Union war effort, helped further impoverish the region.

Right Robert E. Lee turned down command of Union forces to defend his native State of Virginia.

Opposite, below Edward V. Valentine's famous recumbent statue of Lee depicts the wartime leader resting on the battlefield. It occupies a place of honor in Lee Chapel on th Washington and Lee University campus.

Above right After the Civil War, Lee took up the task of rebuilding the South as president of Washington College, now called Washington and Lee University.

Above left General Lee in 1870 and is buried in the Lee Chapel on the campus of Washington College, Virginia.

This photo of the McLean House, where Lee and Grant met to discuss surrender terms, was taken shortly afterward. Today the reconstructed house is the centrepiece of the Appotomattox Court House National Historic Park in Virginia.

The conflict between Johnson, undaunted by reverses, and a Congress drunk with power finally flared openly: Johnson, who tried to circumvent the Tenure of Office Act and fire Secretary of War Stanton for siding with Congress against the President, became the only President in American history to be impeached. Only one courageous vote saved him from being removed from office.

In the State elections which followed re-admission, Republicans capitalized on their popularity with freed slaves to gain majorities in the legislatures of most Southern States. The record they compiled helped establish the South as a Democratic Party bastion for almost a century.

END OF THE OLD SOUTH

The duplicity of the politicians was a far cry from the honest emotion and mutual respect the soldiers had shown for each other at Appomattox. As battle-hardened Confederate soldiers marched up the road to surrender their arms and colors, the Union army was called to attention in a final salute to the bravery of opponents who, though half-starved, had fought them to a standstill for four years. Confederate General John B. Gordon, who began the ceremony with bowed head, straightened in the saddle and returned the salute. The Old South had passed out of existence with those gestures.

The destruction caused by the Civil War extended far beyond the battlefield, even beyond the civilian areas engulfed in warfare. The 'Southern way of life' –the thing the war was supposed to preserve – was sacrificed. Confederates had begun the process themselves by centralizing the government and curtailing individual freedoms in an effort to

Above General Philip H. Sheridan is seated (center) among his staff. This photo was taken in Virginia in 1864. Sheridan later directed the Indian wars of the late nineteenth century.

Right In this 1867 photo, General William T. Sherman and Federal commissioners meet with Indian chiefs at Fort Laramie, Wyoming.

333

create a new nation. Reconstruction finalized the process.

The South had made its case on the field of battle and had failed. A hush descended on Dixie. The war sharply altered Southern society. The dominance of the cavalier evaporated in the smoke of the modern battlefield. The egalitarian nature of combat and the stresses of adversity weakened the exclusionary nature of planter society. New people were admitted to the social and power structure with an influx of Northern immigrants after the war accelerated the process. While the domination of the planters did not end, it was weakened. The trend was accelerated by the growth of industry and increasing importance of the cities.

Most Southerners accepted the new situation. General Lee set a good example for outraged parishioners when a black asserted his right to take Communion in a church in Richmond. Lee went on to devote the remaining years of his life to educating young men of the South.

The Lost Cause replaced The Cause. The Statue of a Confederate soldier in the town square became the new symbol. The South would remain loyal to its memories and its heritage – no section of the nation devotes so much attention to history – but at the same time be as loyal as any section of the nation in two world wars. A further metamorphosis occurred when modern 'progress' became the new standard.

NORTHERN POLITICS

The military influence, not strong in the North prior to the Civil War, dominated Northern politics for a long time afterward. It catapulted General Grant into the Presidency and General Benjamin Butler into the governor's office in Massachusetts. Generals Sherman and Sheridan commanded the wars with the Indians of the Western States later in the century; the names of many of their subordinates had been familiar during the Civil War – General Alfred H. Terry and Lieutenant Colonel George A. Custer among them. The

comradeship of soldiers who fought on the bloody battlefields lasted as long as one of them could don a faded blue uniform and answer muster at the Grand Army of the Republic buildings that still stand in many Northern cities.

Although the Civil War solidified sectionalism, it also—curiously—ended a sort of national provincialism. The war that uprooted more Americans than any previous event in the nation's history gave restless young men a glimpse of life beyond their native horizon. They never forgot the glimpse and soon began a great migration to the western territories. Southerners who had lost everything turned that way to restore their fortunes; Northern youth seeking to fulfil their dreams joined them.

Finally, the Civil War touched the psyche of the nation and initiated a great change as competition within one society replaced competition between two societies.

Opposite Friendship Cemetery, in Columbus, Massachusetts, is the site of the first Memorial Day on April 25, 1866; it is the burial place of four Confederate generals.

Grand Army of the Republic organizations and official ceremonies brought Union veterans together long after the war ended. This parade of veterans occurred about 1880 in Ortonville, Minnesota.

Civil War memorials were constructed in many Northern and Southern communities. This Union memorial is located in Maine.

A stone Confederate soldier stands guard in the center of historic Leesburg, Virginia.

References in bold refer to captions but there may be textual references on the same page.

A

A. Flaglor & Company (Wilmington) 127
Abbott, Fort 110
abolitionists 24, 25, 77, **130**, 299
    movement 23
absenteeism 215-16
Acton 196
aftermath of war 320-37
Alabama 9, 26, 32, 67, 100, 203
    22nd 276
    bread riots 144
    Emerald Guards 46
    military rule 160
    Montgomery **136**
    ports 256
    State Capitol building **203**
    units 255
    wounded soldiers 140
Alabama, CSS 261, 262, **264**, **265**, 270
Albermarle, CSS 264
Albermarle Sound 17, 264
Albuquerque 132, 192, 193
Alcatraz Island **135**, 136
Alexander, Colonel E.P. 91
Alexandria 16, 36, **39**, 53, 256, 258
    Camp Convalescent 83
    occupation 81, 82
Allison *see* Kurz & Allison
Amelia Courthouse 113
Amendment, 14th 327
Amendment, 15th 330
American Red Cross 143
Ames, Adelbert 39
amphibious operations 16-19
Anaconda Plan 72
Anacostia 82
Anchutz Opera Group 81
Anderson, Fort 315
Anderson House 170, **171**
Anderson, Major Robert 9, 10, 13, 14
Andersonville 221, **225**, **307**,

308
    graveyard 275
    National Historic site 308
    prison **223**
Andrew Johnson National Historical Site 281
Andrews, James 288
Angle, The 96, 98, 99
Annapolis 150
Antietam 84-9
    Battle **68**, **85**, **89**, 90
    Bridge 86
    Creek 85
    McClellan, General 117
    National Battlefield Park 85, **155**
    three prase battle 86, 89
antislavery partisans **295**
Apache Canyon 192
Apaches 194
Apple Blossom Festival **65**
Appomattox 61, 114, **122**, **123**
    army's mutual respect 332
    Confederate surrender 319
    Court House **69**, 119, **329**
    Court House National Historical Park 116, **332**
    National Historical Park **121**, 122
    restoration 123
Arbuckle, Fort 257
Archer 272
Arizona 132, 190, 194
Arkansas 174-5
    artillery 169
    political leaders 319
    troops 168, 255
Arkansas, CSS 244, 258, 264
Arkansas Post National Memorial **175**
Arlington 82
arms 224-6
    see also firearms; firepower
Armstrong cannon 88
Army, Federal *see* Federal Army
Army,Confederate *see* Confederate army
Army, Regular 48
army tactics 232
Arnold, Private D.W.C. **44**
Arsenal Penitentiary 152, **153**
    artillery advances 88
    artillerymen 208
    Athens 203
        College 203

Atlanta **131**, 274, **303**
    Battle 288
    bread riots 144
    capture by Johnston 282
    defense **231**
    environs 288-9
    fall 302
    Kennesaw Mountain Battle 285
    Municipal park 288
    Peachtree Street **158**
    railroad **234**
    railroad destruction **327**
    refugees 154
Atlantic Coast 11, 270
Atlantic, South 270
attrition, war of 106-13
Augusta 32, 307
    bread riots 144
Austin 254
Averasboro 316
Avery Island 243
Azores 270

B

Babcock, Fort 254
badges 46-9
Bahamas 30
Bahia (Brazil) 270
Bale, Major General Williams 276
balloons 236
Baltic 9
Baltimore 16, 84, 97
    Butler, General Benjamin 150, **151**
    and Ohio rail line 233,235
    and Ohio Railway bridge 20
Bangor 124
Banks, General Nathanial P. 62, 150
    Brownsville 254
    increase in men 258
    Jackson, attacked by 208
    Port Hudson 252, 254, 255
    Red River Valley 256
    Sabine Pass 257
Barnard, George N. **131**

Barrancas, Fort 14, 15
Barren River 171
bartering 147
Barton, Clara 129, 142, 143, **219**
Bascom 140
baseball 78-9
Baton Rouge 243, 258
    evacuation 244
    monument 244
    raid 247
Battery 5 111
Battery 9 112
Battery, Charleston 12
battery gun **229**
Bayou City 73
bayou communities 242-3
Bayou Teche 242, 243
Beardslee, George W. 293
Beauregard, General Pierre Gustave Toutant 9, 12, 36, 38, **120**
    female attention 140
    residence 239
    Shiloh 181, 183
Beaver Dam Creek 71
Bee, General Bernard E. 36, 309
Beecher Bible **298**
Beecher, Henry Ward **298**
Belgium 224
Belle Island Gardens 19
Bellevue 26
Benjamin, Judah P. 20, 21, 60, 67
Bennett, Lucy 319
Bennett Place State Historical Park **313**
Bennett Place surrender 317, **318**, 319
Benning, Fort 303
Bentonville 315-17
    Battlefield 216, **227**, 316
Berkeley Plantation **71**,72
Bernard, General Simon 239
Berwick, Fort 242
Beufort Arsenal 309
Bibb County 303
Bickerdyke, Mary Ann Ball 'mother' 143, **219**
Bieseker Woods 100
Big Bethel 16, 71
    Battle 312
Big Black River 249, 250
Big Blue Creek 296
Big Round Top 100
Big Shanty Museum 288
'Billy Yank' 40-59
Bird Creek 197
blacks *see* negro

Blakeley, Fort 291
Blakeley Site and Cemetery 291
Blakely, 12inch 88
Blalock, Mrs. L.M. 140
Bleak House 280
Bliss, Fort 193
blockade running 262
Bloody Angle, 106
    see also Angle, The
Bloody Hill 168, 169
Bloody Lane 85, 86, **87**
    see also Sunken Road
Bloody Pond 182
Blue Ridge Mountains 62
Blue Room (White House) 80
blue *see* uniform
Bluff Trail 282
Blunt, General James G. **301**
Bolivar 21
bond $100 **33**
Boonville 150, 167
Booth, John Wilkes **153**
Borden House 177
Border States 27, 149
Border States, western 156
Borginnis, Mrs. Sarah **256**
Bosque Redondos Reservation 194
Boston 30, **50**
    Harbor 223
    Mountain 177
    naval yards 260
Botts, John Minor 162
bounties **52**
Bowen, General John S. 247, **251**
Bowie, Fort 194
Bowling Green 171
Boyd, Belle 19, **83**, 140, **141**
Brady, Matthew **119**
Bragg, General Braxton 15
    Chattanooga, Battle of 279
    Chickamauga, Battle of 275
    Kentucky **188**, 189
    Oakland Plantation 200
    Perryville 187
    reinforcements by rail 233
    Stone's River 200
Brandy Station 101
Brandywine communities 131
Brandywine region 124
Brannan, Captain James M. 16
Brashear City 242
Brashear, Fort 242, 243
Brazil 270
bread riots 144
Breakthrough Point 72
Breckinridge, Major General

John C. 157, 244
breechloaders 224, 229, 278
bridge, pontoon , **38**, 162, 224
Britain *see* Great Britain
British Foreign Enlistment Act 270
Britton's Lane Battle of 186
Brock Road 105, 106
Brooklyn 128
Brooklyn 289, 290
Brooks, Noah 83
Brothers War, the 170
Brotherton House 278
Brown County Historical Museum 196
Brown, Fort 254
Brown family 299
Brown, Joe 49
Brown, John **20**, 21, 299
Brownsville, capture of 254
Brunswick Town State Historic Site **315**
Buchanan, Fort 242
Buchanan, James 9, 14
Buckner, General Simon Bolivar 174
    imprisonment 221, 223
    surrender of command 319
Buell, General Don Carlos **179**
    Perryville 187, 188, 189, 190
    Shiloh 181, 182, 183
'Buffalo Bill' **196**
Buffalo Creek 175
Buford, Brigadier General Abraham 314
bugle calls **54**
Buhlow, Fort 258
Bull Pen 254
Bull Run 36, 37, **38**
    see also Manassas
Bullock, Panthea Coleman **269**
Burbridge, General Stephen G. 158, 160
Burnside, Vallandigham 154
Burnside Bridge 86, **87**
Burnside, General Ambrose E. 17, 89, **93**, 94, 148, 149
    Chicago Tribune closure **87**
    East Tennessee 280
    Fort Fisher assault 212
    Fredericksburg 90, 91
    Potomac, Army of the **282**
    telegraph trains 293
Butler, General Benjamin Franklin 16, 108
    Annapolis 150, **151**
    Baton Rouge evacuation 244
    caricatures 262

Fisher, Fort 312, 315
    food requisitioning 156
    General Order 28, **239**
    New Orleans 238
    politics 334
Butterfield, Major General Daniel 72, 91, 169
'butternut gray' 46

C

Cabinet 25, 33, 130
Cairo (Illinois) 58, 173
Cairo, USS **252**, 268
Caleb Cushing 272
California 134, 136, **157**
    civilian life 134-6
    Column 133, 193, 194
    Volunteers 193, 194
Callaway County 167
Camden-Pine Bluff Road 175
camp life 53-4
campaigns remembered 258-9
Canada 30, 272
Canby, Colonel Edward R.S. 192
cannon 174, 176, 182
    Armstrong 88
    Columbiad 174
    Napoleon 226, **231**, **332**, 282
    Parrott 282, 312, **314**
    rifled 226, **311**
    Whitworth 88
Cannon Walk 12
Canyon de Chelly **191**
    National Monument **195**
Cape Fear River 312
Cape Hatteras 16, 74
Capitol Building (Washington) 54
capture **224**
    see also prisoners
carbine, Hall 278
Carlisle 101
Carnifex Ferry Battlefield 21
Carnton Mansion 302, 303
Carnton plantation 138, 306
Carolinas 113, 309, 312
'carpetbaggers' 328
Carroll, General William H. 160

Carson City 134
Carson, Colonel Christopher 'Kit' **193**
    Apache campaign 194
    Canyon de Chelly **191**
    Navajo stronghold **195**
Carson, Kit Museum 194
Carter House 154, 303
Carter Park (Carthage) 167
Carthage 167
Carver General Hospital **82**
Carver, George Washington **145**
Casemate Museum **18**, 26
Cashtown 97
Casino Park 74
Cass County 150
Cassville 167
Cause, The 334
cavalry **59**
    actions 101
    charge **230**, 231
    Jackson's foot 63
    role 225-6
cavalryman 208
Cedar Bluff 203
Cedar Creek **115**
Cedar Forest 200
Cedar Grove 251
    Battle 77
Cemetery Ridge 97, 98
Centreville **36**, **39**, 77, 78
Chalk Bluff 175
Chambersburg 163
Champion Hill 249, 250, **251**
    Battlefield Foundation 249
Chancellorsville **19**, 27, 90-5, 97
    Battle 94
    General Lee 104
    Tavern 94
    telegraph range limitation 293
    wounded 82, **220**
Chandler, T.C. 94
Charles Lavalle House (1810) 15
Charleston 9, 11, 12, 113, **323**
    Armory **14**
    coastal defenses 309
    destruction **324**
    Fort Sumter bombardment 140
    Harbor **13**
    Housatonic **268**
    South Carolina 8
Charlestown 63
Charlotte 264
Chase, Salmon P. 23
Chattahoochee Arsenal 14
Chattahoochee CSS 303

Chattahoochee River 303
Chattanooga **182**, 187, 200, **205**
    attack distances 208
    Battle 279, 280, 281-2
    great railroad chase 288
    steamboat construction **186**
Cheatham's Hill 284
Chene, Fort 242
Cherbourg 270
Cherokee indians 45, 175
Cherry Hall 171
Chesapeake Bay 272
Chestnut, Mrs Mary Boykin 144
Chicago Board of Trade Battery 200
Chicago Tribune 81, **87**, 148
Chickahominy Bluff/River 71
Chicamauga 274-301
    Battle 275-9, **283**
    Creek **277**
    National Military Park 278
    rail transfer of forces 233
Chickasaws 45
Chimborazo Hospital 140, 142
China 260
Choctaws 45
Christian Commission, United States 129, 142, 216, **221**
Cincinnati 128
Citadel (Charleston) 12
City Point 108, 208
civilian life 124-47
    California and Southern counties 134-6
    feeding the military 140-1
    helping men at front 139-40
    impact of war rurally 138-9
    labor unions, rise of 128-9
    in the North 126-7
    northern morale 130-1
    northern patriotism 129-30
    refugees 131-2
    Rocky Mountains and West 132-4
    the South 136-8
    staunchest rebels 140
    war press coverage 127
    women's changing role 139-40
Clairborne **150**
Clark, Fort 16
Clarke, Captain Jerome 160

Clarke, Mrs. Amy 140
Clarksburg 19
Clarksville 32
Clausewitz, Karl von 27-9
Clem, Johnny 41, **44**, 186
Clifton, Jack **152**
Clinton 255
clothing parcels 139-40
Clover Hill Tavern (Appomattox) 122
Cobb, Fort 257
Cobb's Hill **233**
Coburn, Fort 247
Coburn, Joe 79
Cold Harbor **105**, 106, **109**, **324**
Collins, Commander Napoleon 270
Collis Zouaves **140**
Colorado 132, 193
colors, divisions 47
Columbia, District of **39**, 82, **324**
Columbia-Belmont Battlefield State Park 170
Columbiad cannon 174
Columbus 32, 157, 170-1, 174, 187, 255
    bread riots 144
    fall 303
combat areas, life in 154-7
combat, armed for 224-6
combat tactics 208-12
Commissary Hill 254
Committee on the Conduct if the War 33
communications 233-6
    see also magazines; newspapers; signal corps; telegraph systems
Comstock Lode 134
Confederacy, United Daughters of the 177, 254
Confederate
    Arizona 132
    army 170
        insignia and badges 46-9
        uniform 46
        volunteers 45-6
    Avenue (Gettysburg) 100
    Capital (Richmond) 67
    Cemetery 106
    Cemetery (Franklin)302
    Congress 31, 49, 113,**125**, 160
    Congress, last session of 303
    draft 49
    Generals 119
    government 328

infantry 231
infantry trench 91
Memorial Hall 280
Monument 184
Monument (Fort Donelson) 174
Museum 113
Naval Museum (Chattahoochee River) 303
    navy 261-2, 264, 268
    naivety and nerve 272
    soldier 43-5
    State Guard 150
    States of America 30
    States, occupation of 327-9
Congress 26, 35, **81**, 130, 131, 199
    1861 157
    30th 23
    Confederate *see* Confederate Congress
    conflict with Johnson 332
    Davis, Jefferson 24, 33
    Federal *see* Federal Congress
    fortifications specifications 13
    powers of Commanders 149
    Regular Army increase 48
    removal of president's initiative 324
    seat denial for Southern States 327
    Southern States politics 28
    Stanton, Edwin **329**
    war financing 31
Congress, USS 73, 74
Congressional distrust 329-30, 332
Congressional Medal of Honour 39
conscription 49-53
    riots **126**
Constitution 26, 327
'contrabands' **130**
Convalescent, Camp 83
cooking **55**
'Copperheads' **33**
Copse of Trees 96, 98
Corinth 181, 183, 184, 314
Cornfield 86
Cornfield Avenue (Antietam) **86**
Corondolet, USS 258
corps badges **47**, 48
corruption 156-9
Corydon 163
cotton 30, 156
    exports 31
    mills 243

Cox, General Jacob D. 154, 303
Craig, Fort 190
Craven, Dr. John J. **152**
Cravens House 282
Crawford, General 99
Crawford House 188
Creek indians 45, 175, 197
Croatan Sound 17
Cross Keys 63
Cuba 130
Culpeper **56**, 77, 101
Culp's Hill 97, 100
culture 125
Cumberland, Army of the 278
Cumberland Gap **189**, 280
    National Historical Park 280
Cumberland River 173, 174, 179
Cumberland, USS 73, **75**
Curtis, Brigadier General Samuel R. 176, 177
Custer, General George Armstrong 41
    Alexandria 258
    Indian wars 334
    Rangers execution 224
Custom House 31
Cynthiana 163

D

Dandridge 280
Danville 113
Darling, Fort 108, **110**
Daughters of the Confederacy, United 177, 254
Daughters of the Republic of Texas 254
Dauphin Island 290, **301**
David **271**
Davis, Mrs. Jefferson 303
Davis, President Jefferson 22-33, 67, 68, 136, **152**
    abandonment of Petersburg by Lee 112
    Alabama State Capitol building **203**
    birthplace 187
    'bread riots' 144
    Chattanooga, Battle of 279
    Danville 113

habeas corpus 160
imprisonmentt **18**, 153, 154
Manassas 35
memorabilia 239
military corruption 162
Oakland Plantation 200
peace proposal 85
policy/politics/finances 26
Port Hudson 252
power, manipulation of 25-6
residence 113
Stone Mountain statue 286, 288
Sumter, Fort 9
telegraph communications 292
Thompkins, Sally L. 142
Vicksburg 247
Davis, President Jefferson, sister of 255
Dead Angle 284
Dean and Company 127
Death Valley 100
Decatur 139
December battle (Fredericksburg) 94
Declaration of Independence 72
Deep Cut 77
Delaware, Fort P.O.W. camp 221
delivery system **56**
'Democratic bible' *see Enquirer*
Democratic Party 332
Democrats 23, 66
Democrats, Ohio 148
Department of the Pacific 136, **137**
depots 298
Derenders Monument 196
'Desert Fox' *see* Rommel, Field Marshal Erwin
desertion 215-16
Desperate, Fort 254
destruction 254
detectives 162
Devil's Den 97, 100
Diamond **145**
Dick Robinson, Camp 157
Dictator **111**
Dimmock Line 110
diplomatic relations 30-1
discipline 212-16
disease **55**, **220**
Dix, Dorothea Lynde 143
Dixie 320-37
Doctor's Creek 188, 189
Donelson, Fort 117, 171, 173
Grant's maneuvers 232
Military Park **174**

present day **174**
surrender 223
Dorn, Major General Earl Van 176, 248
Douglas debates *see* Lincoln-N-Douglas debates
Douglas, Senator Stephen A. 23
Dover Hotel 174
Dowling, Lieutenant Richard 254
draft, Confederate 49
draft law (1863) 128
draft, Union 49
Drewry's Bluff 108, **110**
see also Darling, Fort
drummer boys 41
Du Pont Company 128
Duff, Captain James 254
Duffield, Colonel William W. 200
Dug Road 188
Dug Springs 168, 169
Dunker Church 86, **89**

E

8th New York State Militia **233**
87th Indiana 278
East Coast forts 38
East Martello Gallery and Museum 16
East Room (White House) 80
East Tennessee 280-1
military rule 160
East Thomaston 39
East Woods 86
Edwards 249
Edwards Cabin 169
Egypt 30
Elhorn Tavern **176**
Elizabeth City 73
Elliott's Salient 111
Ellsworth, Colonel Elmar Ephraim 82
Ellsworth, George 293
Elmwood Inn 187-8
Emancipation Proclamation 28, 43, 89, 159
Emerald Guards 46
engineers **233**
Engineers, Army Corps of 280

Enquirer 67
entertainment for troops 139
equipment 56
Ericsson, John 72, 74
Erie Railroad 128
Esperanza, Fort 254
Eternal Light Peace Memorial 100
Europe 30, 31, 39, 62
Greenhow, Rose O'Neal 140
powers 85, 96
Southern blockades 262
Evans, Colonal Nathan 'Shanks' 36
Everett, Edward 100
Ewell, General Richard S. 62, 63, 97
Ewell's Corps 114
Ezra Church, Battle of 288

F

1st Maine Heavy Artillery 208
1st Massachusetts Heavy Artillery 216
1st Michigan Light Artillery (Battery A) 190
1st Pennsylvania Cavalry 99, 231
1st Virginia *see* Stonewall Brigade
4th Michigan Infantry **44**
14th Amendment 327
15th Amendment 330
15th Wisconsin 215
45th Illionois Infantry 250
48th Pennsylvania Infantry Regiment 111
Fair Oaks 71
Battle **236**
Fairfield 25
Plantation 94
Fairview 94, 187
Farm Pond 36
Farragut, Admiral David G. 270, 272, **273**
Mobile Bay **243**, 264, **272** 290,291
Morgan, Fort **289**
naval bombardment **241**
Sabine Pass 257

Fayettville-Huntsville Trail 175
Fear, Cape 212
Federal 36, 60, 62, 63
advance 71
army/forces/troops **38**, 66, 167, 170
Congress 134
courts 327
government 328
navy **263**
officers 74
recruiting officers 48
Road 183
target 69
Treasury 49
typical 40-3
'Fighting Irish' **42**
'Fighting McCooks' **118**, 119
Fillmore, Fort 190
finances 26
financing of war effort 31-3
firearms, developments in 278
firepower 229-32
First Manassas *see* Manassas, First
First White House of the Confederacy (Montgomery) 203
Fisher, Fort 212, 312, 313, 315.
Fitzgerald 303
Five Civilized Tribes 194
flag, processional **319**
flag towers **233**
flanking movement 232
Florida 14, 19
forts 14-16
Pensacola Bay **16**
ports 256
State University History Department 14
Florida, CSS 262, 270
food 54-7, 140-1
requisitioning 156
'foot cavalry' 63, 77
Foote, Commodore Andrew H. **173**
Ford's Theater 81, **322**
Forrest, General Nathan Bedford **53**, 173, 186
Alabama 203
cavalry fighting 226
Johnsonville 314
Oakland Plantation 200
fortifications **230**
forts
earthern 224
East Coast 38
Florida 14-16
Pensacola 14
France 30, 39, 62, 68, 270
anti-slavery forces 89

from California 135
Frank Erd building 196
Frankfort 189
Franklin 306
    Battle 138, 302-3
Frederick Forster building 196
Frederick (Maryland) **163**
Frederick W. Kiesling Building
    196
Fredericksburg **38**, 90-5, 104,
    209
    Battle 90, **91**, 148, 293
    defeat 130
    present day 91, 94
    wounded 82
Freedmen's Bureau 323, 324,
    328, 329
Freedom, Goddess of 78
Fremont, Major General John
    C. 63
French Broad River 280
Friendship Cemetery
    (Columbus) **334**
Fritchie, Barbara **163**
front line 53-4
    press coverage 127
Fuller, Captain William A. 288
furloughs 54-7
Furnace Road 94

G

Gaines, Fort 289, 290, **301**
Gaines Mill 72
    Battle (1862) **109**
Gainesville 254
Galveston 73, 257, 270
Garfield, General James A. 184
Garibaldi Guards **41**
Garrison, Lloyd **130**
Gathright House 108, **109**
Gauley Bridge 21
Gay, Mrs. A.H. 139, 147, 155
General 288
General Grant, USS **266**
General Order 27 136
General Order 28 238, **239**
General Order 67 149
Generals (Confederate) 119
Georgetown 19, 163
Georgia 203, 274, 275, 288,
    303

32nd 309
Andersonville 221, **225**
Bascom 140
bread riots 144
coastal operations 17
conscription resistance 49
Decatur 139
'March to the Sea' **118**
Savannah 88
Sumter Light Guards 42
troops 89, 106
veterans 86
Georgia, CSS 270
Germany 39, 41, 62, 81
    settlers in Texas 254
Geronimo, Indian Chief 15
Gettysburg 96-101, 128
    Address **97**
    Battle 131, **228**
    defeat **299**
    failure 119
    Lawrence retaliation 163
    National Cemetery 100
    present day 99-100
    Soldier's National
        Monument **97**
    western 192
    women and the wounded
        143
'Gettysburg of the West' *see*
    Pigeon's Ranch
Gibraltar of the West 170-1
    see also Columbus
Gibson, Fort 197
Gilmore, Fort 108
Glorietta, Battle of 192
Glorietta Pass 193
    Battle 132, **190, 226**
Goddess of Freedom 78
Goldsboro 316
Gone with the Wind 274, 288
Gordon, General George 98
Gordon, General John B. 114,
    122
    Appottomax surrender
        329
    final surrender 332
Gordon-Lee House 278, 283
Gorgas, Josiah 32
Gracey, Captain Frank 314
Grand Battalion, Orleans 47
Grand Gulf 247-8
    Military Monument 247,
        248
Granger, Brigadier General
    Robert S. 291
Grant Drive 105
Grant, General Ulysses S. 27,
    28, 29, 41, 104-23, 146
    against corruption 159
    canals 251

Chattanooga 279
Chickamauga, Battle of
    275
civilian sniping 159
Columbus 170
Fort Donelson surrender
    223
Grand Gulf **248**
Kolb's Farm/Kennesaw
    Mountain 282
McLean House 121
maneuver 232
Mobile attack 294
Mosby's Rangers 224
Port Hudson 252, 255
portrait **116**
presidency 334
prisoner exchange 223
private resource destruction
    247
Raymond, Battle of 249
Shiloh 179, 181, **182**,
    183, 184
siege operations 208
surrender terms **332**
Tennessee 171, 173, 174
Tenure of Office Act 329
Vicksburg 209, **214**, 246,
    250
Western Theater **285**
Winter Quarters 259
Grant Park 288
Granville Rifles (North
    Carolina) 46
gray *see* uniform
Great Britain 62, 68, 69, 72,
    270
    Alabama, CSS **264**
    anti-slavery forces 89
    Boyd, Belle 140
    cannon 88
    Confederacy recognition 31
    firearms 278
    from California 135
    military writers 39
    muskets 224
    navy mercenaries 261
    Parliament 238
    Revolutionary War 315
    Trent Affair **30**
    War of 1812 13, 239
Great Cacapon River 20
Great Central Fair (Philadel-
    phia) **128**, 129
'Great Hanging' 254
'great hog swindle' 158
Great Lakes 187, 272
Great Northern Railroad 255
Great Seal of the Confederacy
    136
Great Valley *see* Shenandoah

Valley
Great Western Railway 242
Green Cay 270
Green, Corporal Johnny 200
'Greenbacks' **31**
Greencastle 163
Greenhow, Rose O'Neal **83**,
    140, **141**
Greenville 280
Gregg and Bowe 127
Gregg, Fort **12**
Grenville **326**
Grierson, Colonel B.H. 247
Grover and Baker (Roxbury)
    127
Groveton Cemetery **37**
guerrillas 223-4
    border states 159-60
Guinea Station **19**, 94
Gulf Coast 256, **273**
    National Seashore 255
Gulf Islands National Seashore
    15
Gulf of Mexico **249**
Gulf Shores peninsula **290**
'Gunboat Quilt' **269**
guns
    battery **229**
    Dictator 111
    Drewy's Bluff **110**
    drill **267**
    Lincoln **70**
    musket 224, **230**, 278
    Rodman **39**
    see also arms; cannon;
        firearms; firepower;
        rifles
    smoothbores 88, 226, 270
Guntersville 203

H

Habeas Corpus, suspension of
    by Confederates 160
Hall rifle 278
Hampton 16, 71
Hampton Roads 72, 73, 74,
    264, 270
Hancock, General 99
Hanover 101
Hardee 53
Harland and Hollingsworth

(Christina River) 127
Harper farmhouse 216, **227**
Harper House 21, 316, **317**
Harper, John and Amy 316
Harper's Ferry **20**, 21, 61, 63, 85, 89
   Brown, John 299
   National Historical Park 21
Harriet Lane 9
Harris, Isham G. 179
Harrisburg 62, 97
Harrison family **71**, 72
Harrison, Fort 108, **109**
Harrison's Landing 72
Harrogate 280
Hart, Nancy 19, 140, **141**
Hartford 49
Hartford 243, **272**, **290**
Harvest Moon 19, 309
hat, kepi-style 46
Hatteras, Cape 16, 74
Hatteras, Fort 16
Hatteras, Inlet 16, 17
Hatteras USS 270
Haupt, General Hermann **236**
Havana 30, 270
Haxall's Mills **324**
Hays, William **192**
Hazel Grove 94
Heiman, Fort 314
Hemp Bales, Battle of the 170
Henry, Dr. Joseph 83
Henry, Fort 171, **172**, 173, 174
   Grant's maneuvers 232
Henry Hill 34, 36, **37**, 77
Henry House 36, 37, **155**
Henry, Mrs. Judith Carter 37, 154, **155**
Henry Schalk building 196
Heritage Days 100
Herndon, William H. 22
Heyward-Washington House 12
Hickmand 187
Hickok, 'Wild Bill' 169
'Hickory' *see* Jackson, General Thomas J. 'Stonewall'
High Point 144
High Water Mark of the Confederacy 100
Highlanders, New York 46
Hill, Fort 250
Hill, General A.P. **89**
Hillsboro's Confederate Research Center 254
Hillsman House 114
Hilton Head **217**
Hilton Head Island 17, 309
Hindman, Major General Thomas C. 177
Hinds Point 159

Hodgenville 25
Hoke, Fort 108
Holly Springs 255
Hollywood Cemetery 113
Holmes, General T.H. 162
Home Guard 158, 257
Hood, General John Bell **120**, 302-19
   Atlanta 288, **303**
   Kolb's Farm/Kennesaw Mountain 284
   railroad destruction **290**
Hood's Texans 105
Hooker, General Joseph 'Fighting Joe' 94, **95**, 97, 153, **154**
   Antietam 86
   Chattanooga 281
   corps badges 48
   Kolb's Farm/Kennesaw Mountain 284
   Potomac, Army of the **282**
Hopewell 208
Hopkins, Mrs. Arthur Francis 142
Hornet's Nest 182
Hospital, Carver General 82
Hotel, United States 81
Hough, Private Daniel 10
Housatonic, USS 12, 268
Howard, General Oliver O. 280, 323
howitzer 13
Hunley, CSS 12
Hunley, H.L. 12
Hunley Museum 12
Huntley, HL 264

163, 223
Indianola 272
Indians 45, 134, **191**, 257
   Apaches 194
   Cherokee 45, 175
   chiefs **333**
   Creek 45, 175, 197
   divisions amongst 197
   insurrection 194-7
   territories 194
   warfare 193-7, **333**, 334
industrial capacity 32
Industrial Revolution 39
infantry 224, 229
   Confederate 231
   firepower 230
Infantry, Museum (Fort Benning) 303
infantry
   rifles **230**
   tactics 230
trench, Confederate 91
Innis House 91
insignia 46-9
   collar 48
   rank 46
Ireland **42**
Irish Brigade 41
Irish Regiment, Third **50**
Irish Zouaves **42**
ironclads **73**, 174, 264, **268**, 272
irregular troops *see* guerrillas
Isbel house (Appomattox) 122
Island Queen 272
issue 31

Champion Hill 249
Cornfield 86
exhausted troops 208
Harper's Ferry 85
Manassas, Second 236
maneuvers 29
men's rations 207
Romney 20
Shenandoah Valley 119
statue 113
Stone Mountain statue **286**, 288
Stonewall Brigade **19**
wounding and death 95
Jackson Mill 19
Jackson railroad 255
Jackson Shrine **19**, 95
Jackson Trail 94
Jamaica **265**
James, Army of the (1864) 108, 143
James, Frank 169, 177
James, Jesse **169**
James River 70, 72, 74, 108, **110**, **144**, **271**
   pontoon bridge 162
Jefferson Barracks **227**
   Historical Park **170**
Jefferson City 167
Jefferson College 242
Jefferson County Courthouse 167
Jefferson, Fort **15**, 16, 153
Jefferson, Thomas **32**, 66, 113, 167
John F. Carr 73
'Johnny Reb' 40-59
Johnson, Fort 9, 12
Johnson, President Andrew 280, 281, **328**
   Congress dispute 327, 329, 332
   portrait 326
   return of property 323
Johnsons Island P.O.W. camp 221
Johnsonville 314
Johnston, Colonel William Preston 183
Johnston, General Albert Sydney 117, 178, 179
Johnston, General Joseph E. 38, **68**, 71
   Atlanta 288
   Averasboro 316
   field uniforms 113
   Kolb's Farm/Kennesaw Mountain 282, 284, 285
   Shiloh 181, 183
   surrender to Sherman 317,

I

Illinois 23, 25
   Central Railroad 159
   Infantry, 39th **229**
   Infantry, 45th 250
Independence, Declaration of 72
India 30
Indian territory 175
   see also Oklahoma, State of
Indiana **25**, 54
   87th 278
   Morgan, General John Hunt

J

Jackson, Andrew 239
Jackson, Camp 150
Jackson cemetery 255
Jackson, Claiborne Fox 150, 166, 167
Jackson County 294
Jackson, CSS 303
Jackson, Fort 309
Jackson, General James S. 190
Jackson, General Thomas J. 'Stonewall' 34, 36, **37**, 72, 94, 140, **163**
   buried **122**

318, 319
Tennessee , Army of 114
Vicksburg 247
Jomini, Antoine Henri 27-9
Joseph Manigault mansion
12
Joseph, Sister **219**

K

Kalamazoo 53
Kansas **20**
  antislavery **295**
  Brigade **207**
  City **294**, 299
  Creeks pilgrimage 197
  militia 296
  slavery 166
  State Militia **207**
  University 300
Kearny, General Philip 48
Kearsarge, USS **264**, **265**, 270
Kelley, Brigadier General 20
Kelley, Colonel B.F. 19
Kelly house (Appomattox) 122
Kennebec 243
Kennesaw Mountain 274, 282,
  284-5, 288
  National Battlefield Park
  282
Kent House 258
Kentucky 22, 24, 25, 157-9
  3rd 314
  Bragg, General **188**, 189
  Morgan, General John Hunt
  163
  raids 293
  Regiment, 9th 200
  southern troop invasion 131
kepi-style hat 46
Key West 15, 16
Kingin, Emory Eugene **44**
Kingston **265**
Kirkland, Sergeant Richard R.
  91, **92**
Knights of the Golden Circle
  154
Knoxville 160, 187, 279, 280
  National Cemetery 280,
  281
Kolb's Farm, Battle at 282,
  284-5, 288

Korean War 281
Kozlowski Ranch 192
Ku-Klux-Klan 329
Kurz & Allison **29**, **106**, **167**
Kyle House 280

L

labor unions, rise of 128-9
Lady Gwin 73
Lafitte, Jean 257
Lane, James Henry **295**, **299**,
  300
Laramie, Fort **333**
Laurel Hill **29**, 105, **106**
Lawrence **162**, 163, **299**, 300
Lawrence Historical District,
  Old West 300
Leavenworth, Fort 298
Lecompte 258
Lee, Brigadier General Albert
  243
Lee Chapel **330**, **331**
Lee, General Robert E. 60, 61,
  82, **85**, **106**, **113**, 114,
  330
  Antietam **89**, 90
  Appomattox **122**, 291, 319
  battleline 100
  black rights 334
  Burnside Bridge **87**
  cavalry actions 101
  Chancellorsville 94, 97, 98,
  99
  commanding 71-2
  defense of home state 45
  defensive structures 232
  field uniforms 113
  flanking by Grant 232
  Fort Stedman 11
  Gettysburg 96, 110
  Jackson, General 95
  McLean House 121
  Manassas 35
  Maryland invasion 162
  newspapers 127
  Northern Virginia, Army of
  117
  peninsular campaign 71,
  72, 77
  Pennsylvania invasion 163
  Petersburg 112, 113-14

portrait **119**
  respect by both sides **69**
  South, rebuilding of **331**
  Spotsylvania **29**
  Stabler-Leadbetter Apoth-
  ecary **259**
  state **330**
  Stone Mountain statue **286**,
  288
  strategy 27, 28, 76
  Stuart, J.E.B, 'Jeb' **120**
  surrender order/terms 122,
  332
  Tennessee 302
  Widow Trapp Farm 105
Lee and Gordon's Mill **277**
Lee Hill 91
Lee, Mrs. Robert E. 147, 303
Leesburg 85, **337**
Leetown 177
Letcher, Governor John 68,
  140, 144
Lewis, Coldwater 190
Lexington **61**, **122**, 170, **171**,
  187, 300
  combat tactics 209
Libby Prison 74, 221
The Liberator **130**
Lighthouse (1825) 15
Lincoln Boyhood National
  Memorial **25**
Lincoln gun **70**
Lincoln, Mary Todd **26**
Lincoln Memorial University
  (Harrogate) 280
Lincoln Museum **322**
Lincoln (place) **150**
Lincoln, President Abraham
  22-33, 45, 54, **68**, 69, 70
  administration 77, 148
  Antietam 89
  Arkansas 175
  assasination 136, **137**,
  153, **322**
  assasination plot 140
  avoidance of malice 324
  balloon demonstration by
  Lowe 236
  Baltimore anti-war riot 151
  birthplace **187**
  blockade 262
  Burnside command 90
  Camp Dick Robinson 157
  Chicago Tribune 87
  dictatorship accusations
  153, **154**
  Ford's Theater 81
  forts 14
  Fredericksburg, defeat of
  130
  Gettysburg Address **97**,100

Grant, General Ulysses S.
  174
  Great Central Fair **128**,
  129
  habeas corpus 135
  inaugural 78
  Inaugural Address 9
  Johnson, Andrew **328**
  Kentucky 186
  Leavenworth, fort 298
  Lee's dismissal 85
  McClellan, General 117,
  285
  military discipline 215
  Mobile Bay, fall of 291
  Monroe, Fort **18**
  Northern blockade 72
  policy/politics/finances 26
  Port Hudson surrender 252
  positive result 89
  power, manipulation of 25-
  6
  spying 83
  Sumner, General E.V. 134
  suppression of new nation
  124
  telegraph communications
  292
  Tilghman's imprisonment
  223
  union dedication 22-4
  Vallandingham, Clement
  148
  Vicksburg 246
  volunteers 16
  Wallis imprisonment 152
  White House receptions
  79-80
  Wood Lake Battle 197
Lincoln, Thomas **25**
Lincoln Train Museum 100
Lincoln-N-Douglas debates 23
Little Blue Creek 294
Little Crow 197
'Little Mac' *see* McClellan,
  General George B.
Little Rock 175
Little Round Top 97, 100
Little Sugar Creek 176, 177
Livermore, Mary Ashton Rice
  221
Liverpool 270
Lloyd Goerge, David 95
loans 31
Locust Grove cemetery 255
Logan County 157
Logan Square (Philadelphia)
  128, 129
London 30
Long Island 126
Longstreet, General James 77,

85, 97, 98 119
Bleak House 280
Chattanooga, Battle of 279
Chickamauga **281**
forces transfer by rail 233
Longstreet's Corps 105
Lookout Mountain **184**, **205**, 278, 279, 281, 282
attack distances 208
Lookout Valley 279
Loring, Brigadier General W.W. 20
Los Angeles Star 134
Lost Cause, THe 334
Loudoun Heights 21
Louisiana 82
Louisiana 30, 31, **150**, 258
Alexandria 53
battles 243-4
North 54
political leaders 319
Redan, 3rd 250
Regiment, Second **241**
Southern 238-44
troops 168
Washington Battery 91
Louisville 187
Louisville and Nashville Railroad 171, **234**
Lowe, Professor Thaddeus S.C. 39, 235, 236, **237**
Lynchburg 113
Lyon, General Nathaniel 150, **167**, 168
body ar Ray House 169
death of 170

M

MacAllister, Fort **304**, 309
McArthur, Arthur 41, 281
McArthur, Douglas 281
McCall, General G.A. 149, 223
McClean House **123**, **332**
McClellan, General George B. 71, 77, 78, **85**, 89, 90
age 41, **44**
Antietam **68**, 90, 117
army 142
Bailey's Crossroads 78
James River 72, 74
Lincoln, President

Abraham 285
Manassas, First 74
Peninsular Campaign 17, 63, 69, 76
strike at Lee 85
telegraph trains 293
McCook, General Alexander McDowell **118**, 119
I Corps 189
McCordle, Mike 79
McCoull House 106
McCraken County 158
McCulloch, Brigadier General Benjamin 168, 169
McDowell, General Irwin 19, 36, 38, 62, 136, **137**, 149
McElroy, Tom **59**
McEvily, William **51**
McGuire, Dr Hunter 113
McHenry, Fort 151
machine guns 224, 229
McLean House 121
Macomb, Fort 239
Macon 32, 144
City Hall 303
Macon, Fort **316**
McPherson, General James B. 118, 155
McPherson Ridge 100
McRee, Fort 15
McTavock, John 303
Madison 288
magazines 293
Magnolia Cemetery 12
Magoffin, Beriah 157
Magruder, General John B. 257
Mahan, Dennis H. 27-9
Mahone, Major General William 111
Main Street (Richmond) 67
Maine 39
Bangor 124
Civil War memorials **336**
Heavy Artillery, 1st 208
naval yards 261
Portland 272
Mallory, Stephen R. 33, **261**
Malvern Hill 108, **228**
Manassas 62, 63, 121
Battle **155**
line 71
present day 37
Manassas, First 34-9, 61, 66, 67, 70, 76, 82
balloon observation 236
Battle **36**, 77,78, 142, 154
battlefield communications **233**
Federal troop retreat **324**
battlefield 34-9, **208**

Greenhow, Rose O'Neal 140
lessons from 38-9
McDowell, General Irwin 136
reebel yell 36
Shiloh 181
spying 83
two-phase battle 36
Manassas Gap Independent Line 36
Manassas, Second **37**, 76-83, 85
ammunition shortage 236
frontal assault 230
Manhattan 298
Mankato 197
Mansfield, Battle of 243, 256, 257, 258
Marbury, Gilbert A. **42**
march, on the 206-7
'March to the Sea' 154, 156, 232, 307
Mardis Gras 131
Mare Island 261
Marietta 288
graveyards 275
Marion, Fort 14
maritime exploits 260
Marksville 256
Marmaduke, Brigadier General John S. 53
Marschall, Professor Nicola **125**
Marshall 319
Martinsburg 140
Marye's Heights 91, **92**, **93** 94, 148
Marye's Heights, Angel of 91, **92**
Maryland 16, 21, **68**, 84, 85, 90, 152
Antietam 89
Artillery, 3rd 139
doctors 83
invasion **85**, 162
and Kentucky 186
legislature 151
military occupation 150-2
western 97
southern troop invasion 131
Maryland Heights 21
Mason, Fort 157
Mason, James M. **30**
Massachusetts
9th **98**
25th **217**
39th 212
Canton 127
Heavy Artillery, 1st 216

Infantry, 12th 77
soldiers 151
Massachusetts, Fort **79**, **249**, 255
Massanutten 62
Massey family 200
Master Armorer's House Museum 21
Matagorda Island 254
Matthews Hill 36
Matthews House **35**
Maury, Matthew Fontaine 16-17, 113, 261
mines 261
Mazeppa 314
Meade, General George G. 91, 97, 98, 99, 101
Meade Station 112
Meagher, Thomas Francis **42**
measles epidemic 54
Mechanicsville 71, 106
Mechum's River station 62
medical care **59**
medical facilities 216-20
medical tent **100**
medicines **126**
patent **55**
Meek's Store (Appomattox) 122
Meigs, General Montgomery 130
Memorial , Eternal Light Peace 100
Memphis 184
Memphis-Little Rock Road 175
'men in blue' *see* union soldier
Mennonites 60
Merrimack, USS 72, **75**
Mesilla 132, 190
Mexico 134
Mexico, Gulf of 239, 270
Meyer, Colonel Albert J. 293
Meyer, Madam Pauline 81
Michigan Cavalry, 3rd, mutiny of 258
Michigan Infantry, 4th **44**
Michigan Regiment, Sixth 53
Michigan soldiers 190, 197, 209
Mid West 154
military discipline 212-16
military essentials 32
military life adjustment 236
Military Museum (Montgomery) 203
military rule 148-63
opposition 160-3
Miller, James H. 221, 309
Milligan, Lambdin P. 149
Mills House **323**

Mine Creek, Battle of 296-9
mines 261
Minie balls 147,278
Minie, Captain 278
Minnesota 194
   2nd 278
   Ortonville **315**
   River Valley 197
   Sioux 194
Minnesota, USS 16
Missionary Ridge 41, **182**,
   278, 279, 281
Mississippi 203, 270, 274
   closure 246-59, 257
   control of 252
   General Grant 171
   northern 184
   ports 256
   Union possession 175, 264
   units 255
Mississippi River 179, 196,
   268, **273**
   clearing 256
   Columbus 170
   Kentucky 187
   New Orleans 238, 272
   Port Hudson **241**
   union fleet at anchor **244**
Missouri 117, 168, 175, 299-
   300
   Cass County 150
   Compromise 166
   control 169
   Diamond **145**
   invasion by Kansas State
      Militia **207**
   and Kentucky 186
   Lane, James Henry 300
   political leaders 319
   River 167
   southern troop invasion 131
   troops 167
Missouri-Kansas border 298
Mitchell, Margaret 274
Mobile 26, 255, 270, 274-301
   attack by General Grant
      294
   bread riots 144
   Emerald Guards 46
   military rule 160
Mobile Bay 264, 289-91
   Fort Morgan **243**
Mobile Bay, Battle of **242**, 270,
   272, 290-1, **301**
Mobile Point, Morgan, Fort
   242
Moccasin Bend **184**, 282
Monitor, USS 72, 73, 74, 108,
   264, **266**
Monroe, Fort 30, **70**, 73, 74,
   151

Davis imprisonment 26,
   152, 153
   Lincoln visit **18**
   union control 16, 54
Montgomery 9, 26, 67, 203
   White House of the
      Confederacy **136**
Monument Avenue **113**
Moore, Camp 54, 255
morale, northern 130-1
Morgan Bay **289**
Morgan City 242
Morgan, Fort **242**, **243**, **289**,
   290
Morgan, General John Hunt
   163, 293
   capture 223
Mormons 133
Morrilton 175
Morris Island 11, **12**
Morris, Lieutenant Charles M.
   270
Morris, Lieutenant George U.
   72
Morrow House 176
Morton, Oliver P. 152
Mosby's Rangers 224
Moultrie, Fort 9, 12
Moultrieville 9
Mount Olivet Chapel 258
Mount Sterling 163
mountain campaigns 19-21
Mouton, General A. A. 243, 258
Mozley Park 288
Mt. Elbe Road 175
Mudd, Dr. Samuel A. 153
munitions 32
Murfreesboro 197, 200, **232**
musket 224, 278
   barrel improvement 229
   smooth bore **230**
Mustang Island 254
mutual respect 212

N

9th Kentucky Regiment 200
9th Massachusetts **98**
9th Ohio Infantry Regiment
   278
Napoleon cannon 226, **231**,
   232, 282

Napoleonic Wars 27, 28
Nashville **139**, 174, 200, 302
Nassau 270
Natchez 255
Natchez Trace Parkway 249
National (baseball) 79
National Cemetery (Bailey
   Avenue) 281
National Cemetery (Shiloh) 183
National Civil War Wax
   Museum 100
National Portrait Gallery
   (Washington D. C.) **326**
Navajo indians 194, **195**
Naval Academy Annapolis 261
naval adventures 270
naval bombardment **241**
naval forces 72
naval hero, Northern 272
naval power, role of 252
naval yards 260, 261
Navy, Confederate 261-2, 264,
   268, 272
Navy Department 72
navy mercenaries 261
Navy, Union 260-1, 262, **263**
negro labor **144**, 145-7
negro rights 334
negro *see also* Ku-Klux-Klan
'negro war' 43
Nelson, General William 'Old
   Bill' 53
Neptune 73
Neuces, Battle of 254
Nevada (Comstock Lode) 134
New Bern **263**
New England 126, 272
   cotton mills 156, 243
   States **324**
New Hampshire naval yards
   261
New Hanover County Museum
   315
New Hope Church, Battle at
   215
New Iberia 242, 243
New Jersey troops, monuments
   to 106
New Lisbon (Ohio) 163
New Market 62
   Battle **211**
New Mexico 132, 133, 190,
   193
   invasion 257
   southern troop invasion
      131
   Territory 194
New Orleans 45, 238-44,
   244, 262, 272
   Buckner's command
      surrender 319

capture 289
   military rule 160
   mint 31
   Orleans Grand Battalion
      47
   present day 239-42
   Washington Artillery
      Battalion 53
New River 21
New Ulm 196
New York 74, 77
   57th **219**
   City 124
      conscription riots
      126
   draft riots 128
   Highlanders 46
   naval yards 260
   Peace Memorial 282
   riots 49
   troops, monuments to 10(
   Volunteer Engineers **21'**
New York Herald **127**, **129**,
   323
New York State
   Militia **42**
   Militia, 7th **44**
   Militia, 8th **233**
New York Times **321**
New York Tribune 128
Newport News 74
Newsom, Ella King 142
newspapers 293
Norfolk 72, 73, 74
   military rule 160
North Braddock Street 65
North Carolina 16, 67, 309
   Bentonville Battlefield
      216
   bread riots 144
   Charlotte 264
   coast closure 315
   Elizabeth City 73
   Granville Rifles 46
   Memorial 100
   military rule 160
   New Bern **263**
   Roanoke Island 57
   scorched earth policy 316
   sons 312
   Sounds 17
   State historical park **317**
   Wilmington 262
North Louisiana 54
northern blockade 72
northern civilian life 126-7
northern invasion 85-6
northern morale 130-1
northern patriotism 129-30
northern politics 334
northern States 330

Northern Virginia, Army of 61, 96, 105, 112, 114, 117, 119
  Appomattox surrender **329**
  surrender **116**, **122**, **321**
  surrender terms 121
Northwest Confederacy 154

O

114th Pennsylvania, the Collins Zouaves **140**
127th Regiment of the Pennsylvania Infantry 91
Oak Ridge 100
Oakland Plantation 200
Ochs Museum 282
Ochs overlook 282
officer uniforms **46**
officers, election of 53
Oglethorpe, General James Edward 307
Ohio
  20th 249
  Army of 187
  Baltimore Railway line/ bridge 20, 233, 235
  Democrats 148
  Division, 10th 190
  'Fighting McCooks' 119
  General Hunt raid 223
  General Morgan 163
  Governor **149**
  Infantry Regiment, 9th 278
  River 302
  troops, monuments to 106
Oklahoma 194
Old Army Road 175
Old Arsenal (Baton Rouge) 244
'Old Blue Light *see* Jackson, General Thomas J. 'Stonewall'
Old Capitol Prison **83**
'Old Jack' *see* Jackson, General Thomas J. 'Stonewall'
Old Military Road 175
'Old Pete' *see* Longstreet, General James
Old Reunion Grounds 177
Old Telegraph Road 176
Old Wire Road 169
On War (Clausewitz, Karl von)

28
Onondaga, USS **271**
Opelousas Railway 242
Opothleyoholo, Chief 197
Orange and Alexandria railroad **236**
Orchard Knob **182**, 279
Order of American Knights 154
Oreto 270
Orleans Grand Battalion 47
Ortonville 315, 334
Osawatomie, Battle of 299
Osceola 300
Outer Banks, North Carolina 16, 17
Outpost (Mahan, Dennis H.) 29
Ozark Mountain village 177

P

Pacific Ocean 134, 270, 281
Paducah 157, 170
Paine, General E. A. 158, 159
Palm Sunday (1865) 121, 123
Palmerston, Lord 30, 31, 238
Palmetto flag 124
Palmito Ranch 319
Pamlico Sound 16, 17
Pappan's Ferry **295**
Parker, Lieutenant Ely S. 41
Parker's Battery 108
Parrott cannon 282, 312, **314**
Parrott gun **12**, 13, 88
Partisan units 158
Passaic, USS **268**
patent medicine **126**
'Pathfinder of the Seas' 261
  see also Maury, Matthew Fontaine
Patrick Henry 262
patriotism 125
  northern 129-30
  songs **137**, 138
Pawnee, USS 9
Payne, Lewis **153**
Pea Ridge 175-7, **176**
  National Military Park 175, **177**
Peace Democrats 25, 152
Peach Orchard 178, 182
Peachtree Creek, Battle of 288
Peachtree Street **291**

Pearce, Brigadier General N. Bart 168
Pelham, Major John 91
Pember, Mrs Phoebe Yates 140
Pemberton, Lieutenant General John C., 246, 247, 249, 250
Peninsula route 71
Peninsular Campaign 17, 54, 63, 66-75, 76, 77
  Dimmock Line 110
  failure 117
  Louisiana 82
  telegraph trains 293
Pennsylvania 85, 97, 101
  Cavalry Battalion, 1st 99, 231
  doctors 83
  hardwood forest 100
  Infantry Regiment, 127th 91
  Infantry Regiment, 48th 111
  invasion 131, 163
Pensacola 14
  Bay **16**
  forts 14
  Harbor **17**
  Historical Museum 15
  Naval Air Station 15
  region 15
Peralt 193
Perryville **179**, 186-90
  battlefield 187, **188**
  present day 189-90
Petersburg 110
  the Dictator **111**
  Lee's retreat 113-14
  military rule 160
  mine digging 250
  mutual respect 212
  National Battlefield 110, **111**
  railroad battery **235**
  siege 208, **230**, **231**
  trenches **112**
Petit John Mountain 175
Philadelphia 62
  Great Central Fair 129
  naval yards 261
Philippi 19, **20**
'Philippi races' 19
Philo Parsons 272
Picacho Pass 194
Pickens, Fort 14, 15, **17**
Pickett, General George E. 96, 119
Pickett's Charge 98, 100
Pickins Governor Francis 9
Pigeon's Ranch (Western Gettysburg) 192-3

Pike, Fort 239
Pinckney, Castle 9
Pineville 256, 258
piping, sleeve 48
Pittsburg 62
Pittsburg Landing 181, 184, 186
Placita Santa Fe 254
Pleasant Hill 258
'plug uglies' 162
Poffenberger, Joseph 86
Point Lookout P.O.W. camp 221
Point Park 278, 282
policy 26
politics 26
  Northern 334
Polk, Lieutenant General Leonidas K. 307
Ponchartrain, Lake 238, 239
pontoon bridge **38**, 162, 224
Pony Express **134**
Pope, General John **77**, 78, 160
Port Gibson 248
Port Hudson 241, 243, 244
  commemorative area 254-5
  siege 252, 233
  surrender 252
Port Royal 62, 63
Port Royal Sound 17
  occupation 309
Porter, Brigadier General Fitz John 71, 72
Porter, Rear Admiral David Dixon 272
Porterfield, Colonel G.A. 19
Portland 272
ports 256
Portsmouth 160, 261
Portugal 270
postal facilities **56**
Potomac 19
  Railway line 94
  River 16, 61, 78, 81, 85, 89, 268
Potomac, Army of the **56**, 70, **80**, 97, 106
  Fredericksburg 90, 94
  under General Hooker 153, **282**
power, manipulation of 25-6
Prairie Grove 177
  Battle **175**
  Battlefield State Park 177
press coverage 127
Price, General Sterling 168, 169
  Hemp Bales Battle 170
  Mine Creek retreat 299

Pea Ridge 176
Westport, Battle of 296
Prince George (Anacostia) 82
prison
    Alcatraz Island **135**, 136
    Andersonvill **223**
    Arsenal Penitentiary 152, **153**
    Libby 74, 221
prison camps, conditions of **224**
Prison, Old Capitol **83**
prisoners of war 221-3
    camps 221
processional flag **319**
Prospect Hill 91
Providence Spring 308
Provisional Government 187
public subscription 31
Pulsaki Arkansas Battery 168
Pulaski, Fort 88, 307, **311**
Purchase area (western Kentucky) 158
Putnam, Sallie A. 142

Q

Quaker merchants 129
Quantrill, William Clark **162**, 163, **299**, 300

R

Raceland 242
Radical Republicans 33
railroad 233, 242, 255
    battery **235**
    chase 288
    destruction **290, 327**
    troop transfer 233
Raleigh 317
Randolph, Fort 258
Rapidan River 77

Rappahannock 105
    River **38**, 77, 90, 94, 212
Ray House **169**
Raymond, Battle of 249
Read, Luietenant Charles W. 'Savez' 272
Reader, Samuel **45, 58, 59, 160, 213, 224**
Reb, Johnny 236
rebel yell 36
rebels 140
Reconstruction Era **239**, 324
recreation 54
Red Cross 143
Red River 256-7
    campaign 243, 258
    Valley 256
refreshment saloon, volunteer (Philadelphia) **127**
refugees 131-2, 154
    problem 147
    in the south **132**
Regular Army 48
religious services **267**
Renshaw, Commander William B. 73
Representatives, House of 23, 24
Republic, Grand Army of the 308, **315, 334**
Republicans 329, 332
    majority 324
    Party 24, 134, 187
Requa, Dr. Joseph **229**
Reverse Cooper Company (Canton) 126
Revolution 26
Revolutionary War 12, **315**
    heroes 119
Reynolds, General J.F. 223
Rhea's Mill **175**, 177
Rhode Island Light Artillery, Battery B 59
Richland 175
Richmond 25, 53, 65, 90, 108, **109**
    at war 67-9
    communication lines 17
    Confederate Capital 35, 67, 274
    evacuation **324**
Fredericksburg, Poytomac railway line 94
    General Lee 72, 105, **106**, 122
    General McClellan 70
    government 19
    Grant's maneuvers 232
    ladies and sandbags 139
    Libby Prison 221
    Lincoln and possession **29**

military rule 160
Monument Avenue **113**
Peninsular Campaign 66, 69, 77
political leaders **68**
powder mill explosion 140
prisoners 221
publications 138
Shenandoah Valley 117
social life 136
State Capitol **32, 67**
strikes 147
surrender **127**
Thompkins, Sally L. 142
troops and civilians 56
war between the states 113
White House **24**
women's war effort 139
Richmond, battle for **110**
Richmond-Fredericksburg Potomac rail line 233
Richmond-Lynchburg Stage Road 122
Ridgely, Fort 196
Rifle Church **298**
rifles 224, 270
    cannon 226, **311**
    Hall 278
    infantry 230, 278
    shoulder-arm 226
Right Gore Angle 13
Rightists 138
Rio Grande River 132, 190
Rio Grande Valley 254
Rivers Bridge State Park 309
Roanoke Island 17, 57, 67, **216**
    occupation 73
Robert E. Lee 248
Robinson House 36, **155**
'Rock of Chicamauga' *see* Thomas, Major General George B.
Rock City 282
Rock Island P.O.W. camp 221
Rockey Mountains 132-4
Rodman casting process **70**, 88
Rodman gun **39**
    15 inch 88
Rogers, Clem 197
Rogers, Will 197
Rogersville 280
role changes 125
Rolla 170
Rommel, Field Marshal Erwin 62
Romney 20
Rose, Major, A.J. 144
Rosencrans, Fortress 200
Rosencrans, General william S. 21, **198**, 200

Chickamauga 275
Roswell 288
Round Mounds, Battle of 197
Round Top 177
Rowen 249
Ruby Falls 282
Ruffin, Edmund 9, **10**, 38
Ruggles, Brigadier General Daniel 182
rural impact of war 138-9
Russellville 280
Ryder, Sergeant Oscar **44**

S

2nd Corps 231
2nd Louisiana Regiment **241**
2nd Minnesota 278
6th Michigan Regiment 53
7th New York State Militia **44**
7th U.S. Cavalry unit **150**
69th Regiment, Company K **42**
Sabine Crossroads, Battle of *see* Mansfield, Battle of
Sabine Pass, Battle of 212, 257-8
Sackett's Harbor 261
sailor, life of 268
St. Augustine 14
St. Charles 175
St. Francis de Sales infirmary 140
St. Francis infirmary 69
St. Joseph and West Coast link **134**
St. Joseph's infirmary 140
St. Louis 134
    arsenal 150
    Jefferson Barracks **227**
St. Louis, USS **268**
St. Nicholas 272
St. Paul (place) 196
Salem Church 94
Salisbury 144, 160
San Augustine 53
San Francisco 134, **157**
    Harbor **135**
San Jacinto 30
San Marcos, Castillo de 14
Sanitary Commission, United States **128**, 129, 142, 216, **220, 221**

Santa Cruz River 194
Santa Fe 132, 192
    National Cemetery 193
Santa Rosa Island 14
Savage Station **219**
Savannah 88
    defense **311**
    fall **304**
    Sherman's arrival 309
    surrender 307, 309
Sayler's Creek
    Battlefield Historical State
        Park 113
'scalawags' 328
Scandinavian mercenaries 261
Schofield, General John M. 118
scorched earth policy 316
Scott, Fort 298
Scott, General **301**
Screven, General 307
scurvy 268
sea, war from the 260-72
Seawell's Point 19
Secession, American War of 28
Secret Service 152
Sedgwick, Fort **231**
Sedgwick, General John 86, 99
Selma 32, **202**
semi-submersible torpedo boat
    271
Seminary Ridge 97
Seminoles 45
Semmes, Captain Raphael 261,
    265, 270
Senate 24, 158
Seven Days battles 74, **228**
Seven Days Campaign 71
Seven Pines 71-142
Seward, Secretary of State 78
Sharp's cornfield 169
Sharpsburg 85, **89**
Shenandoah, Army of the 61
Shenandoah, CSS 270
Shenandoah, Northern 63
Shenandoah Valley 35, 60-5,
    117, 119, 156
    destruction 163
    Hart, Nancy 140
Sheridan, General Philip H.
    115
    Battle of Stone's River **197**
    cavalry 113, 226
    Indian wars **333**, 334
    Mosby's Rangers 224
    Shenandoah Valley 156
    Stone's River 197, 200
'Sheridan's Ride' **115**
Sherman, Brigadier General
    Thomas W. 17, 309
Sherman, General William
    Tecumseh 11, 54, 113, 117,

118, 274-301
Alexandria 258
Atlanta 288, 289
Atlanta refugees 154
Augusta 307
Bickerdyke, Mary Ann
    'Mother' 143
Carolinas 291
Chattanooga, Battle of 281
Chickamauga, Battle of
    275
drive through the South 216
eastwards 302-19
Indian wars 334
Johnsonville 314
Kolb's Farm/Kennesaw
    Mountain 282, **284**
MacAllister, Fort **304**
maneuvers 232
'March to the Sea' 156
P.O.W. execution 221
reinforcements by rail 233
Savannah 303, 309
scorched earth policy 316
surrender by Johnston 317,
    318
Tennessee 302
Tyrone House 259
Western Theater **285**
Shields, Brigadier General
    James 63
Shiloh 47, 117, 178-86, 255
    Church 181
    National Military Park 179
Ship Island **249**, 255
Shirly, Myra Belle 167
Shoal Creek 197
Shockoe Slip 112
Short Hill 21
Shorter, John J. 160
Shreveport 258
Sibley, General Henry Hastings
    192
    Albuquerque abandonment
        193
    Battle of Wood Lake 197
    indian uprising 196
    New Mexico invasion 257
    Placita Santa Fe 254
siege operations 208
Sigel, Colonel Franz 167
    flanking movement 169
Signal Corps, Union 293
Signal Mountain 279, 282
Signal Point 279
Sinking Spring Farm 187
Sioux insurrection 194-7
Sisters of Charity 140
Sitting Bull, Chief **196**
Sixth Street dock (Washington)
    82

Slaughter Pen 197
slavery 166, 167
    anti-slavery forces 89
    antislavery partisans **295**
slaves **130**, **132**, 145-7
    recruitment **133**, 256
    sale of **146**
Slemmer, Lieutenant Adam J.
    14
Slidell, John 30
Smith, General E. Kirby 187,
    319
Smith, Major Leon 73
Smithsonian Institute 78, **80**
    McLean House 121
    spying 83
smoothbores 88, 226, 270
    musket **230**
Snodgrass Cabin **279**
Snodgrass Hill 278
social customs 125
society, appearance of 125
Soldier's National Monument
    97
soldiers and war 206-37
soldiers, wounded 140
Sons of Liberty 154
South, blockading of 72
South Carolina 8, 12, 14, 67,
    309
    Beauregard, General 140
    Charleston **323**, **324**
    Hilton Head **217**
    Hilton Head Island 17
    military rule 160
    Morris Island **12**
South, civilian life in 136-8
South, end of the 332, 334
South Mountain passes 85
Southern California 135
Southern counties and civilian
    life 134-6
Southern Illustrated News 136
Southern Louisiana 238-44,
    242
Southern States 330
    amendment ratification 327
Spangler Spring 100
Spanish Fort 291
spies 83
    border states 159-60
Spotsylvania **29**, **106**, 231
    Courthouse 105, 106
Spring Hall 294
Springfield 25, 167, 168
    National Cemetery 170
    retreat 170
    riots 127
'Square Box' *see* Jackson,
    General Thomas J.
    'Stonewall'

Stabler Leadbetter Apothecary
    259
Stand Watie, General 45, 319
Stanford, Leland 134
Stanton, Edwin M. 23, 152,
    329
    siding with Congress 332
staples 55
Star, Fort 242, 243
Starr, Belle *see* Shirley, Myra
    Belle
State Capitol (Richmond) **67**
State Department 152
State's Rightists 138
State's Rights 25, 187
Staunton 62
Stedman, Fort 111
Stephens, Alexander 315
Steven, Thaddeus **328**
Stevens, Fort *see*
    Massachusetts, Fort
Stevens, Martha 91
Stockade Redan 250
Stokes, Thomas J. 'Thomie' 215
Stone Bridge 36, **37**, 38, 77
    destruction **324**
Stone House **35**
Stone Mountain Confederate
    Memorial Carving **286**,
    288
Stone Wall 91
Stone's River 197-203
    Battle **197**, **198**
    Battlefield **232**
    combat tactics 209
    National Battlefield 197
    present day 200-3
Stonewall Brigade 20, 60, 61
Stonewall's Valley *see* Shenan-
    doah Valley
strategy 27-9
Streight, Colonel Abel B. 203
Stuart, General J.E.B. 85, 101,
    120
    field uniforms
Sturdivant Hall 202, 203
submarines 264
subscription, public 31
substitutes **49**
Sudley Church 36
Sudley Ford 36
Summerfield 21, 140
Sumner, General E.V. 134
Sumter, Camp *see* Andersonville
Sumter, Fort 8-21, 35, 38, 45,
    70, 72, 124, 309
    assault 166
    bombardment 9-10, 140
    counter-attack and
        reconquest 10-12
    drift into war 9

fall of 175
   legacy of war 12
   present day 13
   see also Andersonville
Sumter Light Guards **42**
Sunken Road 86, 91, **93**, 182
supplies 298
Supreme Court 149
Surratt, Mrs. Mary E. 140
surrender, final 319
   Grant's campaign 121-3
Surrender triangle (Appomattox)
   122
Susquehanna River
Sweatt, Leonard 159
Sykes, General 99

T

3rd Corps 48
3rd Irish Regiment **50**
3rd Kentucky 314
3rd Louisiana Redan 250
3rd Maryland Artillery 139
3rd Michigan Cavalry, mutiny of
   258
10th Massachusetts 59
10th Ohio Division 190
10th Texas 215
12th Massachusetts Infantry
   186
20th Ohio 249
22nd Alabama 276
22nd Michigan 186
22nd New York Infantry,
   Company H **42**
25th Massachusetts **217**
32nd Georgia 309
39th Illinois Infantry **229**
39th Massachusetts 212
39th New York Infantry **41**
tactics 208-12, 232
   infantry 230
Tactics (Hardee) 53
Tallahassee 16
Tangipahoa River 255
Taos 194
Taylor, Fort 16
Taylor, Major General Richard
   257, 258
Taylor, Sarah Knox **25**
Taylor, Zachary **25**

Teche Queen 243
Tecumseh 289
telegraph system 292-4
Tennessee 16, 170, 171-4,
   274
   amendment ratification
      327
   Army 114, 187, 215
   East 160, 280-1
   Franklin 138, 306
   Grenville **326**
   Hood 302
   invasion 1864 25
   northern defense line 174
   southern 181, 314
   State House (Nashville)
      139
   Union Army 143
   Valley 203
   western 184, 186
Tennessee, CSS 264, **290**
Tennessee River 173, 179, 182,
   184, 266
   Heiman, Fort 314
   Moccasin Bend 282
Tenure of Office Act 329, 332
Terry, General Alfred H. 315
   Indian wars 334
Texas 256-7
   10th 215
   destruction 254
   Galveston 73
   Invasion 243
   last holdout 319
   military rule 160
   ports 256
   Sabine Pass 212
   San Augustine 53
   troops 119, 132, 168, 190,
      257
Texas, Daughters of the
   Republic of 254
'The Other' Sherman *see*
   Sherman,General
   Thomas W.
Thibodaux 242
Thomas, General George H.
   118
   Chickamauga, Battle of
      275, 278, **279**
   Kolb's Farm/Kennesaw
      Mountain 285
   Stone's River 200
Thompkins, Sally L. 142
Thompson's Creek, Battle of
   255
three phase battle 86, 89
Tiber River 78
Tilghman, General Lloyd 223
The Times 30
Tippee, Mary **140**

torpedoes 261
Townsend, George Alfred 127
training 57-9
   camps 53-4
Trans-Mississippi Department
   162
Traveler 122
Treasury, Federal 49
Tredegar Iron Works 140
trenches, interlocking 224
Trent 30
Trent Affair **30**
Trinity Mountains 203
Trostle Farmhouse **98**
Tucson 133
Tulare Post 134
Tullahoma 200
Tuscumbia 203
two-phase battle 36
Tybee island 307
Tygart River 19
Tyrone house 259

U

Undine 314
uniform 46, 113
   officer **46**
   regulation **48**
Union ambush **209**
Union army 136
   insignia and badges 46-9
   uniform 46
   volunteers 45-6
Union blockade 73
Union dedication 22-4
Union draft 49
Union, Fort **192**
   National Monument 193
Union navy 260-1, 262
Union Soldier 40-3
Union V Corps 91
United Daughters of the
   Confederacy, Tennessee
   Division 174
United States Hotel 81
urban impact of war 138-9
Utah 132, 133
Utassy, Colonel F.G. **41**

V

V Corps 91
Valentine, Edward V. **330**
Vallandigham, Clement 148,
   149, 154
Valley Campaign (1862) 60, 62,
   63
Valley Pike 62, 65
Valverde 190-2
Venus 314
Vicksburg 97, 99, 117, 184
   attack by Grant **214**, 232,
      247
   National Battlefield **251**
   National Military Park 246,
      252
   present day 250-1
   and Shiloh 181
   siege 209, 259
   surrender 249, 252
Viet Nam 183
Vinegar Hill 171
Virginia 30, 32, 85, 108, 274
   Appomattox Court house
      69
   Army 70, 77
   Brandy Station 101
   campaign of 1864-5 28
   casualties **82**
   City 134
   Cold Harbor **105**
   Culpeper **56**
   forces 113
   heroes **113**
   Lee, Robert E. 119
   Lexington **61**, **122**
   Malvern Hill **228**
   map of key positions **293**
   Memorial 100
   Military Institute 20, 61,
      64, **211**
   Monroe, Fort 26, 54, **70**
   Monument 98
   northern 77
   Peninsula 70
   Potomac River 78, 82
   Richmond 67
   Savage Station **219**
   secession 16, 35
   Short Hill 21
   troops 106
   Union Army of 77, 148
   Valley of 61-3
   West 19, **20**, 21
      Harper's Ferry **20**
   Winchester 65

Yorktown 88
Virginia, CSS 72, **73**, 74, 264, **266**
Vizetelly, Frank **127**
volunteer mustering 16
volunteers North and South 45-6

Wachusett, USS 270
Waddell, Lieutenant James I. 270
Wade, Ben 33
Wade, Fort 247
Wajaru Distillery 196
Walker, Brigadier General Lucius M. 53
Walker, Fort 17, 288, 309
Walker, Mary 143
Walker, Mary Edwards **221**
Wallis, Severn T. 151
War of 1812 13, 70, 239
war, financing 31
war aftermath 320-37
War department 149, 152, 156, 189
    actions 152-4
war, ravages of 254
Ward, Commander James H. 268
Ward, Fort **39**
Warren, Fort 151, 223
Warren, General 99
Warrington 15
Washington 24, 38, 73, 77, 85, 90
    Artillery Battalion 53
    at war 81-3
    Bailey's Crossroads 78
    Battery 91
    Capitol Building vaults 54
    club (baseball) 79
    College 123, 331
    defense 70, 84
    Federal Forces 66
    forts **36**, **79**, 88
    migration from 147
    Monument 78
    mormon distrust 133
    naval yards 261
    New Jersey Avenue 78
    Old Capitol Prison -

Park 78
Pennsylvania Avenue 78, **80**
pre war 77-81
    white house receptions 79-81
protection 16, 97
retreat to 78
Square (Charleston) 12
surrender 122
training camps 58
University **331**
in wartime **81**
Willard's Hotel 78
Wasgington D.C. 35
    Carver General Hospital **82**
Washington, George 66, 69
Washington and Lee University **330**

Washington Star 16, 78, 82, 90
Washita, Fort 257
Water Battery **174**
Water Oaks Pond 183
Watt House 108, **109**
weapons *see* arms
Webb, Fort 171
Webner, Frank E. **134**
Webster, Daniel 77
Webster, Fletcher **77**
Weeks, Private Sidney 309
West, civilian life in 132-4
West Coast State 270
West Gulf Squadron 272
West Point 24, 27, 29
    Buckner and Grant 174
    fort 303
    graduates 48
West Virginia 61, 62
    Martinsburg 140
    Summerfield 140
West Woods 86
Western frontier 38
Western Kentucky University 171
Western Tennessee 179
Western theater 166-77
Westernmost battle 194
Weston 19
Westport, Battle of **294**, 295, 295, **297**, 298
Wheatfield 97, 100
Wheeling 21
Whigs 66
    sponsorship 23
White, Fort 19, 309
White House of the Confederacy **24**, 26, 113, **136**
Whitman, Walt **219**
Whittier, John Greenleaf **163**
Whitworth cannon 88

Widow Trapp Farm 105
Wilderness 105, 119
    Battlefield 104
    Exhibit Center 104
Wilkes, Charles 30
Williamsburg, battle at 71
Williamsburg Road 71
Wilmington 262, 312, 315-17
Wilson, Major General James H. 203
Wilson's Creek **167**
    Battle 150, 166, 168-70, **169**
    battlefield 167, **168**
    National Battlefield 168
    present day 168-9
Winchester 20, 61, 62
    Apple Blossom Festival **65**
    exhausted troops 208
    memorial 65
Winder, General John H. 162
Winnebagos 196
Winslow, Captain John A. **265**
winter quarters **57**, 259
Wintergreen Cemetery 248
Winton Spring 177
Wirz, Captain Henry 308
Wisconsin, 15th 215
Wise, General Henry A. 67
Wolsey 15
women and civil war 142-4
women and the wounded 143
women's changing role 139-40

Women's Relief Corps 308
Wood Lake, Battle of 197
Wood, Mayor Fernando 126
Woodson law office (Appomattox) 122
World war II 62, 232, 281
    military uniforms 298
    patriotism 289
wounded 140, 143
Wright, Professor J. Leitch 14
Wyatt, Private Henry Lawson 16, 312

Yank, Billy 236
York River 70
Yorktown 71, 88
    defenses 140

PICTURE CREDITS

The author and publisher would like to than the following organizations and individuals who provided illustrations.

Alabama Bureau of Tourism and Travel, Andrew Johnson National Historic Site, Appomattox Court House National Park, Arkansas Department of Parks and Tourism, John Bowen, Ford's Theater and Lincoln Museum, Fort Point National Historic Site, George Washington Carver National Memorial, Georgia Tourism Division, Gettysburg National Military Park, Gettysburg Tourist Council, Ian Howes, Illinois Historic Preservation Agency (James Quick, photographer), Kansas State Historical Society, Kentucky Division of Tourism, Library of Congress, Lincoln Boyhood National Memorial, Louisiana Office of Tourism, Manassas National Battlefield Park, Maryland Office of Tourism Development, Mississippi Department of Economic Development, Missouri Division of Tourism, National Archives, National Cemetery, Andersonville, National Gallery of Art, National Park Service, National Portrait Gallery, National Trust for Historic Preservation, Newmarket Battlefield Park, New Mexico Tourism and Travel Division, New York Historical Society, North Carolina Division of Tourism, Oatlands Inc., South Carolina Department of Parks, Recreation and Tourism, Tennessee Tourist Development Division, Virginia Division of Tourism, West Virginia Department of Culture and History, West Virginia Governor's Office of Economic Development, Arvis Williams, Zebulon Vance Birthplace.